T0316865

"While the list of leadership books seems to grow almost daily, very few of them will offer the scope and the synthetic approach that this volume provides. The ten essays in this book will assist readers in visiting the broad landscape of the Christian leadership genre, with a way of bringing in the best of secular resources. I will be excited to put this book into the hands of my students."

Jim Singleton, associate professor of pastoral leadership and evangelism, Gordon-Conwell Theological Seminary

"*Organizational Leadership* is the outcome of godly writers whose commitment to biblical authority provides a refreshing theologically sound perspective to the vast field of leadership literature. It is a brilliant confluence of practical advice, moral boundaries for decision-makers and fascinating examples of good and bad practices of leadership. I heartily recommend *Organizational Leadership* to all those aspiring to be a Christ-honoring leader."

Paul A. Kienel, founder and president emeritus, Association of Christian Schools International

"Does Christian faith have anything to contribute to understanding the theory and practice of leadership? Most assuredly, yes! This book offers a much-needed practical theology on organizational leadership, providing perspectives and principles for readers to be 'salt and light' and 'as shrewd as serpents and as innocent as doves' in their formal and informal leadership roles."

J. Stanley Mattson, founder and president of the C. S. Lewis Foundation and director of the C. S. Lewis Study Centre at the Kilns, Oxford

"What I love most about this book is its weaving of Scripture, devotion to Jesus Christ, leadership history and theory, and grounded experience. Its authors provide a marvelous resource that can be read both as a primer and as an advanced study in leadership that is biblically responsible, developmentally accessible, academically engaging and practically valuable."

Mark Labberton, president, Fuller Theological Seminary

ORGANIZATIONAL LEADERSHIP

FOUNDATIONS & PRACTICES FOR CHRISTIANS

Edited by JOHN S. BURNS, JOHN R. SHOUP
and DONALD C. SIMMONS JR.

IVP Academic

An imprint of InterVarsity Press
Downers Grove, Illinois

InterVarsity Press
P.O. Box 1400, Downers Grove, IL 60515-1426
ivpress.com
email@ivpress.com

InterVarsity Press® is the book-publishing division of InterVarsity Christian Fellowship/USA®, a movement of students and faculty active on campus at hundreds of universities, colleges and schools of nursing in the United States of America, and a member movement of the International Fellowship of Evangelical Students. For information about local and regional activities, visit intervarsity.org.

All Scripture quotations, unless otherwise indicated, are taken from THE HOLY BIBLE, NEW INTERNATIONAL VERSION®, NIV® Copyright © 1973, 1978, 1984, 2011 by Biblica, Inc.™ Used by permission. All rights reserved worldwide.

While all stories in this book are true, some names and identifying information in this book have been changed to protect the privacy of the individuals involved.

Cover design: Cindy Kiple
Interior design: Beth McGill
Images: rowing crew: Antar Dayal/Getty Image
    crew race: © spepple22/iStockphoto

ISBN 978-0-8308-4050-2 (print)
ISBN 978-0-8308-9617-2 (digital)

Printed in the United States of America ♾

InterVarsity Press is committed to ecological stewardship and to the conservation of natural resources in all our operations. This book was printed using sustainably sourced paper.

Library of Congress Cataloging-in-Publication Data
Organizational leadership : foundations and practices for Christians /
edited by Jack Burns, John R. Shoup, and Donald C. Simmons Jr.
     pages cm
  Includes bibliographical references and index.
  ISBN 978-0-8308-4050-2 (pbk. : alk. paper)
1. Leadership--Religious aspects--Christianity. 2. Christian leadership. I. Burns, Jack, 1950- editor of compilation.
  BV4597.53.L43074 2014
  253--dc23

2014011065

P	25	24	23	22	21	20	19	18	17	16	15	14	13	12	11	10	9	8	7	6	5	4	3
Y	38	37	36	35	34	33	32	31	30	29	28	27	26	25	24	23	22	21	20	19	18		

CONTENTS

PREFACE

Whoever aspires to be an overseer desires a noble task.

1 TIMOTHY 3:1

—∿—

This book is ideal for those who study leadership, organizations, theology and/or Christianity. The contributors aim to provide a practical theology of leadership from a Christian worldview for emerging and established Christian leaders who want to conduct leadership in a manner consistent with their faith in both religious and nonreligious organizational contexts. The book is also for non-Christians who are eager to see how the Christian worldview manifests itself in leadership perspectives and practices.

More specifically, this book explores various facets of leadership from a Christian worldview so as to equip people, especially Christians, to conduct leadership more authentically than would be possible under alternative paradigms. The hope is that this book will demonstrate that the word *Christian* in front of the word *leadership* proposes something substantively different and qualitatively better than when other adjectives are used or implied.

It may be legitimate to wonder if a book on organizational leadership from a Christian perspective is even necessary given that Christians believe that the whole counsel of God, as revealed in the Bible, provides a complete guidebook to instruct them in all areas of their lives. In addition to the Bible, the Holy Spirit is a helper who engages with believers so that they can accomplish more than they could on their own. The Holy Spirit works in individuals and the collective body found in Christ's church to reveal truth, bear fruit, give courage in a hostile world and glorify Jesus (John 14:16–16:33).

Given all that is readily available to Christians, what can this book contribute to improve Christians' abilities to practice organizational leadership? We offer three justifications for why this book will be a unique and critical asset for those wishing to improve their understanding of Christian leadership.

The first justification is that there is a significant need in the leadership literature for a systematic theology of Christian leadership. In general, the Christian leadership genre falls into two large categories. The first and most common category includes books written by or about successful Christian leaders. These books discuss the anatomy of these leaders' successes and failures, using Scripture to add biblical relevance to the leaders' activity and behavior. It is assumed that readers will be able to generalize the lessons these leaders have learned to their own organizational contexts and experiences. The second category in this genre is more biblically centered. Here authors take a biblical leader like Jesus or Nehemiah and extract biblical principles about leadership from the biblical account of the leader. Readers are expected to extract some sort of universal Christian principles of leadership from these accounts.

We believe that the theology of Christian leadership is too complex to be understood by extrapolating universal principles of leadership from isolated examples from the personal life stories of Christian leaders or isolated teachings from the Bible. The structure of Scripture itself speaks to the need to develop a far more comprehensive biblical foundation for a theology of leadership. While the Bible contains relevant truths specific to leadership, the different genres within the Bible reveal different facets of God's message in a progressive fashion. Systematizing and developing explicit truths and principles germane to Christian leadership from God's progressive revelation of truth serves the intent of Scripture. The Bible provides a commentary on itself when it states that "all Scripture is God-breathed and is useful for teaching, rebuking, correcting and training in righteousness, so that the servant of God may be thoroughly equipped for every good work" (2 Timothy 3:16-17). While the Bible is not strictly a book on leadership, we have found that it develops a comprehensive and profound theology of leadership that provides a foundation for Christian leadership.

The greatest social scientist of all provides a second justification for a book on Christian leadership. King Solomon, who studied life and reported his vast conclusions into over 3,000 proverbs and 1,005 songs (1 Kings 4:32), encouraged people to learn from general revelation to gain wisdom (Proverbs 6:6). While the Bible is all true, all of our understanding about truth is not restricted to the Bible. God has always made himself known through general revelation, the truth about creation that is accessible to all people regardless of worldview. Thus, there is much that can be learned about leadership found in the truths that have been revealed through general revelation (e.g., the social sciences) that can enhance the Christian and non-Christian leadership practices.

The third justification for a comprehensive model of Christian leadership is that while not all Christians are necessarily leaders, all Christians are called to serve in different leadership capacities at different times during their earthly tenure. The apostle Paul in 1 Timothy 3 details the qualifications for the formal leaders of the church, which implies leaders are a distinct subset of the community. Even though not everyone has the gift or calling to be a leader (Romans 12:8; 1 Corinthians 12:28), and not everyone has every gift, Christians are called to demonstrate the responsibilities associated with all of the gifts as necessary. The Christian cannot disengage from evangelism or exercising mercy because he or she claims to not have either of these specific gifts. Christians are called to be "salt and light" in the world (Matthew 5:13-14), which conveys taking a leadership role at strategic times.

This book calls for bold action on the part of Christians who conduct leadership from all kinds of formal and informal positions in organizations. Christians are citizens of heaven and ambassadors to this world. As ambassadors we have a great responsibility to represent our King's wishes here. Kingdom leadership does not begin and end at the church door. Christians are called to conduct leadership in government, commerce, schools, neighborhoods, churches, parachurch ministries and a myriad of other contexts. God has given us many gifts, and our responsibility is to be stewards (not owners) of those gifts and use them to do the King's work.

People from all worldviews can (and perhaps should) learn leadership theories and skills. Christians have a high and unique calling when it comes to conducting leadership. Not only should they learn about leadership theories and skills, but they must also use their knowledge for kingdom work, no matter what kind of organizational context they find themselves in. Christians submit their knowledge and gifts to the King as they walk into leadership by faith and not by sight (2 Corinthians 5:7), trusting in God and not leaning on their own understanding (Proverbs 3:5-6). Christians who conduct leadership lean on a vibrant faith as seen in the fruit and types of works the believer demonstrates (Matthew 7:17; James 2:18).

Regardless of what adjective or set of values is used to frame the study and practice of leadership, the word *leadership* by itself needs to be clarified. In the countless number of words written about leadership by thousands of authors, there is no universally accepted definition for this word. That fact alone makes it a very tricky word to study and write about. It also becomes complicated because the word has common uses that are inexact and rather sloppy when they are applied to a scholarly discussion of the term. For example, leadership can refer to a person or persons in charge of a group or organization ("We will need to get the leadership to agree to this plan") or as an adjective to describe a leader's place in an organization ("I hold a leadership position"). Perhaps the greatest confusion is when it is used as a description to qualify an activity ("What she just did showed real leadership").

Another difficulty in unpacking the term *leadership* is the tendency to emphasize the leader when leadership is discussed or exercised. Certainly leaders have a role in the activity of leadership, but leaders do not conduct leadership on their own. Others are also engaged in the activity of leadership. Indeed leadership is a collective, not a solo, activity. A helpful metaphor developed by legendary business-tycoon-turned-leadership-scholar Max Dupree comes from jazz music! A jazz band usually has a conductor (leader). The conductor doesn't make the music, but the conductor has a very important role and must fulfill that role or the music likely won't happen. Each member of the band also has a role, and each must perform their role or, again, the music will not happen. The conductor and the band members all work together to produce music.

This also happens in organizations. Leaders have roles, but so do the others in the organization. When everyone fulfills their roles, leadership "happens." For this reason, the verb we most often pair with the word *leadership* throughout this book is *conduct*. Hopefully this pairing will remind the reader of the collective nature of leadership. It won't be easy because of the common association of leadership with whatever good behavior leaders practice.

To meet the challenge of combining the Christian worldview with organizational leadership, the book is divided into three sections. Sections 1 and 2 provide the theological and theoretical foundations for constructing a model of Christian leadership. Section 3 outlines specific skills and practices for conducting Christian leadership.

To bless the endeavor, the authors offer the following prayer for the readers as they engage in the study and practice of transformational servant leadership in their personal and professional pursuits. As Paul prayed in Colossians 1:9-12, may God

> fill you with the knowledge of his will through all the wisdom and understanding that the Spirit gives, so that you may live a life worthy of the Lord and please him in every way: bearing fruit in every good work, growing in the knowledge of God, being strengthened with all power according to his glorious might so that you may have great endurance and patience, and giving joyful thanks to the Father, who has qualified you to share in the inheritance of his holy people in the kingdom of light.

May you be blessed as you seek the kingdom of God (Matthew 6:33) and "set your minds on things above" (Colossians 3:2). May you "watch your life and doctrine closely" (1 Timothy 4:16) and "do your best to present yourself to God as one approved, . . . and who correctly handles the word of truth" (2 Timothy 2:15). May you "devote yourselves to prayer" and "be wise in the way you act" (Colossians 4:2-5). May God grant you favor, wisdom, courage and boldness to represent him well in word and deed in your formal and informal leadership pursuits and responsibilities (2 Corinthians 4–5). May you have confidence in he who called you and equips you for every good work (1 Thessalonians 5:24).

THEOLOGICAL FOUNDATIONS *for* CHRISTIAN LEADERSHIP

1

Called to Lead

How Do I Know?

Timothy G. Dolan

—ᚬ—

*I'm really struggling with the whole issue of leadership—
seeing myself as a leader. The truth is, I don't particularly aspire
to be a leader, but I have to be. I am a pastor, you know.
I mean, it goes with the territory.*

*What I could say is that I'm alerted to leadership issues.
I'm seeing writing about it everywhere, and I'm listening
differently. I was one of those people who used to say,
"Why do we keep talking about leadership?"*

QUOTES FROM RESEARCH INTERVIEWS
CONDUCTED BY THE CHAPTER AUTHOR

INTRODUCTION

One of my favorite television shows when I was a kid was *The Twilight Zone*. Each week, host Rod Sterling took viewers to another time and dimension with stories that were bizarre, unusual and sometimes just plain weird. As I was preparing to write this chapter, I happened to flip on the television (always a bad idea when you are trying to get some serious writing done!).

The station I landed on was doing a marathon of old *Twilight Zone* reruns. I thought, *Well, maybe I have time to watch one episode.* And so I did.

The episode focuses on a financially struggling antique dealer named Arthur Castle. Arthur and his wife are barely making ends meet with their little antique shop. One day a woman comes into Arthur's shop and sells him what looks like a worthless bottle for one dollar. Arthur knows it is probably not an antique, but he takes pity on the woman since she obviously is poor and needs the money. When Arthur's wife finds out, she is furious. As they are fighting over the bottle, it falls to the floor and breaks. Lo and behold, out pops a genie. It is not a worthless bottle after all!

The genie offers Arthur four wishes. Arthur's first wish is for a million dollars. Unfortunately, Arthur botches that wish and ends up owing almost all of the money to the IRS. For his second wish, Arthur decides to ask for something "foolproof"—something that cannot be taken away from him (like the million dollars). He decides that one thing is *power*. Arthur says to the genie, "I wish to be a leader. I wish to be the leader of a contemporary twentieth-century country—a country in which I can't be voted out of office." Arthur is savvy enough to know that this kind of leadership could have consequences. But the genie assures Arthur by saying, "You run the risk of consequences no matter what you wish for." And so the genie grants Arthur his wish.

The next thing he knows, Arthur is hunkered down in a German bunker during the final days of World War II, just hours before Berlin is about to fall to the Allies. As one of his lieutenants is handing him a gun to put an end to it all, Arthur, in shocked amazement, realizes what is happening: "I can't be voted out of office. I'm in a bunker. It is the end of World War II—I'm Adolf Hitler!" Fortunately, Arthur has two more wishes, and he quickly uses one of them to become Arthur Castle again.

Clearly, one of the main lessons of this episode of *The Twilight Zone* is to be careful what you wish for! But it is also a reminder that the desire to be a leader and the consequences that go along with it might not always be what we expect. Leadership, and the power and influence that accompany it, does indeed have consequences.

The two Christian leaders I quote at the beginning of this chapter illustrate the complexity and ambiguity of being a leader today. The questions they were wrestling with when I interviewed them for a research project had to do with what it means to be a leader and what effective leadership really looks like. In this chapter, I want to consider two questions Christians need to ask when they are considering leading, either formally or informally: (1) How does one know if he or she is called to be a Christian leader? and (2) What are some of the personal qualities and characteristics that are helpful for a person to possess when aspiring to be a Christian leader?

The Primary and Secondary Calling of God

Discerning one's call to Christian leadership involves understanding the distinction between one's primary and secondary calling.

The primary call of God. Christians frequently use the word *call* to describe the process of being summoned by God to do specific tasks. Often when Christians hear the word, they think of one's work, one's vocation, what we are called to do to make a living. The word *vocation* comes from the Latin *vocare* and simply means "call" or "calling." In his book *The Call*, Os Guinness suggests that all Christians have both a primary and secondary calling. Our primary and most important call is to be a follower of Jesus Christ. Guinness writes, "Our primary calling as followers of Christ is by him, to him, and for him" (1998, p. 31). Kevin and Kay Brennflick, in *Live Your Calling*, believe that this primary call is to "a personal relationship with God through faith in Jesus Christ" (2005, p. 5). Before we are called to *do* something, we are called to *be* someone: a disciple of Jesus Christ (John 10:27).

I am sure many of us have a story regarding God's primary call on our lives. My own experience of this primary call happened when I was a freshman in college. Prior to that time, I saw God as one who was a great unknown—someone I knew was real, but not someone I could know personally. I had a picture of God as someone who was aloof, uncaring and uninterested in me as a person. Over a period of time, I had come to totally reject God, believing that I could make it on my own. Yet, even though I turned my back on God, he never turned his back on me. When I went to college, it so happened that my closest friends turned out to be committed Christians. Looking back now, I know that this was not by my choosing, but by God's divine plan. Slowly, during my freshman year, the Lord softened my heart toward him.

I still remember the night one of these Christian friends explained to me, in simple language, that I was a sinner in need of a Savior—Jesus Christ. He told me that God was not distant and uninterested in me as I had thought all along, but he loved me and had a plan and purpose for me. Soon afterward, I committed my life to Christ, and as I grew closer to him, I knew God was speaking to me. I knew my life had changed forever and I knew in my heart that God had chosen me. That was *my* primary call; to love, follow and glorify him.

Guinness defines God's calling as "the truth that God calls us to himself so decisively that everything we are, everything we do, and everything we have is invested with a special devotion, dynamism, and direction lived out as a response to his summons and service" (1998, p. 29). Ruth Haley Barton, in *Strengthening the Soul of Your Leadership*, defines this biblical idea of "call" as simply "one being (God) reaching out and establishing connection with another (us)" (2008, p. 79). It is important at the outset to remember that most of what God "calls" Christians to be and do is not mysterious; it has already been clearly revealed to us in the Scriptures. For example, in response to the Pharisee's question regarding which is the greatest commandment, Jesus replies, "'Love the Lord your God with all your heart and with all your soul and with all your mind.' This is the first and greatest commandment. And the second is like it: 'Love your neighbor as yourself'" (Matthew 22:37-39). In his Sermon on the Mount, Jesus tells his disciples they are to be salt and light to others. They are to forgive those who hurt them and not lust after others. They are to love their enemies and pray for those who hurt them. They are not to store up treasures on earth, or worry about food or clothes, or judge others (Matthew 5–7). The real issue for most Christians is not *discovering* what God is calling us to be and do but faithfully *being* and *doing* what has already been clearly commanded.

In *The Other Six Days*, R. Paul Stevens affirms this idea of our primary calling to God when he writes that "the Christian doctrine of vocation—so central to the theology of the whole people of God—starts with being called to *Someone* before we are called to do something. And it is not something we choose like a career. We are chosen" (1999, p. 72). The truth is, all Christians are called to be disciples. For some, it is a slow and gradual process; for others, it is more like the apostle Paul's experience on the road to Damascus

(Acts 9). However it happens for us individually, God is the one calling and our task is to respond.

The secondary call of God. The secondary or vocational call focuses more on the particular tasks, functions, work and activities God calls us to carry out. Ruth Haley Barton writes, "God calls us first and foremost to belong to him, but our secondary calling is to answer God's personal address to us. It is to say yes to his summons to serve him in a particular way at a particular point in history" (2008, p. 79). The New Testament makes clear that Jesus calls all Christians, not only to faith in him, but also to serve him in some capacity (Ephesians 2:10).

Sometimes, this secondary calling is to both informal and formal positions as leaders in the church or other organizations. Some well-known examples from the Old Testament of individuals who were called by God specifically to be leaders include: Moses being called to lead his people out of slavery in Egypt (Exodus 3:4-10); Samuel being called to become a prophet to Israel during a time of great sin and apostasy (1 Samuel 3); David being called to be the second king of Israel after the failure of King Saul (1 Samuel 16). In the New Testament, John the Baptist was called to be the unique forerunner of Jesus (Luke 1:11-17); twelve ordinary men were called to be Jesus' disciples and to establish the early church (Mark 1:14-20); the apostle Paul was called to lead God's special mission to the Gentiles (Acts 9:1-19). In each of these instances, and in many others, God has chosen and called specific people, most of whom are quite ordinary, to lead others in doing something specific and unique for him. The call to be a leader has always been contextualized for a particular role, task or function.

The difference between primary and secondary calling is not always as distinct and unambiguous as the above paragraphs might indicate. In reality, these two callings deeply intersect with one another and are usually tightly interwoven in a person's life. One mistake Christians often make when they think about calling is to forget that their first and most significant call is to a person, Jesus Christ, and not to a position. I am convinced that God is more interested in developing us as persons than he is in the particular work we do. A second mistake is the belief that only those engaged in distinctly "Christian" work (e.g., pastors, missionaries, evangelists) are the ones who are really "called." It is unfortunate that many people think that any vocation (e.g., doctor, plumber, carpenter, businessperson, social worker) that is not distinctly Christian is not considered a calling from God. But the Bible reminds us that all work that is useful and honoring to God and others is good work. God's call to be a nurse at a local hospital is just as important as the call to be the pastor of a local congregation (Colossians 3:23; 1 Thessalonians 4:11).

Discerning God's Call to Leadership

How do you know if God is calling you to be a leader? It is important to remember that one does not discern their secondary calling in a vacuum. Rather, this call is discerned and validated by others in the body of Christ. Discerning one's calling is meant to be a communal activity. If one is being called to be a leader it will be obvious, not only to that individual but also to other members of the body. Sometimes people say, "God is calling me to do this or that." And that may be. But input and confirmation from other members of the body helps ground a calling in the larger needs, expectations and judgments of the community to which one belongs.

Whitworth University, where I used to serve, has placed a major emphasis on helping students discover their vocational callings and specifically what it means to be a leader in God's kingdom. For several years my colleagues were involved in a multiyear program funded by the Lilly Endowment that focuses on calling and vocation. They concentrated their attention on five areas where vocation and calling most often get fleshed out: work, family, church, community and the world. Each of these areas is an important setting in which a sense of vocation emerges. In order to help students think about their vocational calling in these various areas, my colleagues developed a list of questions for students to ask themselves as they consider their calling. I believe several of these questions are relevant to our discussion regarding how one knows the context of their calling. These questions focus on spiritual gifts, passions, skills, purposes and convictions.

Spiritual gifts. The New Testament teaches that all believers are gifted by God for some kind of ministry in the church and/or in the world (Romans 12:6-8; 1 Corinthians 12:7). When we discover, develop and use the gifts God has given us, we not only glorify God and build up the body of Christ, but we also understand more fully our "spiritual job description." The first set of questions developed by my colleagues has to do with spiritual gifts. They are: What gifts do you think God has given you? Do other mature believers agree with your assessment?

Os Guinness comments that God normally calls us along the lines of the way he has gifted us. "A sense of calling should precede a choice of job and career, and the main way to discover calling is along the line of what we are each created and gifted to be. Instead of 'You are what you do' calling says: 'Do what you are'" (1998, p. 46). Greg Ogden, in his seminal book *Unfinished Business*, believes that the gifting of the Holy Spirit is critical to understanding where an individual fits in the body of Christ. He says, "The first criteria for identifying equipping leaders is the *recognition* by the body that the appropriate spiritual gifts . . . are operating under the anointing of the Holy Spirit" (2003, p. 190).

While I was serving as a pastor in my second congregation, we decided to start a Stephen Ministry program. Stephen Ministry uses trained lay "Stephen Ministers" to provide care and support to persons in a particular congregation who are hurting or have special needs. I traveled to Berkeley, California, for two weeks of intensive training, but I was not able to convince anyone else in the church to go for the training with me. While I was at the training, it became obvious to me that I would not be able to lead this ministry effectively on my own; it would need the support and involvement of other church members. When I returned home, I determined not to begin this ministry until God called someone to partner with me. As I remember, after nearly a year and a half of praying about this and discussing it with members of the church community, one middle-aged couple in our congregation felt the call to lead this ministry. As a result, they too went for the training in Berkeley and then returned to use their gifts to begin the program.

That was almost twenty years ago. Only in the last year or so has this couple finally passed the Stephen Ministry baton on to others in the congregation and community. Because they made themselves available to God's calling, the ministry grew from a program that was focused exclusively on the needs of our congregation to a ministry that now reaches out to the entire community (and county) where the church is located. And here's the point: it was the willingness of this one couple to heed the call of God and use their God-given gifts of service and leadership that has enabled this ministry to flourish in the way it has. Because they responded to God's call, they became a blessing not only to our congregation, but to the entire community.

While it is essential to listen well to God's voice in discerning God's secondary call on your life, it is also important to understand how God is equipping you for his service. In his book *A Work of Heart*, Reggie McNeal writes, "People who feel called should examine what they bring to the table. A refusal to engage in significant evaluation of competencies and gifts abdicates the stewardship of the call" (2000, p. 109).

There are a number of ways you can discover what your spiritual gifts are. Paul speaks about spiritual gifts and the body of Christ in Romans 12 and 1 Corinthians 12. Participating in a class on spiritual gifts or filling out a spiritual gift inventory can be of some use in helping a person get a sense of his or her gifting. I usually encourage people to try doing different things and then evaluate how well they do and the kind of responses they receive. Start small with an internship or by volunteering with an organization where you can explore your God-given gifts. For instance, you may volunteer to teach Sunday school, organize an event, work in a food bank or serve as a lay leader in worship. If you have gifts in these areas, it will become evident to you and to those around you. Whitworth students are encouraged to do internships associated with their majors and to also volunteer in churches and community agencies. In this way they can explore how their own gift set can be used in a work environment but also how their gifts can be used to meet the needs in the community. Often others see our gifts more clearly than we see them ourselves, so it is helpful to ask others what they think our gifts might be.

What spiritual gifts and abilities do you see in yourself? What gifts do mature Christians identify in you? Is God calling you to use your special gifts to serve as a leader? One of the ways you can determine if you are being called to be a leader in a formal or informal context is by discovering, developing and using your unique spiritual gift mix.

Passions. The second question developed by my colleagues has to do with passion. The question is, "What are you the most passionate about?" *Passion* is not a word that we often use when describing God's calling on our lives. But the truth is that those things we are most passionate about are often things God has laid upon our hearts (Psalm 37:4). And if God has put something on our hearts, then there is most likely a reason for it. Our passions, of course, are not always necessarily from God! Sometimes we can be passionate about things that rise out of our fallen sinful nature. It is always important to make sure that our passions, whatever they might be, are honoring to God (and others) and consistent with the truths of Scripture. Brittany Peters quotes Bob Pierce, founder of World Vision, as praying for this kind of God-directed passion when he famously asked God to "let my heart be broken with the things that break the heart of God" (Peters 2009, p. 8). What Pierce was really asking for was God-given passion!

In his book *Practicing Greatness*, Reggie McNeal writes, "Great spiritual leaders can articulate their passion. They know what makes their heart beat faster. They know what they do that enables them to feel the smile of God. They move towards their passion. They feed it. They are intentional and alive" (2006, pp. 88-89). Parker Palmer suggests that we first come to know who we are, and what our passions are, by "listening to our lives." He writes, "I must listen for the truths and values at the heart of my own identity, not the standards by which I must live—but the standards by which I cannot help but live if I am living my own life" (2000, pp. 4-5).

What is your life telling you? What are your interests, your passions, even if those passions take you outside of your comfort zone? How might God use your life, experiences and passions to serve him as a leader? An important step in discerning whether or not you are being called to be a leader is examining your deep passions. Passion is a prerequisite for authentic leaders.

Skills. The third question developed by my colleagues has to do with skills. The question is, "What skills do you think you already have, as well as what else do you need to develop, in order to be effective accomplishing your vocation?" Sometimes we can be surprised as God calls us to do things far away from our comfort zone and current skill set. Good leaders not only use their gifts and passions in their calling, but they also follow God's direction to develop their skills and abilities. Neither Paul nor Moses thought they had the skills to accomplish what God was calling them to do.

The specific vocational context we are being called to depends on the particular skills God has given us—and how we are developing and using those skills. When I was a kid I had a strong desire to be a cartoonist. I can still remember, at a very young age, drawing miniature comic strips and eagerly following the exploits of Lil' Abner and other cartoon characters in the daily newspapers. For some reason, God gave me this artistic ability, this skill, and I used it with some regularity all the way through my freshman year in college. In college, I wanted to be a political cartoonist. I was drawing political cartoons for the college newspaper. Political cartoonists can have a significant influence on others. But then I became a Christian. And somehow, drawing cartoons didn't seem to be a "real" calling—a way that I could legitimately serve God. So I quit. I am embarrassed to admit that I have not done any significant drawing in almost forty years. When my twenty-eight-year-old daughter ran across some of the cartoons I drew in high school, she said to me, "Dad, you are a good artist. You should draw more cartoons." Her words were convicting, to say the least. It got me thinking about this skill and other skills I have been given and how I am using them (or not currently using them) to serve God.

What skills has God given you or do you feel God is trying to develop in you? In what specific context is God summoning you to develop and use those skills? And parenthetically, as I am discovering as I write this, it might be appropriate to regularly reexamine our skills and abilities even though they may have been lying dormant for a season of our lives. Who knows how God might call you to use them now or in the future?

Purposes and convictions. The fourth and fifth questions on calling, developed by my colleagues while I was at Whitworth, have to do with purposes and convictions. The questions are: What do you believe to be your primary purpose on this earth, and what are your deepest convictions? These questions are similar to the question on passion. What do you believe God has put you on this earth to accomplish? How deeply do you feel you need to accomplish these things before you die?

Os Guinness writes, "Deep in our hearts, we all want to find and fulfill a purpose bigger than ourselves. Only such a larger purpose can inspire us to heights we know we could never reach on our own. For each of us the real purpose is personal and passionate: to do what we are here to do, and why" (1998, p. 3). Kevin and Kay Brennflick suggest that we find our purpose by finding out what it is God wants us to do. They write, "A central part of answering the question, 'what is my purpose in life?' is finding your vocational calling. Within you resides a special combination of gifts—talents, interests, skills, personality traits, and much more—that is the foundation of your vocational calling" (2005, p. 12).

Fortunately, this purpose we are to "find" is not something we need to frantically search for. It is something that naturally emerges out of the gifts, resources and opportunities God gives to us. Parker Palmer is convinced that as we "listen to our lives" and "let our lives speak," we will discover, with God's help, what it is we are meant to do. He writes, "Vocation does not come from a voice 'out there' calling me to become something I am not. It comes from a voice 'in here' calling me to be the person I was born to be, to fulfill the original selfhood given me at birth by God" (2000, p. 10). Ruth Haley Barton agrees with Palmer when she writes, "Our calling is woven into the very fabric of our being as we have been created by God, and it encompasses everything that makes us who we are: our genetics, innate orientations and capacities, our personality, heredity and life-shaping experiences, and the time and place into which we were born" (2008, p. 77).

My wife and I recently spent three weeks vacationing in New England. Every time I travel to that part of the country, where our nation was born, I am reminded of the unique drive and vision of our nation's founders. Many of them were people of deep faith and conviction. We stayed one night in a hotel in Plymouth, Massachusetts, where the Pilgrims landed in 1620. The next morning, we worshiped in the first congregational church the Pilgrims established in the New World. As I wandered through the graveyard behind the church where many of those early Pilgrims are buried, I was reminded of the deep sense of conviction and purpose that drove these Christian men and women to America. They had been persecuted for their faith in England and then in the Netherlands. They wanted to live in a place where they could worship God freely. For this, they were willing to give their all.

While on this trip, I read Rod Gragg's book *Forged in Faith*. I was especially struck by this observation:

> Plymouth Colony grew slowly. Its people were poor, and their hardscrabble struggle discouraged new colonists for years to come. Even so, they remained true to their vision that God had called them to America as New World pioneers with a purpose. They were confident that they had been providentially placed in "New England" to craft a culture that honored and reflected biblical truth. (2010, p. 37)

It was the vision of the Pilgrims' early leaders that got them through the trials and hardships they faced coming to the new world—men like John Robinson, William Bradford, Edward Winslow, William Brewster and John Carver. They were men of deep faith, conviction and sense of purpose.

Greg Ogden suggests that much of God's will is already "written in us" (2003, p. 260). The call of God comes from what Ogden calls a deep sense of "inner oughtness" (p. 262). He writes, "A call has a feeling of positive burden, an inner oughtness, or this I must do" (pp. 262-63).

What are the deep convictions of your life that would undergird any call to leadership God might give to you? Like those Pilgrim leaders, is God summoning you to step out in faith to be a leader in some capacity? It may be something you have resisted doing for a long time. It may even be something you find uncomfortable, challenging and difficult. One of the ways you can determine when and where God is calling you to be a leader is by examining the deep purposes and convictions that give meaning to your life.

ESSENTIAL CHARACTERISTICS OF CHRISTIAN LEADERS

People who have the right gifts, passions, skills, purpose and convictions often make good leaders. But leaders need more than just the right attitudes and attributes. They also need the "right stuff." What are some of the components that make up the right stuff—the essential inner qualities and characteristics—that God looks for in the people he chooses to serve him as leaders? There are many qualities we could consider. Let us review several that are especially important.

Character and integrity. In their book *Leadership Essentials*, Greg Ogden and Daniel Meyer write, "The New Testament, in particular, gives only minimal attention to what a leader does. . . . The Bible is much more concerned about *who* a leader is than *what* a leader does. Why? New Testament leadership is about reflecting the character of the leader and shepherd of the flock, Jesus Christ" (2007, p. 15). The point Ogden and Meyer make is simply this: Christian leaders are first and foremost people of character. It is not so much what they do that makes them stand out, but who they are as individuals. Ogden and Meyer go on to say that leaders with character "fix their gaze on the holiness of Christ and seek to reflect this holiness in the character and conduct of their own lives. This holiness is a blend of moral purity, spiritual produce, sacred purpose and transcendent power" (p. 17).

A synonym for *character* is *integrity*. In his book *Leadership from Inside Out*, Wesley Granberg-Michaelson writes:

> It is not enough that leaders simply have the right skills. People yearn for leadership that is morally seamless, not in a futile quest for leaders whom we expect to be perfect, but in a legitimate expectation that we be led by individuals who seek to embed their lives in faith, who know full well the tenacity of selfish behavior, and also know the slow but sure journey of grace and healing in our lives. (2004, p. 32)

John Maxwell suggests that integrity means being consistent between our words and our actions. "When I have integrity, my words and my deeds match up. . . . Integrity is not what we do so much as who we are. And who we are, in turn, determines what we do" (1993, pp. 35-36).

Granberg-Michaelson also suggests that people who aspire to be leaders must pay careful attention to the three things that tend to trip leaders up— money, sex and power. "Let me suggest where this search for leaders might start: beneath all the other necessary qualities in a leader, we should look for individuals who have demonstrated the inner capacity to deal creatively and responsibly with money, sex, and power in their lives" (2004, p. 16). These three "horsemen of the apocalypse" have been responsible for the downfall of many Christian leaders. In 1 John 2:16 we are reminded that the lust of the eyes (money), the lust of the flesh (sex) and the boastful pride of life (power) have been the downfall of humans since the Garden. We too regularly hear about Christian leaders who have been less than transparent with their money, abused authority or power in some way, or flirted with infidelity or some other moral sin.

As a young pastor in my first call, I participated in a support group for ministers. Each week we sat in a circle and shared with one another some of the challenges going on in our lives and ministry. I remember the day when one of the ministers casually shared with the group that his wife was out of town and that he was planning to sleep with the woman next door that evening. Talk about shock! Of course, he shared this bit of tantalizing information with the group because he was looking for some accountability. He knew once his little secret was out in the open it no longer had the same power over him and therefore he was unlikely to actually go through with it. It was a reminder to me that temptation and sin is always crouching at the door of our hearts and ministries.

In his second letter to Timothy, who was a young pastor in Ephesus, the apostle Paul urges this young leader to "guard the good deposit that was entrusted to you" (2 Timothy 1:14). Part of this "good deposit," I believe, has to do with integrity and character. What I believe Paul is really saying to Timothy is not only guard the message of the gospel that has been entrusted to you, but also your character, heart and integrity.

I read recently that a major Christian magazine gets so many reports of Christian leaders "behaving badly" (ethically and morally) that it has to carefully prioritize which stories to report on. If you or someone you know are one of these Christian leaders behaving badly, then you need to seek help and counseling right away. You also need accountability. One of the most important things struggling Christian leaders can do, besides asking for forgiveness and changing their ways, is submitting themselves to the accountability of other Christians. Fellow brothers and sisters can help Christian leaders be more accountable for their lives and their behavior. Certainly none of us are perfect. If we are honest, each of us is prone to temptation and sin. It is part of the human condition. But for Christians, being a leader is all about integrity and character—saying what we mean, meaning what we say and doing what is right.

Are you a person of integrity? Do you say what you mean, and mean what you say? Do you handle money honestly and with transparency? Do you treat those around you with decency and respect? Do you keep your lusts in check and seek to minimize the destructive power of your own sinful nature? Are you the same person in private as you are in public? Do you have access to a person or group with whom you can be held accountable to God's standards of behavior? One of the ways God's people determine if they are being called to be leaders is by examining whether or not they are people of honesty, character and integrity.

Self-awareness and self-discipline. Another quality that is important for aspiring leaders to possess is a healthy self-awareness regarding their own strengths and weaknesses. Reggie McNeal believes that self-awareness is the single most important piece of information a leader possesses (2006, p. 10). McNeal writes:

Without appropriate self-awareness, hidden addictions or compulsions may guide leaders to behaviors that create huge problems and may dismay, exasperate and bewilder those they lead. Leaders who operate without self-awareness run the risk of being blindsided by destructive impulses and confused by emotions that threaten to derail their agenda and leadership effectiveness. (p. 11)

In their book *Primal Leadership*, Goleman, Boyatzis and McKee argue that self-awareness is one of the key leadership skills of "emotionally intelligent" leaders. They describe self-awareness as "having a deep understanding of one's emotions, as well as one's strengths and limitations and one's values and motives" (2002, p. 40). Self-aware people usually spend a significant amount of time, at some point in their lives, reflecting on who they are. They tend to be especially cognizant of their emotions and how their family of origin, other significant people and life experiences have impacted their thoughts and feelings both positively and negatively. Self-aware people not only know something about their strengths and weaknesses, but are open to constructive feedback. Self-aware people also know what their various roles are and carry them out with dignity and discipline.

One biblical character I have always admired is John the Baptist. It seems to me that John is a perfect example of a self-disciplined, self-aware leader. The Gospels don't tell us much about the personal life of John except that he eats exotic bugs and wears weird clothes. One day he shows up in the desert of Judea, calling people to repentance and baptizing them in the Jordan River. By the time Jesus comes to be baptized, John already has a significant following—a great number of his own disciples. John could have said to Jesus, "Why are you here? This is my turf! These are my disciples! Go somewhere else!" Instead, John realizes that his role as the forerunner of Jesus is just about over. He doesn't have any delusions of grandeur or messiah complexes. He is self-aware enough to know that his function was to *prepare* for the Messiah, not *be* the Messiah. John makes comments that he is not worthy to untie Jesus' sandals and that Jesus' message is more powerful than his own (Mark 1:7). I don't think John is being unduly humble or self-effacing here. I think he truly understands his own strengths, calling and role in the kingdom of God. Therefore, he quietly makes plans to wrap up his ministry and turn his disciples over to the message and the ministry of Jesus. Later on, some of John's disciples come to him complaining that Jesus is gaining and baptizing more disciples than he is. In characteristic fashion, John replies, "You yourselves can testify that I said, 'I am not the Messiah but am sent ahead of him.' . . . He must become greater; I must become less" (John 3:28, 30). It seems to me that John the Baptist is a great example of a self-aware leader who is comfortable in his role. He knows his place in the larger scheme of things.

It is tempting for people who aspire to be leaders to pursue leadership for less than pure motives. Rather than a desire to serve, the real driving motive can sometimes be an unhealthy need for recognition, affirmation or control. Ron Heifetz and Marty Linsky, in their book *Leadership on the Line*, remind us that it is important for potential leaders not only to know who they are, but also to manage the various "hungers"—human frailties—that tug at them. Think of these hungers as the "dark side" of our personalities—the temptations, lusts and desires that pull at us and can bring us down if we are not careful. Heifetz and Linsky write, "We are, all of us, vulnerable to falling prey to our own hungers. Self-knowledge and self-discipline form the foundation for staying alive" (2002, p. 164).

How self-aware are you? How open are you to constructive feedback—both positive and negative? As Paul says, do you have an appropriate view of God, yourself and others (Romans 12:3)? What are some of your unhealthy "hungers"? Do these hungers sometimes get the best of you, or do you have them under control, with God's help? Do you consider yourself relatively healthy mentally and emotionally? Would the people that know you well describe you as self-disciplined?

People skills. I have long believed that having basic "people skills" is a bottom-line prerequisite for anyone who aspires to be a Christian leader. This seems obvious, yet it is amazing how often leaders get into trouble simply because they do not know how to get along with other people. Many studies have demonstrated that the reason leaders often get into trouble is not because of their competence (or lack of it) but because of their poor relationship skills.

An article published in the *Financial Post* in 2006 described a poll that was taken among employers regarding the people skills of recently minted MBA graduates. According to the article, most CEOs of major corporations found that the interpersonal skills of most graduates "were just barely worth a passing grade." Even though most of these graduates were competent and intelligent, they tended to enter the workforce with an "exaggerated sense of their worth and competence," which made it difficult for them to relate well to others (Marr 2006).

I once employed a seminary intern (I'll call him Joe) in one of the churches I served. Joe attended one of the finest seminaries in the country and had the kind of physical presence and personality that immediately drew people to him. When he started working at our church, I thought Joe was going to work out just fine. How wrong I was! After a month or so, it became apparent that even though he had gifts for ministry, Joe did not know how to relate well to others. As the year went on, I spent increasing amounts of my time putting out fires and mopping up after him. It seemed like everything Joe did in the church created hard feelings. Rather than being a helpful colleague in ministry, Joe became a major liability. During that time I came to understand that effective people skills are difficult to teach.

Leaders can have many wonderful gifts and abilities, but if they do not have fundamental, healthy relationship skills, then they are in for a rough ride. Goleman, Boyatzis and McKee (2002) suggest that emotionally healthy leaders exhibit both personal and social competence. Social competence is the ability to manage relationships. This involves both social awareness, especially empathy, and relationship management. Leaders who focus on relationship management are able to guide, motivate and influence others in a healthy way. They also develop others. Managing change and conflict, cultivating relationships, and building collaboration and teamwork are all part of managing the relationships in one's sphere of influence.

What kind of people skills do you possess? How well do you get along with others? Are you a lone ranger, or are you able (and willing) to work as part of a team? How important is being in control for you? Are you comfortable delegating to others? How sensitive are you to the feelings and needs of others? Are you able to get "up on the balcony" (Heifetz and Linsky, 2002) from time to time to see how your words and actions affect others? Would the people who know you best describe you as someone who is open and transparent? One of the ways you can ready yourself to be used as a leader is by paying careful attention to how well you work with others.

Spiritual maturity. A final quality that is important for aspiring Christian leaders to possess is spiritual maturity. This quality brings us back to our primary calling as a Christ follower. Spiritual maturity can be defined in a number of ways. But at its core, spiritual maturity is developed as Christian leaders abide in Jesus Christ. In his classic book *The Divine Conspiracy*, Dallas Willard defines a disciple as someone who apprentices himself or herself to someone else. He writes, "But if I am to be someone's apprentice, there is one absolutely essential condition. I must be *with* that person. . . . If I am Jesus' disciple that means *I am with him to learn from him how to be like him*" (1997, p. 276). A true apprentice is someone who not only learns from the master teacher, but literally follows him or her and does whatever he or she does.

Ruth Haley Barton describes several of the spiritual disciplines that are helpful for spiritual leaders to practice, including times of solitude, regular reading of Scripture, prayer, fasting and observing the Sabbath. These spiritual disciplines, and others like them, help Christian leaders develop the spiritual maturity that allows them to be in a place where God can use them as servant leaders for others. Barton writes, "I cannot transform myself, or anyone else for that matter. What I can do is create the conditions in which spiritual transformation can take place, by developing and maintaining a rhythm of spiritual practices that keep me open and available to God" (2008, p. 12). The most effective Christian leaders are those men and women who are open and available to God. They are not perfect people. But they have heard the call of God on their lives and are doing all they can, with God's help, to not only *do* God's work, but also to *be* the people God calls them to be.

How closely are you apprenticing your life to Jesus Christ? Have you heard the call of God and are you seeking to create the conditions in your life where God can transform you into the man or woman God wants you to be? One of the ways you can discern if you are ready to be used as a leader is to examine your own personal walk with God and your readiness to follow him whenever and wherever he leads.

SUMMARY

Arthur Castle, the antique dealer described at the beginning of this chapter, wanted to become a leader only if he had guarantees that he would never face any problems or opposition. Arthur wanted the privileges and power of being a leader. His motivations were generated from a secular worldview. The Christian worldview teaches about a God-initiated calling to lead. God has called all of us by name, and he has gifted us uniquely to serve him where and when he sees fit. As he calls us to serve him in specific ways, then we really have the honor, as an act of worship, to say to him, along with many other men and women called to be Christian leaders down through the ages, "Here I am Lord, send me!"

REFERENCES

Barton, R. H. 2008. *Strengthening the Soul of Your Leadership: Seeking God in the Crucible of Ministry*. Downers Grove, IL: IVP Books.

Brennflick, K., and K. M. Brennflick. 2005. *Live Your Calling: A Practical Guide to Finding and Fulfilling Your Mission in Life*. San Francisco: Jossey-Bass.

Goleman, D., D. Boyatzis and A. McKee. 2002. *Primal Leadership: Realizing the Power of Emotional Intelligence*. Boston: Harvard Business School Press.

Gragg, R. 2010. *Forged in Faith*. New York: Howard Books.

Granberg-Michaelson, W. 2004. *Leadership from Inside Out: Spirituality and Organizational Change*. New York: Crossroad.

Guinness, O. 1998. *The Call: Finding and Fulfilling the Central Purpose of Your Life*. Nashville: W Publishing Group.

Heifetz, R., and M. Linsky. 2002. *Leadership on the Line: Staying Alive Through the Dangers of Leading*. Boston: Harvard Business School Press.

Marr, G. 2006. "MBA Grads Lack People Skills, Employers Say." *Financial Post*, March 20, p. 1.

Maxwell, J. 1993. *Developing the Leader Within You*. Nashville: Thomas Nelson.

McNeal, R. 2000. *A Work of Heart: Understanding How God Shapes Spiritual Leaders*. San Francisco: Jossey-Bass.

———. 2006. *Practicing Greatness: 7 Disciplines of Extraordinary Spiritual Leaders*. San Francisco: Jossey-Bass.

Ogden, G. 2003. *Unfinished Business: Returning the Ministry to the People of God*. Grand Rapids: Zondervan.

Ogden, G., and D. Meyer. 2007. *Leadership Essentials: Shaping Vision, Multiplying Influence, Defining Character*. Downers Grove, IL: IVP Connect.

Palmer, P. 2000. *Let Your Life Speak: Listening for the Voice of Vocation*. San Francisco: Jossey-Bass.

Peters, B. 2009. *The Hole in Our Gospel Study Guide*. Federal Way, WA: World Vision, Inc.

Stevens, R. P. 1999. *The Other Six Days: Vocation, Work, and Ministry in Biblical Perspective*. Vancouver: Regent College Publishing; Grand Rapids: Eerdmans.

Willard, D. 1997. *The Divine Conspiracy: Discovering Our Hidden Life in God.* San
    Francisco: HarperSanFrancisco.

FOR FURTHER READING

Stevens, R. P. 2006. *Doing God's Business: Meaning and Motivation for the Market-
    place.* Grand Rapids: Eerdmans.

2

LEADERSHIP IN THE CONTEXT OF THE CHRISTIAN WORLDVIEW

Gayne J. Anacker and John R. Shoup

—◊—

You believe that there is one God.
Good! Even the demons believe that—and shudder.

JAMES 2:19

If anyone speaks, they should do so as one who speaks
the very words of God. If anyone serves, they should do so with
the strength God provides, so that in all things God may be
praised through Jesus Christ. To him be the glory and
the power for ever and ever. Amen.

1 PETER 4:11

Does worldview *matter*, particularly within the context of leadership? The answer is an emphatic *yes*. To see this, just consider the stark contrast between two different groups holding radically differing worldviews: the Nazis of twentieth-century Germany and Mother Teresa's Missionaries of Charity. The Nazis believed that the solidarity and supremacy of the Germanic peoples was the most important value for guiding society. Servicing this value was the belief that the human races inhabited a hierarchy—the superior races at the top, and the inferior races at the bottom. The supreme race, the Germanic peoples, were permitted, and even obligated, to rule the others, and that rule included the objective of purifying the human genetic pool by eliminating the inferior peoples. Accordingly, the Nazis systematically exterminated six million Jews and other "undesirable" groups, and this horrific operation continued until the Allies defeated the Nazi regime in 1945. By contrast, Mother Teresa of Calcutta believed in a supreme God of goodness, love and mercy who called her to minister to the poorest of the poor. Her Missionaries of Charity to this day sacrificially and lovingly care for "the hungry, the naked, the homeless, the crippled, the blind, the lepers, all those people who feel unwanted, unloved, uncared for throughout society, people that have become a burden to the society and are shunned by everyone" (Associated Press 1997). Some lessons to note briefly: (1) these two worldviews are very different in their primary principles; (2) those primary principles lead naturally to different principles of action; and (3) the Nazis engaged in mass murder on a world-historical scale only surpassed by Stalin and Mao, while the Missionaries of Charity daily engage in sacrificial and altruistic acts of charity that save lives or bring comfort and mercy to those whose lives cannot be saved. *Worldview matters very much, indeed.*

In this chapter, our primary task is to provide a clear understanding of Christian worldview and its implications for leadership. Preliminary to this we introduce the general concept of worldview and explain its setting in the broader contemporary intellectual landscape. Our conviction in all of this is that a Christian's faith ought to influence both his or her private *and* public dispositions and practices. If it were not to do so, we contend, this would suggest either an incomplete understanding of faith and life or that one's Christian worldview was considered to be of little value.

Good housekeeping, however, requires that we address first the question of how many Christian worldviews there are—one or many; *the* Christian worldview or *a* Christian worldview? The answer, of course, is *both*. Even considering just the most basic worldview concerns (discussed in the next section), there are significant divergences among Christians. We do not wish to diminish those differences, so wherever possible we will avoid using the definite article, thereby honoring the fact that there are many different approaches to fleshing out Christian worldview. Sometimes, however, the context will require the definite article (*the* Christian worldview), and in those instances we should be understood as referring to the vast consensus among Christians on the most basic elements of Christian belief that have defined the essence of the faith. (One special case of bias should be noted, however. Our view of the Bible as the final authority in faith and practice marks the authors as evangelical Protestants.)

WORLDVIEW: THE BASIC CONCEPT

The concept of worldview originated with Immanuel Kant in the late eighteenth century and was then picked up and used by subsequent German philosophers (Naugle 2002, pp. 58-61). While it is distinctively employed in other intellectual disciplines, it was brought into general usage in theology through the work of two influential late-nineteenth-century Christian theologians, Abraham Kuyper and James Orr, and into widespread application in recent evangelical[1] theology through the work of Gordon Clark, Carl F. H. Henry, Herman Dooyeweerd and Francis Schaeffer (pp. 5-6).

Orr has provided the essential meaning of the cluster of German terms used to express this concept. According to Orr, the terms denote "the widest view which the mind can take of things in the effort to grasp them together as a whole from the standpoint of some particular philosophy or theology" (1893, quoted in Naugle 2002, p. 7). To understand this, focus on three key elements. First, "widest view" indicates that worldview is to take in or encompass everything. Second, the phrase "to grasp them together as a whole" indicates that worldview is to bring together one's understandings of the most significant things to create a comprehensive and holistic sense of things. Third, "from the standpoint of some particular philosophy or theology" acknowledges that the person formulating the worldview inhabits some fundamental position about things, and this fundamental position will serve to anchor the whole worldview, significantly influencing its overall character. Moreland and Craig put the matter quite plainly, defining worldview as "an ordered set of propositions one believes, especially propositions about life's most important questions" (2003, p. 13). Colson and

---

[1]Evangelicals (from the Greek "good news") are those Christians (usually Protestant, but increasingly Orthodox or Roman Catholic) who strongly emphasize in their life and theology a personal and intentional commitment to Jesus Christ and his redemptive life, death and resurrection as the basis for their faith.

Pearcey, however, bring this conceptual construct to the level of life and practice, saying, "Our choices are shaped by what we believe is real and true, right and wrong, good and beautiful. Our choices are shaped by our worldview" (1999, p. 13).

In recent decades, in the spirit of Orr's definition, the project of presenting the framework of one's worldview has come to be understood as providing answers to fundamental questions about the world from one's perspective. Some thinkers have shorter lists of questions, some longer, but there is decidedly a general consensus on the sorts of questions to which a worldview ought to provide answers.[2] The following list, a little longer than most, captures all the questions that are generally thought to elicit the key, basic elements of a worldview (see Colson and Pearcey 1999, p. xiii; Dockery 2008, p. 38; Holmes 1983, pp. 31-53; Naugle 2002, pp. 253-330, 349-55; Sire 2004a, p. 20; Stevenson 1987, pp. 5-8):[3]

1. What is ultimate reality?

2. How do we know things/how is knowledge possible?

3. What is the nature and source of the physical world?

4. What is human nature/what is human being?

5. What is the human condition/what is wrong with humanity?

6. What is the solution or response to the human condition?

7. What is the nature of value and morality?

8. What is the nature of history and the future for humanity?

(When referring to a specific numbered question, we will abbreviate "worldview question" with "WQ.")

Given this list of questions, it is plain that in order for worldviews to be taken seriously, the ideas communicated in response to these questions cannot be haphazard or random collections of beliefs. Rather, serious worldviews tend to constitute more or less organized systems of beliefs, exhibiting

---

[2]A Christian philosopher who seriously challenges the centrality of worldview as a cognitive enterprise is James K. A. Smith (see 2009, pp. 17-35, 133-39).
[3]Arthur Holmes does not provide a concise list of worldview questions, but his treatment of Christian worldview in his chapter entitled "The Anatomy of a World View" in fact addresses all of the key questions listed here.

significant coherence (that is, the ideas hang together in a coordinated, rational way). Of course, the basic framework of a worldview can and should be fleshed out as necessary in rich, full detail, in order to demonstrate how it provides a suitable explanatory account for all life and reality.

In order to see what a serious and relatively coherent worldview looks like, we offer a package of responses to these questions that is representative of what many atheists believe about these matters. For convenience, we will call our respondent "Smith," but we need to get the label right. Most thinkers who believe in atheism prefer the affirmative term *naturalism* to the negative term *atheism* as the best label for their view. The idea is that, given that there is no God, it follows that only nature exists, and all of nature is composed of matter alone. Accordingly, the term *naturalism* will refer to the view that only nature exists, and the term *naturalist* to one who believes that only nature exists. And now, the views of Smith, a naturalist:

1. *What is ultimate reality?* Only matter exists.

2. *How do we know things/how is knowledge possible?* Sense experience alone is the basis of knowledge. Physical objects are the only things that exist, so the physical process of sense experience is the only possible modality of knowledge.

3. *What is the nature and source of the physical world?* The physical world exists as a fact, but its existence is inexplicable, making the world a random event. It may be that matter has always existed and will always exist, or matter may have had a beginning, but its existence cannot be explained by anything beyond it, because there is nothing beyond matter by which to explain it.

4. *What is human nature/what is human being?* Human beings are complex physical things that are products of a random physical process. Our minds and our personalities are essentially reducible to the brain—a remarkably elaborate and complex system of electrochemical reactions. We may consider ourselves to be special and important, and we may consider the human race to be special and important to us, but there could not possibly be a cosmic sense in which humanity is special and important, since the cosmos is simply matter alone, and it does not think, feel or desire.

5. *What is the human condition/what is wrong with humanity?* From this naturalist's perspective, this is an odd question. It is like looking at a normal tree and asking, "What is its condition, what is its problem?" Humans are what they are—that is, random products of a blind physical process. They live, experience pleasure and pain, have thoughts, dreams, plans, and emotions, and then they die.

6. *What is the solution or response to the human condition?* Humans can attempt to prolong life, they can attempt to decrease pain, and they can attempt to increase pleasure, but that is all.

7. *What is the nature of value and morality?* Values for this naturalist derive from humans' most basic desires—life and pleasure. All morality ultimately is a conventional human construct to maximize these values. Ultimately, words such as good, bad, right, wrong, just, unjust, moral and immoral have no intrinsic meaning. They have meaning within various humans' ethical systems only as means of guiding and motivating behavior in order to achieve, for an individual or society, the ultimate values of life and pleasure.

8. *What is the nature of history and the future for humanity?* As part of natural history, human history is the unfolding story of this remarkable but accidental and inexplicable part of nature—human life. Human history contains many high moments and many low moments. Humans can attempt to do better, and often do so, but ultimately there is no goal or overarching purpose for history. Apart from their desire, and attempts, to continue their individual and collective lives, there is no future for humanity.[4]

As a first comment, it is good to note that there are numerous different versions of a basic naturalist worldview, Smith's being one variant. All naturalist worldviews will share in common the answers given here by Smith to

---

[4]With regard to the morally relevant worldview questions, WQs 5-7, we have represented this atheist as possessing a greater candor and bluntness regarding his views about the nature of morality than is normally the case with naturalistic atheists. Few atheists care to draw attention to some of the more depressing implications of their views. Their metaphysical views, however, do actually strongly imply these rather stark implications about morality and meaning, but atheists are rarely ready to volunteer these views so bluntly. With the exception of the responses to WQs 5-7, these responses have been suggested by James W. Sire's treatment of the worldview of *naturalism* (2004b), pp. 59-76).

the most basic metaphysical questions, WQs 1-3 and 8 (the questions that concern the ultimate nature of reality), but different atheists provide alternative answers to WQs 4-7, the questions that concern human nature and morality. While Smith's answers reveal him to be a rather frank and blunt thinker on these issues, it is an open question whether the "softer" and more palatable answers of other naturalists can be rationally sustained in light of the metaphysics established by the core naturalist answers to WQs 1-3 and 8.

Next, notice that all Smith's responses here are consistent applications of the basic stance of naturalism to the specific questions, resulting in a high degree of coherence. (It is important to note here that while coherence is a major factor in assessing worldviews, there are other important factors to consider.)

Before moving away from our fictional naturalist, Mr. Smith, we want to circle back briefly to the opening question: *Does worldview matter, particularly within the context of leadership?* Consider that although the daily functional morality of most naturalists is largely the same as the morality of religious people, it is clear that their morality is not "coming from" the same place. And it is clear that Smith and religious people would believe very different things about human nature and human destiny. These differences will likely impact the way that leadership happens. Suppose that Smith is a leader in a large organization employing a very diverse workforce, one that surely includes religious people. As a leader, he will use an array of concepts shared with the others in the organization in order to connect with them to cast a vision to motivate them and harness their energies and resources to achieve the organization's goals. As a naturalist, however, Smith's palette of concepts simply will not include many of the "colors" that connect with the deepest commitments and desires of religious people. Because of these profound worldview differences, he will have greater difficulty in reaching and speaking to some of the strongest motivating desires they possess. To be sure, Smith believes that those religiously distinctive worldview elements (transcendent dimension, loving God, God-given purpose, hope, etc.) simply are not reasonable to believe in, but rational or not, it still follows that those powerful motivating elements will be extremely difficult for him to reach in attempting to connect vitally with those members of his organization.

It is important to be clear about what this example is intended to show. First, it is *not* intended to show that a religious worldview is better than a naturalist worldview. That sort of assessment is very complex and needs to be done carefully (as will be discussed below). Second, this example is not meant to assert that naturalists are inherently poorer leaders than religious people, or that religious people make better leaders than naturalists. In fact, there are many excellent and poor leaders from all worldviews. This example is only intended to show that a significant difference in worldview will have an impact on how important functions of leadership happen within an organization, especially one possessing (with regard to worldview) heterogeneous membership.

TRUTH, RATIONALITY AND WORLDVIEW

Our primary objective is to speak in some detail about Christian worldview and its implications for leadership. Prior to that, however, we must address some key concerns in the general vicinity of epistemology (theory of knowledge). These questions and concerns would arise immediately (and with very good reason) if we were simply to launch into the full consideration of Christian worldview, so it is most efficient to anticipate those questions with a brief, preliminary examination.

First is the question of whether everyone possesses a worldview. This is widely claimed by evangelicals who deal with Christian worldview (see, e.g., Sire 2004b, p. 17; Dockery 2008, p. 36) and may be accurate or inaccurate depending on exactly what is meant. If the concept of worldview properly applies only to the relatively explicit, intentional and comprehensive formulation of views about the ultimate issues (as defined above), then the claim is decidedly false, since many people have no interest in the intellectual work required to achieve this. If, however, the concept of possessing a worldview is sufficiently elastic to include the minimal notion of one's implicit, pretheoretical *attitude* toward life and the world, or having a *hunch*, *suspicion* or *intuition* about ultimate, important matters, then it is arguably true that everyone possesses a worldview. Even those who profess to have no views of any kind on these matters (and there are many such people) still reveal, in the living of their lives, whether they assume that (for example) life is lived before a transcendent authority, or not. This evidence from life can reveal tacit assumptions about ultimate issues. For this usage, more minimal and subjectively toned terms such as *vision, perspective* or *standpoint* are probably more appropriate than *worldview*. One's vision or standpoint might be considered the implicit kernel of a worldview. Ultimately, however, it is best not to think in terms of a two-pole distinction. Instead, the territory between "mere hunch" on the one hand and explicit and comprehensive worldview on the other hand actually constitutes a continuum of more or less well-developed insight and opinion into the nature of things.[5]

An implication for Christian leadership here is that this kernel perspective that is arguably present in everyone's thought or life can be drawn forth, examined, expanded and built on for purposes of connecting with and more significantly engaging the commitment of those with whom one is working or ministering.

The second and third areas of concern—truth and rationality—need to be introduced together, especially where worldview is concerned. Truth and rationality do indeed belong together, but *how* they are understood together in regard to the matter of worldview is critical.

People at all levels have gotten tangled up about truth—for a good reason. They know that truth and rationality are both important, but all too often they do not know how to put the two together, especially with regard to tricky subjects such as worldview. Rather than abandon one or the other, a frequent solution is to twist truth (many different twists have been attempted) so that potential tensions with rationality seem to dissolve. These solutions, however, are never satisfactory, since the various twists that are given to truth always end up producing even graver problems. The only fruitful way to proceed is to get clear about truth first, and then fold in the question of the rationality of worldviews.

As respected Christian philosopher Dallas Willard (1999) has put it, "What truth is is very simple and very obvious." A statement is true if it presents the world *as it is*. In other words, a statement is true if its claim about the world is accurate. For a simple example of this, consider the statement "The broom is in the closet." It is beyond trivial to say that this statement is true if indeed the broom *is* in the closet, and it is false if the

---

[5]Taken altogether, Charles Taylor's usage of "world-picture" seems midway on this continuum (see Taylor 2007, pp. 232, 352-53, 366-67, 651).

broom *is not* in the closet. Note that the truth or falsity of the statement is independent of what we think, believe or wish about the location of the broom. Willard's (1999) definition, in more comprehensive form, says exactly this: "A representation or statement or belief is true if what it is about is as it is presented in the representation or belief or statement." Put plainly, truth is a matter of getting reality right. This understanding of truth has historically been called the correspondence theory of truth, and more recently is referred to as a *realist* view of truth.[6]

Some readers are now surely thinking that this is too easy, too simplistic, especially when dealing with the tricky subjects of God and morality. We hasten to assure those thinkers that there will be complication and difficulty. The difficulty, however, is not with the *nature* of truth. Whether one asserts "The broom is in the closet" or "God exists," one is asserting something about the nature of reality. These two very different statements are alike in being true or false in exactly the same way. They are true if their content (in Willard's words, *what the statement is about*) accurately presents reality, and false if they do not. The difficulty is not with the *nature* of truth; the difficulty lies in *determining* truth, determining whether a statement does in fact get reality right. We turn to this matter in just a moment.

The realist view of truth—that there is a world outside of our minds, independent of our minds, that our minds strive to know accurately—is to be contrasted with a view that can broadly be referred to as a *constructivist* view of truth. This view holds that in large measure, a world outside of our minds cannot be reliably accessed or known in an objective way. In light of this, truth is in large measure constructed by our minds in accordance with our individual or socially aggregated perspectives. (For the clearest presentation of this idea, see Rorty 1979, 1987).

It is not our task in this chapter to argue in favor of a realist view of truth. Rather, our task here is simply to make the delineation between realist and constructivist understandings of truth and clearly indicate that, among

---

[6]This is essentially the view of truth articulated by eminent epistemologist Susan Haack (1998), which she calls "innocent realism" (pp. 156-57). In another more recent, admirably clear book, University of Connecticut philosopher Michael P. Lynch (2004) describes the same position by saying that "truth is objective," and "true beliefs are those that portray the world as it is and not as we may hope, fear, or wish it to be" (pp. 10, 12). Finally, this view is strongly and decisively expounded and defended in Groothuis 2000, pp. 86-92.

those involved in the project of Christian worldview, the overwhelming majority view of truth is the realist view (Colson and Pearcey 1999, pp. 21-26; Dockery 2008, pp. 37-38; Geisler and Watkins 1989, p. 6; Groothuis 2000, pp. 86-92;[7] Holmes 1983, p. 129; Moreland 2007, pp. 68-72; Moreland and Craig 2003, pp. 131-33; Sire 2004b, p. 19; Willard 2009, pp. 56-58). As a way of testing whether truth is about *getting reality right*, try using the word *true* in a sentence that also includes *not* accurately presenting reality. One will see, intuitively, that this makes no sense at all. Consider this sentence, ostensibly about some aspect of Christian faith: "This is the Christian position, and it is indeed true, *but it is not the way reality is.*" No sensible person could ever say something like that, so it follows that truth really does mean *the accurate presentation of reality*. Christian worldview thinkers are presuming, in their work, to present reality as it is. Their view of truth is the realist view.

Now, finally, rationality. For our purposes here, this complex subject can be kept at a very basic level. As a thought experiment, note that the following line is something that no one would ever genuinely say: "This belief of mine is irrational, and I want you to believe it too." We would never say something like this because we know intuitively that we cannot believe things we ultimately believe to be irrational.[8] We can only believe things that, at some level or other, commend themselves to our reason. Nor can we genuinely invite others to believe something that we regard as being in violation of reason. If we urge others to consider believing something that we believe, it follows that it makes sense or seems reasonable to us, at least at some level, and that we believe that others will find it so as well.[9] Accordingly, when introducing others to one's worldview, it is best to acknowledge that not only does one think the worldview is *true*, but also that it is in some measure *rational* to think that it is true.

---

[7]Groothuis uses the term *correspondence theory of truth.*

[8]Of course, those who think that reason is incompetent to apprehend truth, or at least truth concerning ultimate matters, will reject this claim. One famous example of such a thinker was the brilliant but eccentric Danish Christian philosopher Søren Kierkegaard, who claimed that absurdity was the signal hallmark of truth. His approach to ideas, a fideistic-based existentialism, provided a powerful vehicle for mounting a damaging critique of the reigning philosophy of his day. Although Kierkegaard's thinking on this matter is deliciously dramatic, it has not been seen as any kind of basis for a functional, holistic and comprehensive view of truth for all.

[9]This is essentially the sense of rationality presented by Harvard philosopher Robert Nozick (1993, pp. 98-100, 107-9).

Of course, however, nothing is clearer than the fact that reasonable people disagree constantly about the most important matters, and disagreements about the ultimate issues—reality, God, morality, meaning and purpose—are among the most hotly debated. The apparent lack of progress toward rational consensus easily leads many people to believe that reason is incapable of penetrating these matters in a decisive way to determine truth— to determine the way things truly are. This popular view is understandable, but it is not actually true itself. When properly understood, and diligently and patiently applied, reason can indeed make progress in determining truth concerning the ultimate issues.

We first need some understanding of why some might think that reason is impotent with regard to ultimate issues. Our reasoning faculties are most effective with rather concrete matters that are decisively settled by a straightforward series of observations, or observations combined with simple logical inferences. For example, the scientific method has been sharpened over the centuries to produce situations where the observation of an experiment's outcome will either tend to confirm or decisively disconfirm a clear, clean hypothesis. The ultimate issues, however—those issues constituting worldviews—are at once both highly complex and abstract. There is (almost by definition) no straightforward series of observations that will confirm or disconfirm a statement about an ultimate issue.

Consider the meaning of life (whether we have one, and if so, so what?). This concept enfolds all the richness of human existence (our nature, our capacities, our identity, our hopes, our fears, our dreams, etc.) and all this set in the context of the ultimate nature of reality as a whole. We know intuitively that there is no simple series of observations or a simple logical inference that will produce a decisive answer to questions about this. Instead, any adequate answer to the question of the meaning of life will involve a multifaceted inquiry involving all manner of evidence.

Here is a moment for leadership. It seems that we can expect that reasoning about ultimate issues will be difficult, and the results will come far more slowly, and partially, than we would like. Progress requires strong logical skills, perseverance, diligence, sensitivity to the subtleties of human life and culture, humility, and courage. Why humility? These matters are complex, and the evidence is sometimes so partial and subtle in nature that it is often subject to alternative interpretations. The important question, however, is *whether the alternative interpretations are equally plausible or rational*; it is this task of refined judgment to which we are called. Why does all this take courage? It would be easy to avoid controversy and effort by saying that all worldviews are equally true or rational (heaven forbid!) Such a position is open to numerous logical challenges, but it also has the fatal flaw of committing us to saying that the worldviews of, for example, Mother Teresa and the Nazis are rationally indistinguishable. Such a grotesque and absurd outcome compels us to commit to articulating the grounds of reality that warrant rational judgments concerning good and evil. To be sure, the pleasant face, good humor and high social standing of today's moral nihilism make this difficult, but that is why the distinctive concept of Christian leadership in this key area is critical.

So how do we go about rationally arguing for truth on the important but difficult matters involved in Christian worldview thinking? There are serious divisions among Christian thinkers concerning this question, but most would agree, at least in concept, with the following understanding, significantly requiring both humility and breadth.

Humility is crucial. As discussed above, worldview thinking is simply not susceptible to the rational decisiveness we crave in these matters of ultimate concern. In these sorts of discussions, we rarely see matters as easy to settle as whether or not the broom is in the closet. It is usually not possible to say "Idea X is therefore decisively proven to be false," or "Idea X is therefore proven to be absolutely true." We need to be prepared for partial or intermediate answers such as the following:

Negative-tending conclusion statement types

- Idea X is unlikely to be true, given these considerations.[10]

- Idea X is significantly challenged by a couple of important considerations.

---

[10]For a real-life (and startling!) example of this sort of statement, consider the claim made by New York University philosopher of mind Thomas Nagle, an ardent atheist, who recently published the view that he can no longer believe in materialist reductionism (the assumption that all reality reduces to physical processes). He states, "For a long time I have found the materialist account of how we and our fellow organisms came to exist *hard to believe*, including the standard version of how the evolutionary process works" (2012, p. 5, emphasis ours).

Affirmative-tending conclusion statement types

- Idea X has some merit, given these considerations.

- Idea X is a more satisfactory way of viewing subject A than idea Y.

- Idea X is the best explanation available for subject A.

Although statements of these kinds are nondefinitive—they reveal that the matter is open for further debate—still, they are actually very good news. Assuming adequate rational support for them, statements of these kinds would show that rational progress toward truth is distinctly possible in the realm of ultimate concerns. Consider that if enough of the conclusion statements about a worldview's elements (WQs 1-8, for example) were *negative-tending*, it would mean that the worldview as a whole would be unlikely to be true. In the other direction, a worldview for which numerous (adequately supported) conclusion statements about its elements were *affirmative-tending* would be more likely to be true. It actually can be entirely reasonable to say things like the following statements:

- It is highly implausible to think that worldview A is true.

- Worldview A is more likely to be true than worldview B.

- Worldview A is more likely to be true than any other worldview.

In light of these possible outcomes, while reason can give strong indication, it is quite the case that for *all* worldviews there is plenty of room for faith.

Here, now, is the critical question: *Can careful inquiry about the ultimate issues of worldview achieve results that will allow even these nondefinitive conclusions?* The answer is a strong *yes*. Careful, thoughtful inquiry indeed does show that there are distinctly better and worse answers to all the worldview issues, and these answers can mount up sufficiently to warrant the judgment that a given worldview is the most rational worldview to believe. Further, Christians need not be afraid that Christianity will fare poorly in this sort of inquiry. Indeed, Christianity does very, very well when considered carefully as a worldview. This is where *breadth* comes in.

While this chapter is not tasked with actually engaging in explicit apologetics (defense of the faith, from the Greek word *apologia*, "to give a defense"), we can briefly indicate what it would look like to attempt to show the rationality of a Christian worldview. The overall enterprise would constitute a very large "cumulative case" argument, comprising many different strands of reasoning, all combining their rational weight, in varying degrees, to support the conclusion that the Christian worldview in question presents reality as it is.[11] Some strands of the overall cumulative case argument are instances of linear arguments[12] aimed at establishing reasonable belief for specific elements of Christian worldview such as the existence of God, the reliability of the Bible, the reality of Christ's resurrection and so on, or defending Christianity from specific negative attacks. Other strands employ reasoning in the form of *argument to the best explanation* to show that laudable elements of culture or ways of life are most consistent with Christian worldview, or that dysfunctional elements of culture are inconsistent with a Christian worldview. A high-level application of this approach is to show that critical elements of human experience, values and essential concepts (consciousness, self-consciousness, thought, reason, love, truth, goodness, justice, hope, meaning, purpose, etc.) really only make sense within a Christian worldview.

In all of this, the objective is to make a rational determination of truth according to the primary standards for rational inquiry—evidence and coherence—and considered in the light of this objective, Christian worldview fares very well indeed. The linear and explanatory arguments aim to provide abundant direct evidence that central features of Christian worldview are true. This is reinforced by coherence considerations—namely, that the entire web of belief constituting Christian worldview exhibits mutually reinforcing rational connections between the elements of the worldview, showing that the set of beliefs is not random or haphazard, but organic and comprehensive.[13] To show that Christian worldview covers thought, life and experience organically, coherently and comprehensively is a powerful marker of truth.

An analogy may be helpful. Consider a large meeting tent. It is of no value as a tent unless the fabric is elevated off the ground, so the tent poles are

---

[11]The work of Douglas Groothuis (2000) has been most helpful to us in this section, especially pp. 175-82.

[12]The term *linear arguments* is a less technical way of referring to rather straightforward deductive or inductive arguments, or combinations thereof.

[13]For a good discussion of the concept of coherence in Christian worldview thinking, see Holmes (1983, pp. 51-53).

essential. But even when elevated, the fabric of the tent will not perform its function well unless the fabric itself is of high quality, durable, reinforced well in critical places and properly fitted to withstand the strain of the poles and anchor ropes. The tent poles can be thought of as the analogs for the arguments providing good evidence of the truth of critical elements of Christian worldview. The quality, durability and reinforcement of the tent fabric as a whole can be thought of as the analog for the coherent nature of the "fabric" of belief in Christian worldview. And ultimately, the final test is that Christian faith speaks to the heart of individuals and makes sense of their lives. To speak metaphorically, the tent of Christian worldview is doing very well. Now, let's look at the fabric itself.

LEADERSHIP AND CHRISTIAN WORLDVIEW

What makes Christian leadership unique is Christian worldview. Christian worldview comprises a remarkable set of beliefs that offer the very best answers possible to the worldview questions. It is not, however, just a set of beliefs; *it is a way of life*. To be a Christian is to live all of life in a new way, according to new principles—God's principles. About three thousand years ago, King David wrote:

> Blessed are those whose ways are blameless,
>> who walk according to the law of the LORD.
> Blessed are those who keep his statutes
>> and seek him with all their heart. (Psalm 119:1-2)

Note "ways," "walk," "keep" and "seek him with all their heart." In this passage, David clearly teaches that following God is a way of life. Accordingly, Christian leadership should not only be considered to be a systematic way of thinking about and conducting leadership, but one which most certainly encompasses a prescription of what *kind of person* we should become in order to be one who leads effectively as a Christian. In the following, then, look not only for teaching on what a leader should *do*, but on how a leader should *be*. (The *doing* comes from the *being*.)

As we begin to unfold Christian worldview and its leadership implications, a qualification is in order. While Christian leadership argues for ethics informed by Christian principles, neither this chapter nor this book argues for a theocracy, either at the micro or macro level. A leader's formal position is not a throne from which to mandate conformity to his or her beliefs. The challenge for Christian leaders is discerning when and how to render appropriately the things due Caesar and due God at the same time (Matthew 22:21) while living in a world they are technically not part of (John 17). The apostle Paul uses the metaphor of an ambassador in 2 Corinthians 5:20 to illuminate that while the Christian lives in a foreign land, he or she represents, in life and word, the Master of his or her country of citizenship. Paul continues this metaphor in Philippians 3:20 when he states, "Our [Christians'] citizenship is in heaven."

We are now ready to consider the elements of Christian worldview and their implications for leadership. Given the specific nature of Christian faith, it is most appropriate to begin by addressing WQ 2, the epistemological question: *How do we know things/how is knowledge possible?* Christians generally embrace the standard modalities of knowing, including sense experience as well as reason, and in patterns of reasoning—both induction and deduction.[14] In addition, however, Christians believe that there is a God who has created both human beings and the physical world, and two important concepts follow from this belief. First, according to Christian worldview, the ability of humans to know the world is not accidental. Rather, Christians believe that God has created both humans and the world such that the human modalities of knowing are effective in coming to know the world. Knowledge is the result of design, not accident. Second, Christians believe that God has deliberately revealed himself and his ways to us, known broadly in theology as the doctrine of revelation.

General and special revelation. God desires us to know him and his purposes, so he has revealed himself to us in various ways, which theologians cluster under the heading "general and special revelation." Special revelation encompasses "those acts of God whereby he makes himself and

---

[14]*Induction* is reasoning that is aimed at providing rational support for a conclusion such that the conclusion is viewed as being logically probable (as opposed to being improbable). An example conclusion from such an argument would look something like the following: "Therefore, it is highly likely that the Dow Jones Industrial Average will remain above 14,000 for the remainder of 2013." *Deduction* is reasoning that is aimed at providing rational support for a conclusion such that, given the premises, the conclusion follows with logical necessity. An example of such an argument is the following classic: (1) All men are mortal; (2) Socrates is a man; (3) therefore, Socrates is mortal.

his truth known at special times and to specific peoples" (Thiessen 1979, p.7). The incarnation of Jesus, Scripture, the Holy Spirit, the church and prayer are all avenues of special revelation, but preeminently, it is the Bible (the objective record of God's most dramatic and specific revelation of himself and his ways, discussed below) in which God makes himself known in the contemporary world.

This is in contrast to general revelation, typically "addressed to all intelligent creatures generally and accessible to all; it has for its object the supplying of the natural need of the man and the persuasion of the soul to seek after the true God" (Thiessen 1979, p. 7). God has revealed much of his own nature as well as truths about humanity and morality throughout his creation (Romans 1:18-20). Historical and contemporary leadership models, "reading" humanity through the lens of social science, are knowingly or unknowingly based on data that has derived from God's general revelation. Since all truth is God's truth, models incorporating reliable inferences from this data will contain elements of truth and are therefore applicable to Christian models of leadership. This does not mean that all the results of social science are true. Far from it! It only means that social science, if done carefully and judiciously, can attain to truth, and that this truth will be a result of God's general revelation.

A Christian worldview will incorporate truths found in both special and general revelation. The nature of special revelation, and particularly the Bible, requires that it has priority over general revelation when reconciling incompatible truth claims. For example, an interpretation of data from general revelation could suggest to some that an unborn fetus does not qualify as a life. Many Christians, using special revelation found in Psalm 139, believe life begins at conception. While some questions of interpretation can be raised in this case, the general principle is that Christian worldview reconciles competing worldview claims by giving the Bible the last word when it speaks clearly on a matter of reality, morality, faith and practice.

As with general revelation, interpretations from special revelation can be in error. This is not saying the Bible has errors, just that people can make erroneous conclusions from the Bible. Extreme historic examples include Hitler and American slaveholders, who both used biblical texts to justify their various atrocities. A comprehensive and systematic understanding of all Scripture cannot possibly be viewed as supporting mass murder or the enslavement of some humans by others. A sound worldview is predicated on a full and accurate interpretation of information provided in both general and special revelation.

The Bible. The Bible is the most complete and detailed source of knowledge we have concerning God and his ways, so it is a major part of a Christian answer to WQ 2. Theologian Clark Pinnock has said, "The Bible is the golden grail of all philosophical thought because it affords a perspective upon life and history which originates beyond the flux of human situation. It is, therefore, the clue to the meaning of life and reality, the only sure antidote to the rootlessness of modern man cut off from his transcendent ground" (1971, p. 230).

The Bible is able to afford this "perspective upon life and history" because, as Paul states, "all Scripture is inspired by God and profitable for teaching, for reproof, for correction, for training in righteousness; so that the man of God may be adequate, equipped for every good work" (2 Timothy 3:16-17 NASB). The doctrine of inspiration implies that the Bible serves as the final authority in inferences about the nature of reality, morality, faith and practice. Paul admonishes Christians to be laborers in the Bible in order to handle accurately the "word of truth" (2 Timothy 2:15).

Two examples show how Scripture serves as final authority over human reasoning. First, Machiavelli, in his theory of political leadership for the effective prince, certainly thought that historical observation abundantly proved that *the end justifies the means*, but this all-too-human conclusion is overridden by the biblical admonition to let everything be done in a just and loving manner (Micah 6:8; 1 Corinthians 16:14). Second, the biblical principle of stewardship of resources (1 Corinthians 4:1-2) overrides policies and practices that justify the exploitation of human and physical capital to enhance the bottom line. In both cases, God's special word to us in the Bible draws us to a higher mode of human life than seems possible when we are left to our own, human, resources.

The implications of the doctrine of biblical authority for Christian leaders are many. One, they are to be scholars of the Bible who handle the Word of truth accurately (2 Timothy 2:15) and long for the Word of God as their sustenance (1 Peter 2:2). Second, they must seek to implement relevant biblical principles in all of their decisions and actions. For example, as modeled by Christ, Christians are to treat people with dignity and grace, even their enemies (Matthew 5:44). Christians are to stand for justice and mercy, especially for those who are vulnerable to injustices, such as orphans and widows (James 1:27). Christians are to conduct all business practices with integrity by letting their "yes" be "yes" (Matthew 5:37). Even when a specific concern is not directly addressed in the Bible (surgical procedures, for example), knowledge of broader biblical principles (in this case, the importance of health, personal prudence and comfort) can assist Christian leaders to make wise, godly choices throughout the full scope of life.

In summary, careful attention to the Bible's teachings and principles equips leaders with authoritative understanding of the purpose and nature of life, the proper ordering of priorities and values, and principles for healthy relationships and lifestyles. A classic Old Testament example can be seen in the case of the four young men—Daniel, Shadrach, Meshach and Abednego— taken from Judah and deported to Babylon, where they were forced to enter a royal imperial leadership training program. They profited from listening to God's Word and followed God's dietary laws, refusing to eat the king's food at the risk of losing their privileged positions. Because they were faithful to God's Word, far from suffering, they flourished in their training and became favored counselors to the king, demonstrating God's blessings that can be found in obedience (Daniel 1).

The nature of God. WQ 1 asks *What is ultimate reality?* and Christian worldview's answer is "God." Christian teaching on God answers not only that first worldview question, but it also provides the basis for distinctively Christian answers to several of the other questions as well. We can offer here only the briefest possible overview of the doctrine of God,[15] the central element of Christian worldview, and we will approach this overview from the perspective of addressing worldview questions the answers to which are strongly driven by the answers to WQ 1.

To begin, the most important thing to say about God is that he is spirit, eternal, changeless and self-existing. God's being is wholly other than physical being. Because he is immaterial, without body or parts, his being does not

---

[15]See Grudem (1999) or any number of other excellent works of theology for a full treatment of the nature of God.

suffer the limitations that attend physical matter. God is eternal; there has never been, nor will there ever be, a time when he did not exist. God does not change; since he is perfect and complete in his being, any change would diminish him. God is self-existing, self-causing, if you will. God's existence does not depend on anything except himself. This is an important part of the meaning of God's statement to Moses when speaking from the burning bush: "I AM WHO I AM" (Exodus 3:14). God is absolute being.

These attributes, when put together with the attributes of omnipotence (all-powerful) and omniscience (all-knowing), constitute the basis for understanding God as creator and sustainer of the physical universe, Christian worldview's answer to WQ 3. His act of creation begins the Christian story: "In the beginning God created the heavens and the earth" (Genesis 1:1). For worldview purposes, a few points are crucial. First, God's perfect, eternal and self-sufficient being predates the physical world, so the physical world is metaphysically separate from God's being. It is *dependent* on God, but it is *not* God. Second, "in the beginning" there was nothing but God, and then he created world, out of nothing except from the speaking of his command: "And God said, 'Let there be light'" (Genesis 1:3). Third, the creation narrative concludes with the remarkable statement, "God saw all that he had made, and it was very good" (Genesis 1:31). Creation is good, *very good*, but it is not God. It is not to be worshiped. Rather, its Creator is to be worshiped.

The next key aspect of God's nature to be considered is best captured by the combination of the following three attributes: God as personal, God as relational and God as all-loving. To say that God is personal is to say that essential to his being is thought, emotion and volition. Next, God is a relational being, evident in the Trinity of distinct persons—Father, Son and Holy Spirit—a community in relationship constituting the unity that is God's being. And as John the disciple of Jesus states, "God is love" (1 John 4:16). That is, love is of the essence of God's nature, and is the chief characteristic of all his actions. Now, this has relevance for WQ 4, *What is human nature/what is human being?* Consider an important aspect of the doctrine of creation, that human beings are created "in the image of God" (Genesis 1:27). This is an extremely rich doctrine, part of which is the implication that all human beings mirror elements of the Creator himself as being persons with a spiritual dimension, relational beings, moral agents and beings who find love to be so critical to their lives. Christian leaders will understand that in building community and in fostering loving relationships among those in their groups, they are building upon and developing human factors that are part of the very fabric of all reality.

The last key aspect of God's nature to be considered in connection with Christian worldview is the moral nature of God, his holiness and perfect goodness. This aspect provides, for Christian worldview, part of the answer to WQ 7, *What is the nature of value and morality?* God's holiness (in the moral dimension) speaks to his purity and complete freedom from all evil thought or deed. To say that God is all-good (omnibenevolent) is to say that in all his relationships, his actions are entirely focused on the good of the other. Both of these attributes characterize the very essence of God's nature, so that means that the goodness and morality toward which we strive in our lives have their standards in the very nature of God. Goodness and morality are objective and real. It is well understood that society requires genuine leadership (intellectual and organizational) in the realm of morality. It is good to know that leadership in this dimension helps draw people toward the heart of God.

The incarnation. The incarnation of God in the person of Jesus Christ (John 1:14) is the heart of Christian faith, providing the key element of Christianity's answer to WQ 6. In Christ, we have a suffering servant who makes redemption possible and provides eternal life to those who believe (1 John 5:11-13). As we learn from the story of Nicodemus in John 3, one who believes in Jesus is "born again" into a new life centered on a personal relationship with Christ (John 1:12), with a new nature that is oriented toward God, allowing the believer to begin to live a life that honors God.

THE BIBLICAL NARRATIVE

It is difficult to grasp the essence of the Christian worldview without knowing "the biblical story," at least in short form. It also richly sets up many important leadership lessons that flow from Christian faith. In light of this, we offer an overview of the central story of the Bible. This narrative can be seen to contain important parts of Christian worldview's answers to WQs 5, 6 and 8.

God created a place for humans to worship him without distraction and in pure uninterrupted fellowship (the Garden of Eden, Genesis 1–2). In an event referred to as "the fall" (Genesis 3), sin entered the world when humans chose to disobey God (they had been forbidden by God to eat of the tree of the knowledge of good and evil), corrupting their relationship with God and with creation. The good news is that God provided the payment for sin, as well as the promise to redeem individuals, mankind and creation. This payment was Christ's atonement on the cross and the defeat of death through his resurrection—"Christ died for our sins according to the Scriptures, that he was buried, that he was raised on the third day according to the Scriptures" (1 Corinthians 15:3-4). The book of Revelation ends with the utopia provided in Genesis 1 and 2 restored in the form of a new earth and Jerusalem in which the redeemed can now safely eat from the tree of life that was originally in the Garden of Eden. (This vision of restoration provides an important part of Christian worldview's answer to WQ 8.) Table 2.1 illustrates the symmetry and continuity of the Christian message from Genesis through Revelation in which Christ's atoning work is central to the plot.

Table 2.1.

A. Genesis 1—A specific place to dwell with God

B. Genesis 2:15-17—Garden of Eden, trees
   Genesis 3:15—The first hint of a Messiah

C. Genesis 3:22—Adam and Even kicked out of the Garden of Eden lest they eat from the tree of life

Everything in between Genesis 3 and Revelation 21 is about restoration/transformation in establishing the kingdom of God.

A. Revelation 21:1-2—New heaven and new earth

B. Revelation 21:10-27—New Jerusalem

C. Revelation 22:1-2—Tree of life

As a result of the fall, everything between Genesis 3 and Revelation 21 is about transforming broken individuals and relationships and establishing the kingdom of God (the central plot of the Bible narrative). God's transformation in people's lives can be thought to have two elements or two moments— redemption and sanctification. An analogy may be helpful. Imagine that a man has pawned a valuable but broken and tarnished antique clock in a pawnshop. In order to fully transform the clock into its proper, exquisite condition, the man must purchase it back (redeem it) and then repair and restore it to its rightful beauty and proper running condition. Sanctification is, for followers of God, the process of being repaired and brought back to beauty and order by God. We will discuss redemption first, then sanctification.

Redemption begins the work of transformation, when God restored the relationship between himself and individuals by paying the penalty exacted by sin ("For the wages of sin is death"—Romans 6:23). The first hint of the gospel is in Genesis 3:15-21, in which God promised a deliverer and provided an animal sacrifice to cover the original sin. As the Old Testament unfolds, more information on the nature of God and his redemption plan is revealed, all of which point to the coming Messiah, foreshadowing Christ's death on the cross and resurrection from the dead.

As revealed in the biblical narrative, God created people to have fellowship with him, when something went amiss. Humanity's fall into sin, and its implications for life and society, constitutes Christian worldview's answer to the second half of WQ 5, *What is wrong with humanity?* Rather than leaving mankind in an eternal state of separation, God's holiness and mercy converged to make the payment for sin possible and began the work of restoration and transformation of individual believers. This entire story, from the fall through Christ's redemptive work, can be viewed as God's progressive revelation of himself and his plan of salvation, his revealing of himself through history in progressively more detailed and specific ways, yielding greater knowledge and understanding of the deepest things. The first glimmer of insight comes with God's provision and covering for sin as early as Genesis 3:21, through the Abrahamic (Genesis 12:1-3) and Davidic (2 Samuel 7:4-17) covenants, and the unfolding message of the Pentateuch, prophets and writings. All of this documents God's plan of redemption to its ultimate fulfillment in Jesus Christ (Luke 24:44-47), the key element of Christianity's answer to WQ 6.

Those who have saving faith in Christ trust in his work on the cross as payment for their sin and acknowledge Jesus Christ as Lord. In 2 Corinthians 5:17, the apostle Paul talks about the transformation of individuals that comes with believing: "Therefore if anyone is in Christ, he is a new creature; the old things passed away; behold, new things have come" (NASB). Having been justified by faith, as a new creature, the believer is in the process of being transformed from the inside out in what is known as the doctrines of regeneration and sanctification.

Regeneration, the element of redemption that happens within the life of the believer, takes place the moment one receives Christ as articulated in John 1:12: "But as many as received Him, to them He gave the right to become children of God, even to those who believe in His name" (NASB). The believer receives the Holy Spirit at the moment he or she is born again (John 3:1-16; Ephesians 1:13) to become a new creature as told in 2 Corinthians 5:17. At the moment of saving faith, the believer inherits a new self (Colossians 3:10). Even though the believer has a new self, the sin nature is still present. The apostle Paul documents the struggle between the new and old self in Romans 7:14-23, a "war" between the good that we are called to as new creatures and the sin nature that remains in us (for now), dragging us into sinful behavior.

The doctrine of sanctification deals with the continual process of becoming more Christlike. The metaphor of bearing fruit is used to describe the evidence of sanctification in which both God and man are agents in the process. Christians are told to work out their deliverance (salvation) in "fear and trembling," knowing that it is God who is at work in their lives, "both to will and to work for His good pleasure" (Philippians 2:12-13 NASB). Paul reiterates this theme in Galatians 5:16-25. As God's Spirit works in us, as we increasingly "walk by the Spirit," we are led to resist the temptation to sin and to become filled with the fruits (virtues) of Christ himself: "love, joy, peace, patience, kindness, goodness, faithfulness, gentleness, self-control" (Galatians 5:22-23 NASB). This call to walk in the Spirit, acquiring the virtues of Christ, is also a key element of Christianity's answer to WQ 7.

In summary, God created a perfect world that became broken. He is now in the process of returning that broken world to its original intent. God in his wisdom saw fit to create and use people in that plan.

God's plan to use his followers in the process of restoration sets the theme for the Christian's existence. There is a job—the ministry of reconciliation; and there is a title—*ambassador*. Paul explains:

> All this is from God, who reconciled us to himself through Christ and gave us the ministry of reconciliation: that God was reconciling the world to

himself in Christ, not counting people's sins against them. And he has committed to us the message of reconciliation. We are therefore Christ's ambassadors, as though God were making his appeal through us. We implore you on Christ's behalf: Be reconciled to God. (2 Corinthians 5:18-20)

This ministry of reconciliation is for all followers of God, so we are now able to see clearly the distinctive feature of *Christian* leadership. As Christians lead, their leadership should be interwoven with the higher calling of carrying out the ministry of reconciliation in a fallen world. Reconciliation with God essentially calls for the transforming work of redemption and sanctification. Christian leaders, then, must serve others by using their gifts and talents to facilitate transforming redemption and sanctification in the lives of those they lead. Accordingly, a model of Christian leadership as *transformational service* mirrors the central theology of a Christian worldview.

Another implication for Christian leadership from the biblical narrative is that conflict and deceit exist. Leadership is not easy in a fallen world. When Jesus sent the disciples out, he warned them to be "as shrewd as snakes and as innocent as doves" (Matthew 10:16). An adequate model of Christian leadership should recognize that the world is a tricky place, requiring leaders to be judicious (the meaning of "shrewd" in this context) in how they engage others, with the highest ethics ("as innocent as doves").

A CHRISTIAN LEADERSHIP MODEL

A Christian model of leadership is one in which leadership perspectives, practices and habits are congruent with the tenets and habits of the Christian faith. Whether a leader is in a secular or a Christian organization, the Christian leadership model equips leaders to serve transcendent purposes utilizing the transforming power of the Word of God, the example and mind of Christ, the Holy Spirit, the community of believers, and prayer to walk in truth and in a manner worthy of the Christian calling (Ephesians 4:1; 5:1).

A model of Christian leadership first requires at least one participant in the group to be a Christian to fully render the resources available from special revelation. It requires the Christian to walk by the Spirit and to be devoted to prayer, Bible study and the church. The following chapters will further develop a model of Christian leadership. Each chapter uses truths from both special and general revelation to develop relevant leadership principles and practices that align with the whole counsel of God. The truths we reveal in these chapters will be best understood when the reader takes advantage of all the ways God uses his special revelation to reveal truth. Pray for the guidance of the Holy Spirit as you grapple with these chapters. Discuss these ideas with your Christian community and mentors. Explore the Scriptures beyond those that we provide on these topics.

A guiding metaphor for the model of Christian leadership is *ambassador*, as used in 2 Corinthians 5:20. The essence of the metaphor of Christian leadership is transformative service in an alien context. Implied in the metaphor is, first, a particular end—the ambassador serves at the will of the king to further the king's agenda. Second, implied in the metaphor is the means of service, which brings us to a second key metaphor in our model, that of a steward. The ambassador is the steward, not the owner of the resources of his or her king and country. The steward's job is to use those resources (gifts) to advance the king's interests (e.g., truths from special and general revelation, which in the Christian context are transformative). Third, implied in the metaphor are the challenges of a Christian model of leadership—suffering or sacrificial service associated with living in a foreign, war-torn land and judiciously balancing the interests of the sending king with the dynamic demands of the situations in the host country.

By way of summary, the following items are foundational elements for a model in Christian leadership that logically follows from a Christian worldview:

1. Be a Christ follower.

2. Be filled with the Spirit.

3. View your engagement in an organization as a holy calling, a vocation from God.

4. Understand that your vocation is carried out as an ambassador of Christ, a citizen of heaven.

5. Know that you are a steward, not the owner, of the gifts and talents God has given you, and their purpose is to do kingdom work.

6. Experience Christian fellowship on an ongoing basis.

7. Know and apply relevant biblical principles for every word and action.

8. Pray without ceasing.

9. Actively participate in the body of Christ, his church.

10. Align truths from general revelation with special revelation to guide practices.

11. Walk by faith and not by sight (i.e., trust in the Lord and do not lean on your own understanding).

Life and leadership are too complex for a single book to address all the different contingencies that a comprehensive model of leadership needs to address. This book provides a foundation for individuals to construct their model of Christian leadership. In addition to the foundational elements, a model of Christian leadership recognizes that a person has to have relevant competencies associated with education, training and experiences for corresponding leadership positions and roles.

This book helps groom emerging leaders by aligning relevant competencies found in both general and special revelation to form the beginnings of a comprehensive model of Christian leadership. As God works in the life of individual readers, the model becomes more robust as God uses the truths revealed in these chapters to address individual circumstances.

TEST CASES FOR CHRISTIAN LEADERSHIP

Implementing a model of Christian leadership is not easy, in part because as implied in the metaphor and subsequent chapters, balancing the multiple and competing demands associated with different kingdom priorities and values often allows for more than one legitimate solution to a challenging situation. We offer the following examples as a means to think through the initial features of a Christian model of leadership.

A franchise owner who is committed to a model of Christian leadership is confronted by a new requirement to sell greeting cards and gifts that promote and even celebrate a variety of vices and lifestyles. The owner is wrestling with a difficult decision. Should he acquiesce to the new conditions of his franchise agreement or limit his revenue stream by not carrying a full inventory of retail at the risk of losing his business by violating the new conditions of the franchise agreement?

1. What biblical principles justify expanding his inventory to include objectionable items?

2. What biblical principles justify not expanding his inventory?

3. How can prayer, the mind of Christ, the Holy Spirit and church help with the decision?

4. What additional truths from general revelation (sound business and legal practices) can help with the decision?

5. How do both decisions involve a step of faith?

It is not uncommon for leaders to terminate individuals, whether because of right-sizing or incompetence. In a litigious society, a far-too-common practice, even in Christian organizations, is to surprise the employee with the announcement of his or her termination on his or her last day and escort the fallen colleague out of the building. The justification for the clinical treatment is to avoid dialogue in which comments by the employer could potentially be used in an employee wrongful termination lawsuit. In lieu of candid discussion and even a time of prayer in Christian organizations, the new cold-shoulder treatment fails to treat the hurting individual with dignity and compassion.

1. What biblical principles justify implementing an abrupt exit strategy?

2. What biblical principles justify implementing a more gracious exit strategy?

3. How can prayer, the mind of Christ, the Holy Spirit and church help with the decision?

4. What additional truths from general revelation (sound business and legal practices) can help with the decision?

5. How do both decisions involve a step of faith?

REFERENCES

Associated Press. 1997. "Mother Teresa—In Her Own Words." *Washington Post*, September 5. www.washingtonpost.com/wp-srv/inatl/longterm/teresa/stories/words.htm.

Colson, C., and N. Pearcey. 1999. *How Now Shall We Live?* Wheaton, IL: Tyndale House Publishers.

Dockery, D. S. 2008. *Renewing Minds: Serving Church and Society Through Christian Higher Education.* Nashville: B&H Publishing Group.

Geisler, N. L., and W. D. Watkins. 1989. *Worlds Apart: A Handbook on World Views*, 2nd ed. Eugene, OR: Wipf and Stock.

Groothuis, D. 2000. *Truth Decay: Defending Christianity Against the Challenges of Postmodernism*. Downers Grove, IL: InterVarsity Press.

Grudem, W. 1999. *Bible Doctrine: Essential Teachings of the Christian Faith*, abridged ed. Edited by Jeff Purswell. Grand Rapids: Zondervan.

Haack, S. 1998. "Reflections on Relativism: From Momentous Tautology to Seductive Contradiction." In *Manifesto of a Passionate Moderate: Unfashionable Essays*. Chicago: University of Chicago Press.

Holmes, A. F. 1983. *Contours of a World View*. Grand Rapids: Eerdmans.

Lynch, M. P. 2004. *True to Life: Why Truth Matters*. Cambridge, MA: MIT Press.

Moreland, J. P. 2007. *Kingdom Triangle: Recover the Christian Mind, Renovate the Soul, Restore the Spirit's Power*. Grand Rapids: Zondervan.

Moreland, J. P., and W. L. Craig. 2003. *Philosophical Foundations for a Christian Worldview*. Downers Grove, IL: InterVarsity Press.

Nagle, T. 2012. *Mind and the Cosmos: Why the Materialist Neo-Darwinian Conception of Nature Is Almost Certainly False*. Oxford: Oxford University Press.

Naugle, D. K. 2002. *Worldview: The History of a Concept*. Grand Rapids: Eerdmans.

Nozick, R. 1993. *The Nature of Rationality*. Princeton: Princeton University Press.

Orr, J. 1893. *The Christian View of God and the World as Centering in the Incarnation*. Edinburgh: Andrew Eliot.

Pinnock, C. 1971. *Biblical Revelation: The Foundation of Christian Theology*. Chicago: Moody Press.

Rorty, R. 1979. *Philosophy and the Mirror of Nature*. Princeton: Princeton University Press.

———. 1987. "Science and Solidarity." In *Rhetoric of the Human Sciences: Language and Argument in Scholarship and Public Affairs*, edited by J. S. Nelson, A. Megill and D. N. McCloskey, pp. 38-52. Madison: University of Wisconsin Press.

Sire, J. W. 2004a. *Naming the Elephant: Worldview as a Concept*. Downers Grove, IL: InterVarsity Press.

———. 2004b. *The Universe Next Door: A Basic Worldview Catalog*, 4th ed. Downers Grove, IL: InterVarsity Press.

Smith, J. K. A. 2009. *Desiring the Kingdom: Worship, Worldview, and Cultural Formation*. Cultural Liturgies 1. Grand Rapids: Baker Academic.

Stevenson, L. 1987. *Seven Theories of Human Nature*, 2nd ed. New York: Oxford University Press.

Taylor, C. 2007. *A Secular Age*. Cambridge, MA: Harvard University Press.

Thiessen, H. 1979. *Lectures in Systematic Theology*. Grand Rapids: Eerdmans.

Willard, D. 1999. "Truth: Can We Do Without It?" Dallas Willard website. www.dwillard.org/articles/artview.asp?artID=66; *Christian Ethics Today: Journal of Christian Ethics*, April, p. 12.

———. 2009. *Knowing Christ Today: Why We Can Trust Spiritual Knowledge*. New York: HarperCollins.

3

Toward a Biblical Theology of Leadership

Rick Langer

—⚏—

The study of leadership in human institutions has spawned an enormous literature in the past several decades. A host of leadership models have been suggested; a wide variety of survey instruments have been crafted; a multitude of consulting firms have arisen to help people implement the various models that have been put forward. Interest in leadership is not confined to business, education and government; it is prevalent in Christian circles as well. As Beeley and Britton note, "We seem to be living in one of the many times in the history of the church when many are sensing an acute need to recover a sense of the basis of Christian leadership, in order for the church to be able to fulfill its core apostolic mission" (2009, p. 3).

But however much Christianity and the secular culture share an interest in leadership, there are certainly concerns that are unique to the Christian context. For example, a Christian might wonder if leadership is really a properly human task at all. If all authority belongs to God, does not human leadership always entail a usurpation of divine authority? And if human leadership is permitted, what sort of leadership is most in keeping with a prior and foundational commitment to the Christian faith? What are the characteristics of a distinctively Christian leadership model? How does Christian leadership translate into a business or educational or governmental setting? If Christian values conflict with business outcomes, which will win?

In addition to these questions, a Christian must also ask what he or she should make of modern leadership literature. Does it matter at all? Does the reading of such literature simply distract a Christian leader from a focus on Scripture? Do leadership skills acquired by training simply lead one away from dependence on the Spirit? Questions of this sort are not merely curiosities, but rather they are essential to everyone who seeks to follow Christ and serve faithfully in a leadership capacity.

LEADERSHIP AND DIVINE REVELATION

If one seeks to develop a distinctively Christian perspective on leadership, one must first decide what counts as a legitimate source of this sort of knowledge. Should it derive from special revelation through Scripture alone? This sounds like a good path to distinctively Christian thought, but the theological foundation of this claim is unclear. Is God revealed in his Word only, or is he also revealed in his world? The answer to this question depends almost entirely on what one means by "world." In certain contexts, *world* is a near synonym for *sin* or *the world system* or *worldliness*. If this is the case, there would seem to be little or no benefit in augmenting a study of the Word with the study of the world except by way of negative illustration. However, it is also clear that Scripture uses the term *world* as a synonym for *creation*. In this sense, studying "the world" would mean studying the created order—what might be called general revelation. Since leadership is an observable human phenomenon, various approaches to leadership would certainly offer themselves as objects of systematic study.

The merits of such studies should not be discounted, nor should they be dismissed as just a modern fascination with all things scientific. Calvin and Luther both valued general revelation as manifested in Greco-Roman teachings on leadership skills and civil government. As Calvin put it:

> If we reflect that the Spirit of God is the only fountain of truth, we will be careful . . . not to reject or condemn truth wherever it appears. In despising the gifts, we insult the Giver. How, then, can we deny that truth must have beamed on those ancient lawgivers who arranged civil order and discipline with so much equity? Shall we say that the philosophers, in their exquisite researches and skilful description of nature, were blind? (1993, 2.2.15)

There is every reason to think that if the insights of the ancient philosophers were valued during the time of the Reformation, the equivalent would be true in our contemporary setting. There is much to be learned from the "exquisite researches and skilful description of nature" found in contemporary studies of leadership. We should not reject or condemn truth, regardless of where it appears, understanding that the light of truth ultimately shines from God himself.

No doubt appealing to secular studies must be done with caution. Calvin warns those who read the pagan philosophers that "many monstrous falsehoods intermingled with those minute particles of truth scattered up and down in their writings as if by chance" (1993, 2.2.18). Truth is not easy to come by since even our most careful observations are tainted by sin, conditioned by our culture and shaped by the language in which they are expressed. But that does not make careful observation worthless; it just means that the thoughtful observer will have to do his or her best to sift the findings of leadership studies to separate as much as possible the actual observations from the more deeply theory-laden interpretations.

It is worth pointing out that a similar problem is found in our study of Scripture. Though the Word of God contains propositional statements, they are not formulated into a theory of leadership (or economics, or government). Theory building will always depend on interpretation and cultural constructs. In a Christian setting it is also conditioned by a theological inheritance from previous generations or perhaps a confessional framework. A Christian understanding of leadership will necessarily go beyond the pure data of Scripture and include human interpretation, practical application and rational reflection. Theoretical constructs will have layers of theory and culture that must be distinguished from the underlying foundation of Scripture. Ultimately, attempts to construct a biblical theory of leadership will always be fallible, even if Scripture is not.

As we discussed in the previous chapter, it seems, then, that our best approach to developing a truly Christian view of leadership is to include the best findings of both special and general revelation. These findings will need to be carefully scrutinized in light of Scripture, the leading of the Holy Spirit, prayer and the community of believers, but they must also withstand the scrutiny of real-world implementation. The mutual refinement of Christian reflection and real-world observation is essential to the faithful rendering of a Christian vision of leadership.

THEOLOGICAL FOUNDATIONS OF LEADING AND FOLLOWING

The theological roots of any biblical understanding of leadership must grow in the soil of God's authority. There is no authority that is not from God (Romans 13:1). Therefore, human authority is always a delegated authority. God appoints people for particular tasks at particular times (Daniel 4:25, 32, 36). He raises up one person and puts down another (Psalm 75:6-7). Even those who do not know God or recognize him as God are possessors of delegated authority and serve divinely appointed purposes (Isaiah 45:1-7). This does not mean that every act of every leader is good, for God sometimes appoints human leaders as a judgment upon their subjects. Such was the case with evil kings during the Old Testament monarchy, and also when the Babylonians conquered Israel and sent them into exile. Leadership serves divine purposes—by intention or by accident.

Anchoring leadership in God's appointment also implies that there is no such thing as tenure—God appoints for the time he ordains, but there is no guarantee that amount of time coincides with the leader's desires. I am reminded of a Christian friend I once asked about lessons he had learned during his many years as a leader. His immediate response was, "I've learned not to hold on too tightly. It isn't mine anyhow and it will only get ripped out of my hand." This was a man who learned by experience that Christians who are leaders are untenured and subject to the purposes of a God whose ways are not our ways and whose thoughts are not our thoughts.

The delegated nature of human leadership also means that leadership is associated with a certain context. We are not leaders or followers because of gifts or abilities, but rather we are appointed to lead or follow in a particular place and time. We are placed within a certain horizontal context—the social setting or institution in which we serve. This context answers the question of whom or what we are responsible *for*, and will therefore direct much of our leadership task. We are also placed in a vertical context—a chain of authority that answers the question *to* whom we are responsible. This reminds us that delegated leaders are accountable leaders. Leaders cannot lead independently of the purposes of God, who providentially appoints them. Delegated leaders never have the leader's own projects or self-fulfillment as their proper object. Leadership is a sacred gift given for a purpose, and like every other gift, God will demand an accounting for how well that purpose was fulfilled (Matthew 25:14-30).

Leadership and redemptive history. A brief consideration of our place in redemptive history reinforces this view of leadership. Unlike most ancient Near Eastern creation epics, the biblical creation does not arise out of chaotic conflict within a pantheon of warring gods. Instead, creation is made in an orderly fashion and by divine intention. Plants are made as food for the animals. Seas are made for fish to swim even as the sky is made for birds to fly and the ground made for animals to crawl. The stars mark out the season—a sort of divine clock, as it were. In the original creation, human beings are made in God's image. The stated implication of the image is that humans are granted dominion over the created order—ruling as God's likeness or presence. We are to multiply, fill, rule and subdue the earth. Indeed, since human beings are ill-equipped to live in many climates, filling the earth will demand that we subdue it. We are often required to transform our environment in order to render it habitable. But our transformative powers are not intended just to serve human purposes. In Genesis 2, there is a clear synergistic relationship between humanity and creation. God waited to plant a garden because a garden needed tending and there was "no one to work the ground." Furthermore, the animals are brought to the man in order to be named. Clearly human beings are a part of the created order, but it is also clear that we have a special role as stewards over the created order on God's behalf. Creation itself seems to have been made in springtime, so to speak. As C. S. Lewis observes, creation was good, but immature. It was not born full-grown because part of God's intention was that human beings share in the oversight of that maturation process (1972, p. 195; Stackhouse 2008, pp. 46-47).

These facts entail a certain stewardship vision of human leadership. The world is populated with objects that have purposes of their own, not merely the raw material for human passions. We have done well by the object of our stewardship when it blossoms into what it was meant to be, not when we subdue it according to our own will and personal desires. This stewardship component is exactly what is missed in many critiques of human dominion relative to the created order. Lyn White's (1967) famous critique, *The Historical Roots of Our Ecological Crisis*, demonstrates this mistake: "Christianity, in absolute contrast to ancient paganism . . . not only established a dualism of man and nature but also insisted that it is God's will that man exploit nature for his proper ends." This is exactly what humanity is *not* supposed to do. The created order has ends divinely embedded within it. Steward leadership does not allow us to exploit these things for our own purpose but rather to bring this diversity of purposes into harmonious relationship. In a world full of musical instruments, we are called to conduct an orchestra that brings out the beauty and design of the instruments, not run a pawn shop that converts the instruments into cash for our personal disposal.

Our stewardship function within creation does not end with the fall. We continue to tend the garden but now in the face of opposition. We also tend a host of other aspects of the created order that have broken loose from their moorings because of the fall. God may have appointed a boundary for the sea, but in a fallen world we may have to build dikes and levees to assure that the sea stays within those boundaries. In fact, the curse is a reminder of the accountable nature of steward leadership. We have often failed as steward leaders because we have violated our appointed boundaries. The result was a curse on us as leaders and also upon all that was under our stewardship responsibility. The curse made it harder to fulfill our divinely ordained responsibilities, but it did not revoke them. We are still commanded to multiply and fill, except now that job will be attended by pain in childbirth. We are still commanded to tend a garden and subdue the earth, except now that task will be done by the sweat of our brow and complicated by thorns and thistles.

In addition to the foundational themes of creation and fall, the redemptive story of the kingdom also has implications for human leadership. The coming kingdom was inaugurated in Christ, is currently foreshadowed in his church and will ultimately be made manifest in a new creation upon his return. As we steward the created order, we are not simply serving our immediate needs, but we are also reordering things according to God's kingdom purposes. We are not necessarily building the kingdom, but we are offering foretastes. We work to make this world glimmer with the light of the next, that those who have eyes to see and ears to hear may come to the

King in this present age. Again, we do not lead for our own sake and we do not reorder creation for our own purposes. Our authority is delegated and our purposes are preappointed. We lead only as kingdom agents in our present age.

And in the final age, the picture of the new heavens and the new earth is expressed in the image of the New Jerusalem. The story that began in a garden ends in a city—but a city with a garden at its center. A city is perhaps the quintessential expression of human culture building—the ultimate exercise of our world-transforming abilities. In our present age, cities are often places of squalor and oppression, but that is in no small part due to the failures of humans in many functions, including leadership. One day, we will reign with Christ and rule in full accordance with his intentions. We will be faithful stewards; we will embrace our boundaries and pursue our tasks with zeal. The end result is that the city and the garden will meet in final embrace. The garden of creation will find a well-tended home in the human habitation of a city.

These considerations make clear that human leadership is deeply entwined in the narrative of salvation history, but this does not exhaust the biblical material on leadership. The Bible also abounds with examples of leaders, followers, metaphors of leadership and even direct teachings about leadership itself. To complete a biblical background for leadership, these aspects of biblical teaching must also be considered.

Biblical teaching on leadership. The Bible uses various terms and metaphors to refer to human leaders, one being *king*. Often the position of king has a negative connotation. In 1 Samuel 8, when the Jewish monarchy is first being established, the warning given regarding kings is negative. The desire to have a king is viewed as a rejection of God himself. The nature of human kings is predicted to be violent and exploitive, a prediction quickly confirmed in actual practice. The ongoing development of the monarchy is a tragic tale of conflict and division. It is marked by a very small number of good kings and a very large number of bad ones.

The best of the human kings was David, and he is actually far more closely associated with a different term for a leader: the *shepherd*.[1] This description is used by God of the sort of leader David was to be for Israel (2 Samuel 5:2).

---

[1] For a very readable and helpful summary of biblical teaching on the image of shepherd leadership, see chapters 1 (Old Testament) and 2 (New Testament) in Witmer 2010.

It is also applied to the leaders of the tribes of Israel relative to their people
(2 Samuel 7:7). These very positive connotations for the shepherd-leader
foreshadow the later teaching of Christ regarding servant leaders. Shepherding as a model of leading is also an important theme for the prophets
Ezekiel and Jeremiah (see especially Ezekiel 34 and Jeremiah 23). The picture
is one of an empathetic leader who is sacrificially committed to the welfare
of the flock, and harsh words of judgment are given to those who fail to
reflect this sort of attitude. Shepherding includes a very personal attachment
to the sheep and a loving concern that is modeled by God himself toward
his people in Psalm 23.

Two other Old Testament kinds of leaders deserve mention. In contrast
to the king, the prophet led without human authority. Instead, the prophetic
role was dependent almost entirely on a charismatic giftedness on the part
of the prophet. He or she served as a check and balance to the king and to
the priest, often condemning them for failing to live up to God's standard
for the leaders of his people. An interesting counterpoint to the gift-based
prophet is the priest. The priest's role was to be an intermediary, representing
God to the people and the people to God. In contrast to prophets, the
priesthood was an inherited office held independent of any giftedness or
ability on the part of the priest. His role was structured into the theocracy
by divine appointment and very explicit instruction. In many ways, the
priest served a managerial role, faithfully tending divinely given structures
and schedules of worship.

In the New Testament, the dominant metaphors for leadership seem to
be drawn from family life. Paul refers to himself and his hearers as brothers
and sisters. Elders are chosen in part because of their proven family and
household management skills (Banks and Ledbetter 2004, p. 41). These
metaphors again reflect a very strong personal relationship between the
leaders and followers. They also have overtones of equality in personal
worth and dignity, even if there are distinct differences in leadership functions and responsibilities. The family metaphors also reflect the fact that the
household was not just a place where family members dwelled together, but
it was also a place of commerce that included slaves and other workers. In
this regard, the household becomes a natural proving ground for New Testament church leaders and followers.

The servant or shepherd metaphor is also prevalent. *Pastor* is a term with strong shepherding connotations, and Paul often uses the language of service or even slavery to express his view of his position as a leader. Though the term *priest* is occasionally used in the New Testament, it is uncommon and associated with all believers rather than a particular subset of leaders (Banks and Ledbetter 2004, p. 40).[2] It is really not a leadership term. Also absent from New Testament discussions of leadership are the abundance of formal Greek leadership terms. According to Banks and Ledbetter, "If we begin by looking simply at the basic words Paul uses in speaking about [leadership], what strikes us first is the infrequency of terms related to those at the top, to formal power, and to organization. Of more than three dozen terms used of people in leadership positions in his day, the only high-ranking one Paul uses is in reference to Christ (Col. 1:18)" (p. 38).

It is also noteworthy that biblical leaders commonly receive their roles unexpectedly, are unwilling to embrace their roles or view themselves as ungifted and unworthy of leading. Moses is a notable example of this—offering almost two chapters full of excuses for his inability to lead. Gideon exhibits a similar reluctance. Saul hides in the luggage hoping he will not be found. Jeremiah views himself as too young for the task. Paul viewed himself as the least worthy of the apostles because of his sinful background. All of this is a striking contrast to the modern American tendency to aspire to lead and to assume that a call to lead is unnecessary or else universally given. Biblical leaders are called to the position—and conceptually, a call must come from outside oneself. Talking to oneself is bad enough, surely calling oneself is even worse! Common contemporary visions of a desire to lead are often built around the inner passions of the person who is to become a leader. This is true of not only secular models but also many Christian models that are deeply influenced by our prevailing culture. Laurie Beth Jones in her book *Jesus, CEO: Using Ancient Wisdom for Visionary Leadership*, for example, offers a model of leading based on Jesus. Though she

---

[2]Banks and Ledbetter specifically state that "the language of priesthood appears only metaphorically in Paul's writings, never of a literal person or group, in regard to a wide range of devotional, compassionate, financial, and evangelistic activities (cf. Rom. 15:16, 27; 2 Cor. 9:12; Phil. 2:17, 25, 30). Paul's point is that the kinds of ceremonial activities God required of only some people in the Old Testament are now required of all Christians. This desacralizes and democratizes the role of those who have a significant part to play" (2004, p. 38).

makes many references to Jesus and includes servant leadership as part of her model, it is striking how self-oriented and gift-centered this vision of leading is. Consider these recommended "affirmations for leaders":

- "I proudly say I AM, knowing clearly my strengths and God-given talents. I repeat my strengths to myself often, knowing my words are my wardrobe."

- "I release others so that I myself can fly."

- "I judge no one, knowing that judging others causes major energy leaks in my life."

- "I shape my own destiny. What I believe, I become. What I believe, I can do" (1995, pp. 295-302).

This is not only a self-centered leadership model, it is also a nonvocational model in the sense that it is not rooted in a divine calling. It is an appointment without a call; a drum major in search of a band.

The matter of calling is not only important to leaders, it is also important to followers. Part of the reason for assuming everyone should be a leader is a conviction that everyone receives a call from God. Unfortunately, we have a hard time imagining that a calling could be a call to follow. We mistakenly assume that following a calling entails leading. This is a profound violation of the theology of giftedness and Paul's teaching that everyone is apportioned a place in the body according to the will of the Holy Spirit. It does not matter if one is appointed to be a head or a foot; the point is that one is appointed, and that appointment comes from the Holy Spirit "to each one individually just as He wills" (1 Corinthians 12:11 NASB). Indeed leadership cannot happen unless the head and foot work together for God's purposes.

The fact that both leaders and followers are recipients of a divine call and divine gifts leads to a very synergistic view of leadership in the New Testament. The leader-follower relation is one of mutual respect and regard. The writer of Hebrews reminds his hearers of the general obligation of all Christians to share with one another and to do good to one another. He then addresses followers specifically, reminding them that leaders are called by God to do their job and will give an account to him. Therefore, followers are to obey and submit to their rulers in order that their calling might be a joyful one and not a sad one (Hebrews 13:17). It seems both leaders and followers are to be concerned for the welfare of the other.

Similarly, Paul exhorts the Philippians to receive and honor Epaphroditus, a person who was appointed by the congregation to fulfill a special task. He discharged his duty well, and therefore, he was to be honored (Philippians 2.29).[3] He identifies individuals in Corinth who have devoted themselves to service of the saints, a noteworthy description of a leader, and then encourages the congregation to be subject to such men and to give them recognition (1 Corinthians 16:15-18). Perhaps most important of all, Paul's discussion of spiritual gifts in Ephesians 4 makes it clear that the most central task of leaders is to release and encourage a gifted laity to do the work of the ministry (Ephesians 4:11-12). In summary, leaders and followers have a deeply respectful mutual obligation to one another. Christian leadership requires faithfulness to God's calling and mission and it requires the joint effort of gifted and Spirit-filled leaders *and* followers.

To return to leaders themselves, the reluctance and lack of giftedness found in certain biblical leaders that was mentioned earlier does not mean that being a leader is incompatible with giftedness. It is clear that many biblical leaders were naturally gifted people who fit quite easily into their roles as leaders. This certainly seems to be the case with Daniel, a young man of aristocratic roots and substantial personal gifts. It also seems that Joseph was well suited to lead, was gifted as a household manager and a strategic thinker, and also possessed substantial charismatic gifts such as receiving visions and interpreting dreams. David was the youngest of his brothers but became a leader in their stead partly because of his initiative in the face of Goliath's taunts and his ability to inspire others to follow his lead.[4] Perhaps the main point is that biblical leadership is not tightly dependent on natural gifts or abilities. These gifts seem secondary to divine calling and appointment, but when a person does possess these gifts, there

---

[3]The theme of honoring leadership is prevalent throughout Paul's epistles (see also 1 Corinthians 16:18; 1 Thessalonians 5:12; 1 Timothy 5:17).

[4]Banks and Ledbetter include examples of lesser-known New Testament leaders, noting that "proven experience and a good reputation in managing workers were therefore also qualifications for leadership in the church. It is not inappropriate to assume that this is the background for people singled out by Paul such as Titius Justus (Acts 18:7), Aquila and Priscilla (Rom. 16:3), Gaius (Rom. 16:23), Nympha (Col. 4:15), and Philemon and Apphia (Philem. 1–2)" (2004, p. 41).

is no question that they will be used for kingdom work.

It is also clear that there are a diversity of models and personalities of leaders in the pages of Scripture. Eventually, David held a clear and structured position. He was backed by institutional structures and military might. Prophets like Nathan led in a very different way. They were dependent almost entirely on their personal giftedness and had no appointed office. John the Baptist is labeled the greatest person born of woman, but held no office and lived in the wilderness. His primary activities seemed to be preaching and baptizing; his primary asset was most likely his charismatic personality. Timothy seems to have been called and gifted to be a leader, and held what might now be called a pastoral office, but his primary qualifications seemed to be relational. He was like no one else in terms of the depth of his love for, and interest in, the welfare of those he served.[5] His loving and compassionate heart made him one of Paul's most trusted leaders. Paul himself leads in different ways depending on the situational context (Banks and Ledbetter 2004, pp. 41-43).

The diversity of Christian leaders is even more striking as one ventures outside of the pages of Scripture and into the annals of church history. There are models of egalitarian and communal leaders—both in the church of the catacombs and in monastic settings. There are the strongly hierarchical and institutional leaders that emerged in the Roman Catholic tradition. There are the silent, almost antileader practices that emerged from the Quaker tradition. There are fiercely democratic leaders who are central to congregational forms of polity. All of these models, and countless more, have not only proven to be functional in practice, but they are all rooted in various interpretations of biblical teaching.[6]

One dominant theme in this diverse set of Christian leadership practices is what is variously called servant, shepherd or steward leader (Greenleaf 1977; Howell 2003; Kuest 2006; Laniak 2006; Malphurs 2003; McCormick and Davenport 2003; Phelps 2009; Rinehart 1998; Rodin 2010; Witmer 2010). As was noted above, this model of a leader is rooted

---

[5]Banks and Ledbetter (2004) give a helpful summary of the importance of these relational qualities among Paul's associates in general.

[6]See chapter two of Banks and Ledbetter (2004) for a helpful summary of various forms of church leadership.

in the earliest parts of the Old Testament and continues all the way through the New Testament. It is explicitly taught by Jesus as his distinctive approach to leading, and he contrasts it with the way the Gentile world led. He even tells his followers to view themselves as "slaves" of others (Matthew 20:27). The shepherd leader is suggested not only as a model for Israel's kings, but also a picture of God himself and his role relative to Israel. It is manifested dramatically in the image of the suffering servant used by Isaiah to depict the Messiah. And as mentioned above, it is implied by the almost absolute rejection of the traditional Greco-Roman leader paradigm in the language of the New Testament authors. In addition to the emphasis on the steward leader, other important themes emerge from scriptural teaching:

1. Leading is a normal human activity. We are ordained and equipped by God to lead relative to the rest of the created order and in a wide variety of settings. At times, for some people, this includes the leading of other people in order to accomplish divinely ordained purposes.

2. Filling the role of a leader always depends on God's delegated authority. There is no authority for a leader that does not derive from God's providential appointment. All those who serve as leaders should view themselves as holding their positions by the grace of God and should be aware that God can change or remove a leader at any time.

3. Human leadership is not just a management task; it is often a transformative task. The creation was immature, so to speak, and part of the human function was to facilitate its growth. Human leaders and followers are often sent to change or alter conditions that are not pleasing to God— be that slavery in Egypt or slothfulness in Crete (Titus 1:5, 12-13).

4. While granting that leadership is often transformative, there is a very substantial place for managerial functions in kingdom work. All well-run organizations require management skills. Through history, those who performed these management tasks were always faithful and accountable stewards of what was entrusted to their care (1 Corinthians 4:2).

5. Leaders do not exist independently of followers. Both are divinely appointed to their place in an organization. Both are divinely equipped and

gifted. Successful completion of a God-given mission defines Christian leadership. It will always be a joint effort of gifted leaders, gifted followers and divine provision.

BIBLICAL LEADERSHIP AND CONTEMPORARY LEADERSHIP THEORY

Given the diversity of examples of biblical leadership, it is difficult or impossible to identify a single biblical model of leadership—at least in terms of the way we conceive of leadership models today.[7] Furthermore, given the fact that many biblical leaders and followers were appointed against their wills while others seemed to be naturally gifted to lead and follow, it would be somewhat surprising if either leaders or followers were always associated with a particular personality or gift mix. At least in the pages of Scripture, the common theme seems to be the calling of God, not gifts or personality of those who are called as leaders and followers.

This does not mean, however, that the study of leadership is pointless. The fact that one's call to leadership is divine in origin does not mean one leads or follows in the absence of human skills. Leadership theories, systematic studies of what makes an organization function and the wisdom of human experience can all contribute to making leaders and followers more effective. Therefore, in evaluating leadership models in light of biblical revelation, I am inclined to avoid looking for a single theory that is "most biblical." Rather, given the biblical themes regarding leadership discussed above, it would be prudent to look for models that are permissible in the sense of not violating the boundaries of biblical teaching, and that are profitable in the sense of focusing on making leaders and followers more effective in areas that are valued from a biblical perspective. Given the brevity of this chapter, I will not attempt this on a whole set of leadership models, but rather consider "transforming leadership," a particularly influential model, and allow it to serve as an example of the kind of reflection that might be carried out on other leadership models as well.

---

[7]Beeley cites Aitken regarding the ambiguities inherent in the biblical material, cautioning leaders "to maintain a prudent wariness of relying wholeheartedly on particular models or techniques of ministry, tempting as they may seem." He also points to James Bartz who warns against "assuming that 'one size fits all' when it comes to understanding the giftedness and nurturing required to produce effective ministers" (Beeley and Britton 2009, p. 8).

The transforming leadership model is defined partly by contrast with "transactional leadership," which focuses on an exchange between leader and follower, the goal of which is to produce some mutual benefit. The two participants in this exchange are not changed as persons, they merely obtain some desired good. In contrast, transforming leadership transforms both the leader and the follower according to some sort of moral vision. The participants are motivated and reshaped according to this vision. Transactions are not excluded from transforming leadership, but it is not dependent on them.

Much attention has been given to the distinguishing marks of the transforming leader, the most common formulation being that of Bernard Bass, who offers four essential characteristics of the transforming leader: idealized influence, inspirational motivation, intellectual stimulation and individualized consideration. What should be made of these distinguishing features of transforming leadership from a biblical perspective?

Idealized influence. This feature of transforming leadership focuses on the leader's ability to model desirable behaviors (exceptional capabilities, persistence, determination, ethical conduct) and to inspire followers to emulate their leader.

Inspirational motivation. Transforming leaders motivate and inspire by providing meaning and challenge to their followers' work. They possess and communicate to others a compelling vision of a future state.

Idealized influence and inspirational motivation are exhibited by biblical leaders, at least in certain instances. In the case of Jesus, the Sermon on the Mount clearly casts a compelling vision of a possible future and a compelling moral vision as well. Furthermore, Jesus clearly modeled this vision in his own life. He was willing to suffer and turn the other cheek; he practiced solitary prayer and often explicitly attempted to avoid drawing attention to himself; he fulfilled the law, being perfect even as his heavenly Father was perfect. In all these ways and hundreds more, Jesus embodied the moral vision that he taught. He explicitly serves as a model for his disciples, whom he tells to serve as he himself served, to love as he loved, to do the works that he did and to teach others to do the same (John 14:12; Matthew 28:19-20). Very similar statements could be made about the apostle Paul, who also inspires imitation and constantly refers to the correlation between his own practice and his teaching (Philippians 3:17; 1 Thessalonians 1:5; 2 Thessalonians 3:7). He, too, casts a compelling vision of the future—drawn in large measure from Jesus' own vision. Indeed, his life and practice are shaped by the resurrection—the ultimate tangible manifestation of the desired future that has already broken into the present (Philippians 3:12-20). The power of the resurrection combines with a clear focus on the mission of proclaiming the gospel to form the foundation of Paul's theology of leadership (Strawbridge 2009).

Bass's model of charismatic and inspirational leading is not only found in the pages of Scripture, but it was also taught and modeled in the early church. A powerful example is found in the instruction of Gregory of Nazianzus to those in pastoral ministry:

> The aim of our treatment (*therapeia*) is to provide the soul with wings, to rescue it from the world and give it to God—to protect what is in God's image if it abides, to take it by the hand if it is in danger, or to restore it if it is ruined: to make Christ dwell in the heart by the Spirit, and in short to deify and bestow heavenly bliss upon those who have pledged their allegiance to heaven. (Beeley 2009, p. 17)[8]

This is not a transaction, it is a transformation. The minister is called to lift the eyes of the congregation toward their final calling and destiny. With that end clearly in view, they offer transformational "treatment" to their congregations in the present, reshaping their daily practice according to the model of the heavenly vision.

Intellectual stimulation. As Bass and Riggio note, "Transformational leaders stimulate their followers' efforts . . . by questioning assumptions, reframing problems, and approaching old situations in new ways" (2006, p. 7). The emphasis seems to be on the leader's ability to encourage others to see things differently and thereby inspire their followers to try things they otherwise would not try.

It is clear that this sort of task was central to Jesus' mission. Once again, in the Sermon on the Mount, the central content of the moral vision is built around a new way of seeing, understanding and applying the Jewish law. Jesus constantly uses the phrase, "You have heard it said . . ." and then he offers a new vision or understanding introduced by the phrase, "but I say to

---

[8]Beeley is quoting Gregory of Nazianzus, *Oration* 2.22.

you . . ." In so doing he was directly in opposition to traditional rabbinical teaching that always relied on the appeal to tradition, at times contrasting the teachings of various rabbis who made up the tradition. Normal rabbinical teaching was a series of appeals to previous teachers. In contrast, Jesus simply declares a new vision by appeal to his own authority—"but I say to you." The effect of this approach was to leave his hearers marveling at his teaching because "he taught as one who had authority, and not as their teachers of the law" (Matthew 7:29).

The mind is also central to Paul's vision of transformation. He calls the Romans to be transformed by the renewal of their minds (Romans 12:1-2). He wants the Colossians to set their minds on things above, not on earthly things (Colossians 3:1-4). The Ephesians are encouraged to be renewed in the spirit of their minds (Ephesians 4:23-24). What is striking in these passages is not just that Paul is calling his followers to a radically different lifestyle—to live as new men and to put off the old man—but that he emphasizes the absolutely central role that the mind plays in this process. Sound, biblical teaching should produce a transformed mind. This mind, as he tells the Corinthians, no longer views things "from a wordly point of view," but rather from the perspective of new creation (2 Corinthians 5:16-17).

This focus of Jesus and the New Testament writers on a renewed mind has contributed to the centrality of teaching and preaching in the historical mission of the church. Transformational teaching and preaching is at the center of gospel ministry, is reflected in how the early fathers led, was dramatically manifested in the Reformers and continues to be central to the mission of the church today (Beeley 2009). This sort of teaching, when done well, is a clear example of the perspective-changing "intellectual stimulation" that characterizes transforming leadership.

Individualized consideration. Transforming leadership requires attention to the individual needs of the follower. This is often manifested in mentoring relationships, careful listening and sensitivity to personal concerns. It will often include individual consideration in appointing necessary tasks, using the tasks as an opportunity for growth in the followers and not merely using the followers as a means to accomplish a particular task (Bass and Riggio 2006, p. 7).

Jesus is an unmistakable example of such an approach to leading in that

his approach to launching the kingdom mission was fundamentally relational and transformational. His primary focus was on the twelve disciples,
with whom he lived in daily contact for over three years. He was known by
them as a teacher, mentor and friend. Paul exhibited a similar pattern of
leading among his missionary team members. Furthermore, his letters are
also full of instances of assigning people particular tasks for transformative
purposes. For example, he sent Onesimus, the runaway slave, as a messenger
to his previous master (Philemon 10-16); and he sent Epaphroditus back to
the Philippians both as an encouragement to them and as an opportunity
for them to honor him for his sacrificial service (Philippians 2:25-30).

Also related to individualized consideration is the shepherding metaphor
for leadership. It is built distinctively around a concern for the sheep. The bad
shepherd is concerned for his own well-being, the good shepherd is concerned for the sheep (Ezekiel 34:2-6). Jesus offers a distinctive mark of a good
shepherd: the sheep recognize his voice and he calls the sheep by name (John
10:3-4). In Luke, Jesus offers the parable of the lost sheep—the one missing
sheep from a flock of a hundred compels the shepherd to seek. Paul also exhibits individualized consideration in his constant pattern of naming people
individually and greeting them personally at the end of his letters. This is often
associated with calls to pray for these people's needs, praise of their successes
or requests to meet their tangible needs with hospitality (Romans 16:1-16;
1 Corinthians 16:10-18; Philippians 2:19-30; Colossians 4:7-18).

When it comes to spiritual gifts, Paul reminds his readers that the Holy
Spirit apportions these individually. A flourishing Christian community requires the exercise of all of the spiritual gifts. They are necessary to the
proper function of the whole, and all have been placed there by the wisdom
and design of God himself (1 Corinthians 12:7-31). There are no little people
in the body of Christ. Leaders have their roles and responsibilities, but
Christian leadership cannot happen if the rest of the body does not act, each
using their gifts for transformative purposes. All of these factors, and many
more, contribute to a picture of biblical leadership that is deeply committed
to individualized consideration.

So what does this material show regarding transforming leadership and
the biblical vision of leadership? It seems there are many important points
at which the two visions coincide. This does not prove that transforming

leadership is *the* biblical vision of leadership, or even *the most* biblical. It does show, however, that its most central tenets are compatible with the biblical worldview, that these tenets were often manifested by biblical leaders and that biblical discussions of leadership and metaphors for leaders resonate with many of the concerns addressed in discussions of transforming leadership. It is a model that is both permissible by biblical standards and supportive of central biblical values. I would desire to claim nothing more than that for this model. Transforming leadership is a contemporary cultural artifact. It answers questions in a particular way because it comes to the table with particular concerns, many of which are unique concerns of our historical moment. These concerns will change as our culture changes. Ultimately, I would expect other models of leadership to rise to preeminence and transforming leadership to be left behind or dramatically altered in the process. But granting all these facts, it has proven to be a good way to talk about the practice of leadership and the qualities of effective leadership within our cultural moment. And it fits well within the boundaries of biblical leadership practices, offering helpful handholds for those who seek to climb the mountain of leadership at this present time.

While different models of leadership may come and go, as long as they capture the essence of the Christian worldview outlined above and in the previous chapter, they are candidates for a Christian model of leadership. Any proposed alternative model of Christian leadership should at a minimum include the foundational biblical principles described above.

Concerns for Further Discussion

It would be well to close by addressing some remaining questions and concerns about the relationship between biblical leadership and contemporary leadership studies. Though these two often complement one another, there are some substantial areas of conflict or confusion that should be addressed.

Contemporary North American culture is extremely materialistic, deeply attached to the bottom line and output oriented. That tends to push to the fringes fundamental biblical concerns that are communitarian, spiritual and ethical. I would argue that biblically, one always looks out the windshield at spiritual, moral and relational destinations, and material things are seen through the side window on the way to these goals. Almost all of the leadership literature has the exact opposite orientation. It looks out the wind-shield at materialistic, bottom-line outputs and uses them for navigation while it glances out the side window at the ethical, relational and spiritual landscape as it goes by. It is welcome to see ethical concerns included in discussions of leadership, but the mission of the corporation, organization or institution that is being served will still be used to judge the effec-tiveness of leadership. Modern corporations are not built as engines of spiritual production. Spiritual growth does not pay the light bills. Fur-thermore, though leadership does acknowledge the importance of an in-spirational vision, it is not clear what boundaries can be placed on such visions, unless they are grounded in biblical ethical standards. Absent such standards, it seems enormously pliable, and one could make a case not only that Jesus was a transformative leader, but so were Jim Jones, Genghis Kahn and Adolf Hitler (Mendez-Morse 1992; Yukl 1989, p. 226). It is easy for such models to become a formula for success regardless of the goals for which they are deployed.

Another concern is the tacit assumption that Christian leadership will always prove effective by secular standards. In other words, we assume that if Christians succeed in doing leadership in a biblical fashion, they will also succeed in doing leadership in a way that contemporary culture will deem successful.[9] But why is this so? Does not the world value very different things than the Christian? Is not the gospel opposed to the boastful pride of life—the very thing that many businesses are built around exploiting?

To take a specific example, Jim Collins's seminal works *Built to Last* (1994) and *Good to Great* (2001) are both built around meticulous research on comparison companies. He closely pairs these companies in terms of business sector, size and market opportunities, then identifies the distin-guishing marks of the failed and successful companies so that other com-panies can learn from the successful ones (or from the bad examples of the failed ones). The measure of success is the financial bottom line— roughly speaking, the market value of the company. But is the long-term balance sheet a proper biblical goal? Are production, consumption and

---

[9]For a classic expression of this view, see Barton's (1925) attempt to demonstrate how all the founda-tions of modern business success are found in the life of Jesus. A more contemporary version of the same assumption is Jones (1995).

growth necessarily biblical values? Perhaps a biblical worldview would seek goals like health, beauty and sustainability. If so, is there any reason to think that pursuing these goals is also the fastest way to production, consumption and growth?

Similarly, Collins suggests one of the important features of successful companies is a "big, hairy, audacious goal"—a BHAG (Collins and Porras 1994, pp. 93-94). This approach to goal setting has found an enthusiastic reception in many Christian circles. For example, a Christian institute dedicated to finding "best practices" states:

> Christian leaders need to dream big because with God we can achieve big. With a BHAG, there is always the risk that everything will crash and burn. That's what makes a BHAG a BHAG. And that's what trust and faith are for, to give us the courage to strive for the audacious. BHAGs take courage and are not for the faint-of-heart. They are exactly what we need to achieve God's vision. (Lopus 2010)

But is faith really given so we have "the courage to strive for the audacious"? And furthermore, why should Christian leaders pursue a big, hairy, audacious goal as opposed to, for example, a noble, righteous, enduring goal—an NREG instead of a BHAG? They might, for example, choose to honor Christian principles before the secular missions of their companies. They might also choose to pursue somewhat different goals (NREGs rather than BHAGs) by somewhat different means. And most importantly, it is possible that this tradeoff might not be rewarded in the bottom line because they do not have an unqualified commitment to the bottom line.

And would this be a bad thing? It is provocative to consider if the world would be a better place if human leadership were at times less efficient in producing and consuming goods. Not inefficient, but simply less efficient. Would fewer people actually be hungry? Fewer goods might be produced, but is our primary problem a lack of goods or a host of other social ills that swirl around the production and consumption of goods? How much famine is caused by war as opposed to weather? How much violence in the world today is a side effect of an unrelenting drive for growth and expansion? In an era of globalization, cultures often don't get acquainted, they collide, and the collisions have violent ramifications. It is concerning that Christians commonly assume that authentic discipleship will lead to successful leadership measured by the "bottom line" of this current world order. Perhaps part of our problem is not in finding the proper skills for effective bottom-line leadership, but rather finding alternatives to bottom-line vision.

I am by no means certain what the answers to all of these questions are, but it is good that they be asked. Part of the task of formulating a distinctively Christian theory of leadership must include identifying distinctively Christian goals and purposes, and then being willing to pursue those goals and purposes even at the expense of success in the eyes of the world.

CHAPTER SUMMARY

1. Human leadership is not a usurpation of divine authority but rather is often a means by which God accomplishes divinely ordained purposes.

2. Learning from systematic, scientific study of leadership practices is an appropriate complement to the study of leadership in the Scriptures. Both contribute to a fully formed Christian vision of leadership.

3. Biblical leadership is most strongly tied to divine calling rather than a particular set of human gifts or abilities. A divine call to lead or follow often comes independently of a desire to lead or follow.

4. The shepherd-servant-steward leader is probably the most consistently positive image found in biblical discussions of leaders. This image conceptually involves a divinely appointed purpose and a focus on the benefit of those who are led. The leader in this image always answers upward to God for the way the task of leading is discharged.

5. Transformative leadership is a contemporary model of leadership that is compatible with biblical teaching. There are many aspects of the ministry of Jesus and Paul that fit closely with the model of transformative leadership.

6. Deep questions remain about contemporary leadership models and their compatibility with the core values of a biblical leader and follower. One of the dangers of exclusively using secular leadership models is that they are often tied to goals that do not necessarily reflect biblical values. A biblical leader may be compelled to maximize something other than the bottom line or organizational success.

REFERENCES

Banks, R., and B. M. Ledbetter. 2004. *Reviewing Leadership: A Christian Evaluation of Current Approaches.* Grand Rapids: Baker Academic.

Barton, B. 1925. *The Man Nobody Knows: A Discovery of Jesus.* Indianapolis: Bobbs-Merrill Co.

Bass, B. M., and R. E. Riggio. 2006. *Transformational Leadership.* Mahwah, NJ: Erlbaum.

Beeley, C. A. 2009. "Theology and Pastoral Leadership." *Anglican Theological Review* 91 (1): 11-30.

Beeley, C. A., and J. H. Britton. 2009. "Introduction: Toward a Theology of Leadership." *Anglican Theological Review* 91 (1): 3-10.

Calvin, J., and Beveridge, H. 1993. *Institutes of the Christian Religion.* II.2.15. Grand Rapids: Eerdmans.

Collins, J. C. 2001. *Good to Great: Why Some Companies Make the Leap—and Others Don't.* New York: HarperBusiness.

Collins, J. C., and J. I. Porras. 1994. *Built to Last: Successful Habits of Visionary Companies.* New York: HarperBusiness.

Greenleaf, R. K. 1977. *Servant Leadership: A Journey into the Nature of Legitimate Power and Greatness.* New York: Paulist Press.

Howell, D. 2003. *Servants of the Servant: A Biblical Theology of Leadership.* Eugene, OR: Wipf & Stock.

Jones, L. B. 1995. *Jesus, CEO: Using Ancient Wisdom for Visionary Leadership.* New York: Hyperion.

Kuest, R. D. 2006. *Uncommon Leadership: Servant Leadership in a Power-Based World.* Fullerton, CA: Hope International University Press.

Laniak, T. 2006. *Shepherds After My Own Heart: Pastoral Traditions and Leadership in the Bible.* Downers Grove, IL: IVP Academic.

Lewis, C. S. 1972. *Miracles.* New York: Macmillan.

Lopus, L. 2010. "Big Hairy Audacious Goals for Christian Workplaces." Best Christian Workplaces Institute website, July 28. http://blog.bcwinstitute .com/?p=66.

Malphurs, A. 2003. *Being Leaders: The Nature of Authentic Christian Leadership.* Grand Rapids: Baker Books.

McCormick, B., and D. Davenport. 2003. *Shepherd Leadership: Wisdom for Leaders from Psalm 23.* San Francisco: Jossey-Bass.

Mendez-Morse, S. 1992. "History of Leadership Research." In *Leadership Characteristics That Facilitate School Change.* SEDL website. www.sedl.org/change /leadership/history_of_leadership_research.html.

Phelps, O. 2009. *The Catholic Vision for Leading Like Jesus: Introducing S3 Leadership—Servant, Steward, Shepherd.* Huntington, IN: Our Sunday Visitor.

Rinehart, S. 1998. *Upside Down: The Paradox of Servant Leadership*. Colorado Springs: NavPress.

Rodin, R. S. 2010. *The Steward Leader: Transforming People, Organizations and Communities*. Downers Grove, IL: IVP Academic.

Stackhouse, J. G., Jr. 2008. *Making the Best of It*. New York: Oxford University Press.

Strawbridge, J. 2009. "The Word of the Cross: Mission, Power, and the Theology of Leadership." *Anglican Theological Review* 91 (1): 61-79.

White, L. 1967. "The Historical Roots of Our Ecological Crisis." *Science* 155 (3767): 1203-7.

Witmer, T. 2010. *The Shepherd Leader*. Phillipsburg, NJ: P & R Publishing.

Yukl, G. A. 1989. *Leadership in Organizations*, 2nd ed. Englewood Cliffs, NJ: Prentice Hall.

THEORETICAL FOUNDATIONS *for* CHRISTIAN LEADERSHIP

4

The Leadership River

A Metaphor for Understanding the Historic Emergence of Leadership Theory

John S. (Jack) Burns

—⟋⟍—

Good leadership is a channel of water controlled by God;
he directs it to whatever ends he chooses.

Proverbs 21:1 (*The Message*)

Why Study the Historic Emergence of Leadership Theory?

People who study leadership are action oriented and want to learn skills they can use to fix the problems they see in their organizations. Action-oriented people often act as if theory should be relegated to the ranks of academics because it is irrelevant for those who are doing the hard work of conducting leadership in organizations. Clearly, the reason you are reading this book is because you want to learn things that will help you optimize the way you conduct leadership. The authors hope the readers of this book will find ideas that will help them think better about their organizations both with regard to the theology of Christian leadership as well as with regard to God's general revelation of truth found in emerging theories about organizations and leadership.

Since this is a book about Christian leadership, a reader might argue that an in-depth exploration of leadership theories might be irrelevant because a book about Christian leadership should focus its exploration on how Jesus conducted leadership. Scott Rodin, another contributing author for this book, wrote in *The Steward Leader* that the "What Would Jesus Do" (WWJD) approach to leadership is too simplistic and, worse, obfuscates Jesus' real mission:

> How would you rate a leader if you were given the following information about his work: he chose ill-prepared people who did not understand his mission; he so frequently spoke in veiled and unclear language that the people he came to lead seldom understood what he was saying, and most left him in frustration; he concealed his true mission from even his closest associates until the very end of his term; he angered those in authority who could have been an asset to his work; he made such outrageous claims about his abilities that all but a handful of followers turned against him; one of his own team members testified against him; when he left for a time, his team was in total disarray and completely demoralized; and it was left to those who followed him to reassemble the team, recruit new members, and build an organization. How excited would you be to lift this person up as your model for leadership? . . . My point is that Jesus came to be the Lord of our life, not our example of good leadership. (2010, p. 88)

As God, Christ's country/home/citizenship is in heaven. He came as a selfless servant to steward God's gifts, including the gifts of love and grace, in order to redeem creation. This theology informs our role as Christians to live as redeemed citizens of heaven and as Christ's ambassadors on earth. This applies to all areas of life, including how Christians conduct leadership. Christ's ambassadors are stewards of the gifts they have been given by the Master. As we employ these gifts in our leadership capacities, we are called to use them consistent with the Master's purposes and values.

The purpose of these next two chapters is to explore the historic and emerging theories of management, leadership and organizational development. The historical roots of leadership, God's general revelation, complement truth from special revelation and help develop a comprehensive model for Christian leadership. North American culture has a bias for new ideas, often ignoring the fact that great minds of the past have generated important knowledge that has laid a foundation for emerging ideas as well as a means of assessing them. C. S. Lewis labeled this bias "chronological snobbery" (1955b, p. 201). Emerging contemporary theories of leadership have been built on ancient theoretical foundations. Serious exploration of contemporary leadership theory must begin by examining the major schools of leadership that have mixed and mingled over the centuries to bring us to our present understanding. Indeed, old and new theories found through general revelation are important to understand because Christians believe that through God's general revelation throughout the ages it is possible to glean his truth; this honors the fact that all truth comes from God.

LEADERSHIP SCHOOLS

The leadership literature is vast, and for decades scholars have experimented with ways to organize the literature into some sort of coherent form. We believe students learn theories best when they are able to assign discrete concepts to similar families of ideas. These families of ideas can be described as "leadership schools." As with every other way scholars have attempted to organize the voluminous leadership literature, there are limitations to this particular approach, including the tendency to overgeneralize ideas so that they "fit" into a particular school. Despite the limitations, this framework provides a useful way to learn the general tenets of each school and how these various theories have emerged, interacted and built upon one another throughout history.

Timelines are useful pedagogical tools for learning about the historical development of theories. Unfortunately, timelines have severe drawbacks because they suggest that epochs are discreet with little overlap or interaction with each other. Leadership schools are not bound by discrete epochs, but have continuously ebbed and flowed over the ages with regard to their influence. To address the limitations of timelines, a river metaphor has been used successfully as an instructional tool in leadership courses and workshops for more than a decade (Burns 2000).

A river is an amazing thing. When one casually observes a river, it appears to be a fixed, constant feature of the landscape. Yet when examined closely, a river is always changing and never quite the same. Standing on the bank, one can be swept away by a current of questions about a river: Where did all of that water come from? How long did it take for a particular drop of water to get to this place, and what will be its fate as it continues its journey? What is going on deep beneath the surface? This metaphor brings to mind similar questions about leadership theory, including: From where does a particular leadership theory come? What can one learn from the innumerable influences that give it the properties observed today? What constrains the theory? What trends and patterns are emerging as it continues its journey? Indeed not only as we study leadership, but also as we conduct leadership, we are constantly reminded of the dynamic and turbulent nature of leadership theory and practice.

OVERVIEW OF THE LEADERSHIP RIVER SYSTEM

Every metaphor has its limitations. This metaphor is somewhat complicated because it illustrates an incredibly vast array of theories. We caution the reader to not get caught up in the "geography" of our river metaphor, missing the message it illustrates. The metaphor will describe five major contributing influences:

1. Word/Christ—God the Creator

2. Political science

3. Business management

4. Industrial Revolution/management

5. Christ/God the basis for moral leadership

Emerging in and around these major influences, the metaphor will describe ten major leadership schools:

1. Power

2. Divine right

3. Scientific management

4. Trait theory

5. Human relations

6. One best way

7. Situational/contingency

8. Excellence/quality

9. Transforming

10. Christian leadership

Figure 4.1 is a map that depicts the geography of the Leadership River system. It is important to note that this metaphor illustrates an imprecise chronology for the development of leadership theory. The first third of the river system represents centuries of time reaching back to creation. The last two-thirds of the river system represent roughly the last two and a half centuries of primarily European and North American influence on leadership theory.

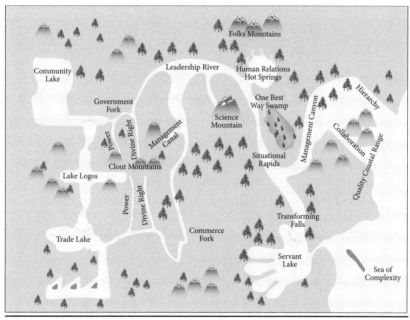

Figure 4.1. Leadership River

The Headwaters Lakes: The first three contributing influences. The source of the entire river system, a deep cross-shaped alpine lake, is called Lake Logos. John 1 speaks about how the Logos (Word/Christ) was God and was with God and that through the Logos all things were created that were created. Thus, the Truth that emerges in the theories examined along the course of the river comes from the Creator of Truth, Christ.

Living water from Lake Logos tumbles over northern and southern waterfalls into a northern and a southern lake. These two lakes represent the foundational academic disciplines that have contributed to contemporary leadership theory: political science and business management.

The northern lake is named Community Lake. Human beings were created to be social beings living in community with one another, even as the relational community of the triune God lives in relational community with creation. Community Lake represents the ageless need for humanity to effectively administer and govern human social and political interaction. The river that flows from Community Lake is called the Government Fork.

The southern lake, also fed by Lake Logos, is called Trade Lake. Trade Lake represents humanity's enduring need to engage in the exchange of goods and services. The most primitive shores of Trade Lake reveal the initial economic activity of humans: hunter/gatherer economies. On more developed shores of Trade Lake, we see the next stage of economic evolution: agricultural societies. Here the hunter/gatherer nomads learn how to domesticate animals and grow food. The river that flows out of Trade Lake is named the Commerce Fork. Along its banks, villages spring up around clusters of farms. In the villages a tiny mercantile/producer class of masters and apprentices emerge who produce and sell goods and services for the surrounding farms and other village inhabitants.

Government Fork and the first two leadership schools. As Government Fork emerges from Community Lake, the raging Power Tributary immediately storms into it. Melting glaciers from the Clout Mountains give rise to this furious stream. The *power* school of leadership identifies seven power bases: position (legitimate), expert, connection, reward, coercive, referent and information (French and Raven 1960). The successful utilization of power from any available power base will not only propel a person into a position as a leader, but it will also serve to sustain the person in their position. It is impossible to identify the earliest exercise of power by one human being over another. It seems to have always been with us.

Through the ages, many have philosophized about power, including Friedrich Nietzsche, who described how the "will to power" was the highest aim for leaders of the masses he called the "herd." Thomas Hobbes concluded that in order to keep people from killing one another, they should form a social contract to authorize a leviathan leader to use totalitarian power to keep peace. Machiavelli, writing around 1500, is one of power theory's most famous observers. In *The Prince*, Machiavelli advises that the primary job of the prince was to first become, and then remain, the prince by whatever means it took to do so. It did not matter if the prince had to break the people's moral laws like murder or perjury. The highest and only moral obligation for the prince was to remain as the prince! If the prince could rule by giving the people graces, and for appearance's sake going along with their religious beliefs, that was acceptable. Yet Machiavelli advised that it would be important for the prince to kill or maim someone every now and then, just so the people wouldn't cultivate rebellious thoughts, thinking the prince was too soft or too much like them. By the same token the prince was advised not to be too cruel or the people might believe death would be a preferable release from their oppression, and they would thus have nothing to lose and everything to gain if they were to rebel or become martyrs.

Power differentials emanating from the seven power bases are found in all human social arrangements. Power can be used both positively and negatively. Examples abound that illustrate the positive use of power: democracies elect officials who are authorized by the electorate to use power to ensure stability and help advance society; parents draw from various power bases to help keep children safe as they mature into adults; law enforcement officers (position power) are authorized to use their power to maintain public safety. Unfortunately, history also has a long record of the use of Machiavellian abusive power. Abusive power is employed in order to manipulate and control people for the benefit of the power wielder. Contemporary examples range from despotic dictators down to playground bullies.

Christians are sometimes uncomfortable with the discussion of power because of its corruptive potential and apparent antithesis of doing everything from a motivation of love. Yet love without power may merely generate good feelings. Power without love can lead to tyranny. As a result, a Christian model of leadership recognizes that there is a wise, meek and judicious use of power that contemporary leaders need to include in their repertoire when conducting leadership.

Soon after the Power Tributary charges into Government Fork, it is joined by a regal tributary that blusters forth from Entitlement Heights called the Divine Right Tributary. Examples of *divine right* leadership are found in the Old Testament, in the ancient history of Egypt and in the political system of the European Middle Ages. It has been taught by philosophers like Plato and refined by management theorists like Max Weber. The divine right school assumes that society is arranged in a rigid hierarchy. In these structured societies, certain members by birthright, and/or because of some innate quality, and/or through some kind of divine mandate, are ordained with the right or responsibility to lead the rest of the society. Leaders are usually replaced at death, by abdication or through contest (usually revolution, but sometimes election) where victory is assumed to be a sign of divine ordination.

The influence of this ancient stream in the Leadership River can be seen through historic examples including the laws of primogeniture—which ensure the orderly inheritance of property and titles—nineteenth-century social Darwinism that reinforced classism, and the historic American cultural deference to leaders who have been to the "right" schools or who come from the "right" families. The divine right and power schools combine to form a very simple definition of leadership: leadership is whatever the "ordained" leader does, and the effective use of power ensures that the leader remains "ordained."

Although throughout history people have abused the notion of divine calling and leadership, as we have mentioned in earlier chapters, divine calling is a part of the special revelation that informs the Christian model of leadership. The biblical example of God's selection of Moses as the leader of Israel is but one example of a leader divinely called to their position.

Tributaries on the Commerce Fork. As the Commerce Fork leaves Trade Lake and begins its long journey through a high plateau, it is also joined by a Power Tributary and a Divine Right Tributary. The character of these tributaries is identical to their twin northern streams that flow into the Government Fork. European and North American social and economic history illustrate how the combined influence of power and divine right on the Commerce Fork ensured that for centuries societies remained rigidly hierarchical and that there was very little social mobility or extensive economic development. This rigid social/economic order was unquestioned because it was assumed to have been divinely mandated. The top of this hierarchy often controlled both the theological and political structure as well as the economy. For centuries, most Europeans were peasants bound generation after generation to a feudal lord's land, a system that was usually supported by the church.

The tiny mercantile class in the villages was also constrained by the same theological, political, social and economic rigidity as the serfs on the farms. People in the mercantile class would hold the same occupations generation after generation. Entry into the trade guilds was controlled by masters of particular crafts. In this system, the job of the master was to teach a skill or a craft to a handful of apprentices (usually younger male relatives). The job of the apprentice was to obey the master, learn all that could be learned and eventually "hang out their own shingle" by opening their own shop or taking over the master's operation. In this system, with a limited span of control between masters and apprentices, there was no need for professional management to control production.

The influence of the power school and divine right on commerce continues today even though most of the world has long since abandoned the abuses of European medieval economic arrangements. Even today success in business is often seen as a "blessing" (ordained by God) and power is sometimes abused to ensure that the blessing continues! In all kinds of economic endeavors, power is sometimes used to try to gain a monopoly position and limit government or any other kind of regulation or interference. For example, global cartels try to control prices of commodities like oil, software giants try to control software applications and computing platforms, and media moguls have vast global empires that attempt to control information and entertainment. Monopolists attempt to curry favor from governments and other authorities in order to gain more power and control.

The fourth contributing influence: The Industrial Revolution and the emergence of management. A worldview shift ushered in by the European age of Enlightenment began the gradual erosion of the power/divine right stranglehold on European culture. The Enlightenment spawned evolutions in theology (Reformation), politics (democracies), society (equality, liberty and mobility), knowledge (science) and commerce (international trade, technology, industrial revolution).

The Industrial Revolution, which began slowly in the late seventeenth century, was fed by the creation of capital, banking and expansion of trade beyond local, national and continental borders. Technological innovations shifted the production of goods from the small shops of master craftsmen to factories in ever-growing industrial cities. Eventually laborers migrated from farms and even across national borders and continents to work and live in the emerging urban industrial centers. Laborers performed jobs on the assembly lines of the new mass-production era of manufacturing. The need for increased span of control of workers in factories created a new kind and class of worker: the professional manager.

The Industrial Revolution is the source of the Management Canal. The Industrial Revolution and the management that controlled it became wildly successful. The manmade Management Canal is such an influential tributary that it overwhelms the Commerce Fork, radically changing and dominating the entire character of that river.

Formation of the Leadership River: Confluence of Government Fork and Commerce Fork. Shortly after the Industrial Revolution, the Government and Commerce Forks merge and form the main channel of the Leadership River. Because of the influential augmentation from the Management Canal, Commerce Fork is much larger when it converges with Government Fork. The management influence on the newly formed Leadership River is profound, forcing the water from Government Fork deep below the surface. Even political terms reflect management's influence: political *boss*, campaign *manager* and *school superintendent* surface. It is not until 1978 that leadership will finally emerge as a unique academic discipline.

The third and fourth leadership schools, illustrated by the Scientific Management Tributary. The European Enlightenment of the sixteenth century set in motion a gradual worldview shift away from authoritarian Christian theism. This shift was a catalyst for the growth of science and mathematics in Europe. Advances in mathematics and physics increased knowledge about the physical world. Biologists discovered the sources of diseases, and medicines to cure them. The scientific method of testing a hypothesis under controlled experimental conditions was applied to all kinds of practical problems, and ever more sophisticated technology that emerged from many of these investigations revolutionized how humans lived and worked. As a result of astonishing achievements over a few centuries, a worldview based on reason, empiricism and faith in science began to dominate Western civilization.

In North America, the Industrial Revolution was rolling under a full head of steam by the end of the nineteenth century. At that time, the icy waters of the Scientific Management Tributary made a controlled descent from Science Mountain into the Leadership River, giving birth to the third leadership school on our journey, *scientific management* (also called Taylorism). Fredrick Winslow Taylor began to experiment with combining the scientific method and management. Perhaps his most famous experiments took place at the Bethlehem Steel Works Midvale Plant, where he conducted shoveling experiments to determine that the optimal shovel load was always 21.5 pounds. He then set out to design shovels for different kinds of materials that, when fully loaded, would weigh 21.5 pounds. Further calculations would determine how many pounds of material a worker should shovel to earn a day's wages.

In the scientific management school, the entire production process is dissected into small subunits of effort. The manager's job is to experiment to discover processes that optimize efficiency of each subunit of work, and then, based on these experiments, develop comprehensive lists of procedures for workers to follow in order to maximize productivity. Managers train workers to perform each individual task, monitor the workers' performance and develop incentives to improve efficiency and productivity. In this scheme, which continues to assume organizations are best run as rigid hierarchies, managers view workers as analogous to the machines with which they work. Good managers continuously fine-tune the entire system, human and mechanical, seeking greater efficiencies.

"Task" is the construct associated with scientific management. The task construct occurs on a continuum (see figure 4.2) that expresses the degree of organizing structure that managers provide to workers regarding their duties. When managers dictate the exact procedures workers are to follow, they are called high-task managers. Conversely, low-task managers leave workers to their own devices to get the job done. Taylor believed that optimal performance was assured by high-task management, where workers were ultimately treated as if they were tiny cogs in the giant industrial machine. Though more humane at the beginning of the twenty-first century, scientific management is still around. Total quality management is a successful recent example of the application of scientific principles to the management process.

Much like power, the study of the traits of leaders has been around since the beginning of time (e.g., Plato, Odysseus, Plutarch). Our fourth leadership school, the *trait* school, is found in the deep shadows of Science Mountain. Beginning in the late 1800s, social scientists believed that through scientific investigation it would be possible to discover the

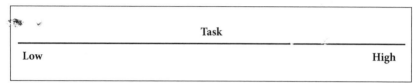

Figure 4.2. Task Construct Continuum

characteristics that suited people for various roles in society. For example, phrenologists examined the shape of the skulls of criminals and characteristics such as distance between a person's eyes in order to develop a typology that would help them predict a propensity toward a life of crime. Similarly, social scientists studied successful historic and contemporary leaders and attempted to discover common traits that were assumed to have contributed to success. Early on these researchers did not recognize that their methodology was flawed since the pool of leaders they used was made up of white males from European and North American cultures. Lists of traits developed from this pool reflected this bias. Recognizing this limitation, later social scientists continued to develop lists of leadership traits from ever more diversified pools of successful leaders. These various lists were often in conflict with one another. To resolve these conflicts, lists either became too broad to be effective, or so narrow that exceptions were obvious.

In 1948 legendary leadership scholar Ralph Stogdill reviewed 124 studies published between 1904 and 1947. He found that the lists of traits of leaders exceeded those of the average member of a collective group, and he concluded, "The qualities, characteristics, and skills required in a leader are determined to a large extent by the demands of the situation in which he [or she] is to function as a leader" (1948, p. 63). Thus Stogdill suggested that leader traits were not as crucial to the leadership equation as the environmental context where leadership is conducted. Just as most social psychologists have abandoned phrenology for predicting criminal potential, most leadership theorists have abandoned the quest for discovering a universal prescriptive list of leadership traits.

The fifth leadership school, illustrated by the Human Relations Tributary. As the river winds past the Folks Mountains, a pleasant hot springs becomes the source of the Human Relations Tributary, which warmly enriches the Leadership River. Mary Parker Follett's great pioneering work was rediscovered by feminist management scholars more than fifty years after her death. Unfortunately, most scholars do not give her credit as the founder of the human relations theory of management; that honor is erroneously given to Elton Mayo, a Harvard scholar from Australia who led the team that conducted the famous Hawthorne experiments beginning in the late 1920s.

In the early 1920s, Mary Parker Follett observed poor women at the Roxbury Neighborhood House in South Boston as they came together in groups to work on complex neighborhood social problems. She observed how these women drew inspiration from the cross-fertilization of ideas that emerged in a group setting to develop creative solutions for significant problems. She knew that in an industrial setting, the high-task managers of these same women would prevent them from coming together in groups to solve even minor productivity issues. Follett began to experiment in workplaces, examining the efficacy of groups in solving productivity challenges apart from the authoritarian management structure. She became an important management consultant until her death in the early 1930s (Boone and Bowen 1987).

Elton Mayo's Hawthorne studies signify an important turning point in the management literature. Mayo departed from the practice of treating workers like cogs in a giant machine and advised managers to view workers as people with very human needs and aspirations. Mayo and his associates stumbled onto these radical ideas quite by accident through the famous Hawthorne Lighting experiments. In the original experiments, they hypothesized that productivity would steadily increase as illumination in the plant increased, until finally productivity would level out at a point where greater illumination would not generate greater productivity. Workers, fully cognizant of the fact that the researchers were there to conduct some sort of an experiment, quietly conspired with one another to figure out what the experiment was and to make the experiment fail! Once the workers saw what was happening to the lighting and deduced what the researchers were trying to do, they began to influence one another by independently regulating productivity regardless of what was happening with the lights. Thus, the experiment failed to produce the hypothesized results.

Mayo learned at least two enduring and significant lessons from these failed experiments. First, people perform differently when they are being observed in an experiment (dubbed the "Hawthorne Effect" in the literature of psychology), and second, that people in groups can influence one another both positively and negatively when it comes to productivity. This second finding gave rise to a set of new experiments designed to see if productivity would increase if workers developed shared feelings of positive regard for their managers and the work environment. Research demonstrated that positive regard and productivity increased when managers demonstrated consideration for human needs of workers and developed nurturing relationships with them. *Human relations* theory abandoned the task construct in favor of a new construct labeled "consideration" (see figure 4.3). High-consideration managers learned to listen to workers to discover and address workers' needs, whereas low-consideration managers tended to treat workers like Taylor's "cogs in a machine."

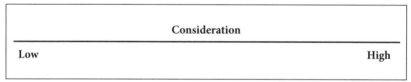

Figure 4.3. Consideration Construct Continuum

Douglas MacGregor, writing in the 1950s, wrote about Theory X and Theory Y management contrasting high-task and high-consideration management styles. Theory X managers are high-task managers who hold negative beliefs about workers, including: workers are lazy, will steal from the company, are not trustworthy and dislike working. MacGregor found that when managers hold Theory X assumptions about employees, their management style is controlling and autocratic, and more importantly, workers "live up" to managers' negative expectations.

Conversely, Theory Y managers are high-consideration managers with positive beliefs about workers, including: workers are industrious, capable, motivated, curious and have exceptional ability. Theory Y managers are far less controlling and autocratic, listen to workers' concerns and are more likely to engage in collaborative relationships with workers (Boone and Bowen 1987). MacGregor found that Theory Y employees also "live up" to the positive assumptions of their managers.

The sixth leadership school, illustrated by the One Best Way Swamp. Scientific management theory with its emphasis on managing the task dimension, and human relations theory with its emphasis on consideration, became competing theories. In the midst of this conflict, part of the river diverts into a narrow channel to form the One Best Way Swamp. Beginning in the 1950s and as late as the 1980s, swamp-dwelling theoreticians proposed that one ultimate and all-inclusive optimal way of management could be discovered. Robert Blake and Jane Mouton (1964) are perhaps the most famous of the *One Best Way* theorists. These two scholars made an admirable attempt to refute the either/or nature of the task-versus-consideration argument by suggesting there was a both/and solution that they believed would yield the one best way to manage.

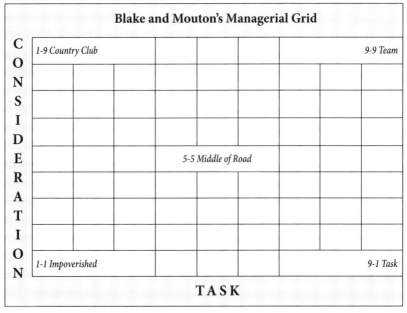

Figure 4.4. Adapted from Blake and Mouton (1964)

To represent their theory graphically, Blake and Mouton developed the 9x9 Managerial Grid (figure 4.4). The horizontal axis of the grid represents the task construct. The vertical axis represents the consideration construct. They labeled management styles represented at critical points on the grid as follows: 1-1 Impoverished, 1-9 Country Club, 9-1 Task, 5-5 Middle of the Road and 9-9 Team. The objective for Blake and Mouton was to use sophisticated assessment instruments to diagnose current organizational practices and plot them on the grid. Then, these consultants could recommend steps to move the organization to the best way to manage, the 9-9 "Team" position on the grid. Blake and Mouton had significant professional success as authors and business consultants. Meanwhile, other scholars were busy developing theories that demonstrated that the One Best Way theories were of limited efficacy.

The seventh leadership school, illustrated by the Situational Rapids. The majority of the Leadership River is not diverted into the quagmire of the One Best Way Swamp. It continues on its course and, beginning in the 1970s, picks its way through the Situational Rapids, a series of outcropping rocks that separate the river into several different channels. *Situational/contingency* theorists assert that in different kinds of circumstances different kinds of management styles are appropriate. Victor Vroom and Arthur Jago suggested that managers need to be able to employ five management styles, ranging from autocratic/authoritarian style to group-generated/delegation management style. They developed a complex decision tree made up of a series of eight yes/no questions for managers to use to determine which of five management styles were appropriate for a particular situation (Vroom and Jago 1988).

Paul Hersey and Kenneth Blanchard (1988) gained notoriety as situational theorists. Like Blake and Mouton, these theorists combine the constructs of task (horizontal axis) and consideration (vertical axis), as seen in figure 4.5. Unlike Blake and Mouton's Managerial Grid, however, Hersey and Blanchard posit that there is no one best way to manage, but that there are four equally appropriate management styles that result from various combinations of the task and consideration constructs. Though managers may have a preferred style, they must be adept at employing each of the management styles as necessary.

At times managers must use the "telling" leadership style that is high task (specific instructions and close supervision) and low consideration (little need for a nurturing leader/follower relationship). Other situations require a manager to draw on a leadership style that is relatively high task (specific

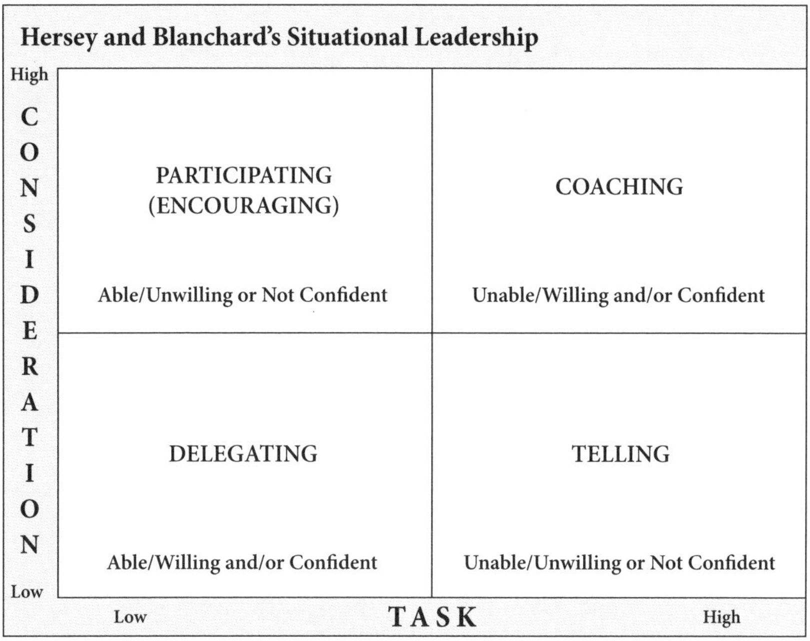

Hersey and Blanchard's Situational Leadership	
PARTICIPATING (ENCOURAGING) Able/Unwilling or Not Confident	**COACHING** Unable/Willing and/or Confident
DELEGATING Able/Willing and/or Confident	**TELLING** Unable/Unwilling or Not Confident

(Vertical axis, top to bottom: High — CONSIDERATION — Low. Horizontal axis, left to right: Low — TASK — High.)

Figure 4.5. Adapted from Hersey and Blanchard (1988)

instructions and close supervision) and high consideration (high nurturing relationship between leader and follower)—this is called "coaching." Another leadership style is "participating" (encouraging), which is employed in situations that require low task (specific instructions and close supervision are not needed) and high consideration (high nurturing/supporting/encouraging relationship between leader and follower). Finally, there are situations where "delegating" is the appropriate management style, with low task (specific instructions and close supervision are not needed) and low consideration (nurturing relationship between leader and follower is minimal).

Each of Hersey and Blanchard's four management styles is appropriate when used in the proper situational context. To determine the situational context, the manager performs an assessment of the follower's ability, willingness and confidence to perform a particular task in a particular situation. If followers are unable and unwilling or not confident, telling is the appropriate management style (e.g., drill sergeant and army recruits at basic training). If they are unable but willing and/or confident, then coaching is the appropriate management style (e.g., freshman quarterback who wants to be the varsity starter). When workers are able but unwilling or not confident, then participating (encouraging) is the appropriate style (e.g., a junior partner in a law firm tries her first solo case). If followers are able, willing and confident, then the appropriate management style is delegating (e.g., a hospital administrator's supervisory relationship with a surgeon). This elegant management theory has great utility especially with small or homogeneous groups where followers' abilities and willingness are consistent (Hersey and Blanchard 1988). Indeed Christ seems to have used situational leadership in his various interactions with Peter. At times Jesus was quite confrontational with Peter, telling him precisely what to do (Matthew 16:21-23), and after the resurrection, Christ delegated tremendous responsibility to him (John 21:17).

The eighth leadership school, illustrated by the Quality Coastal Range and the Management Canyons. Just downstream from the Situational Rapids and looming deep below the surface is the beginning of a submerged jetty that eventually makes its way to the surface and rises to form the Quality Coastal Range. This jetty separates the river into two distinct channels. Most of the water that originated in the Commerce Fork, the Management Canal and the various management tributaries that have joined the Leadership River now flows into the Management Canyons.

One of the major influences on the various combinations of management schools in the bays of the Management Canyons is from the Quality Coastal Range. These mountains appeared in the early 1980s as the United States was emerging from a deep recession. In 1982, Thomas Peters and Robert Waterman published the landmark book *In Search of Excellence*, which examined several American companies that had been successful despite the poor economy. Their goal was to identify successful (excellent) management practices that could be assimilated by struggling US businesses. About the same time, W. Edwards Deming (1986) was gaining an American audience for the principles of total quality management he had been teaching in Japan for over thirty years. In the mid-1980s, *excellence and quality* became the management mantra of the resurging American economy.

For the next thirty years, thousands of management books and articles were published that describe what was being learned in the Management Canyons. Some theorists and authors who explore the Management Canyons are somewhat confused about terminology, labeling as "leadership" ideas that actually describe management. Indeed the management literature is the product of numerous combinations of influence from the schools we have discussed upstream. Management is a critical component in organizations, for organizations must be managed well or there is no opportunity for leadership to flourish.

The critical point here is that management and leadership are distinct disciplines even though they have many overlapping foundational influences. Beginning in 1978, leadership began to emerge as a distinct academic discipline in the social sciences. Leadership scholar Joseph Rost published a review of the major twentieth-century writings in leadership up to 1991 and drew the following conclusion regarding the confused application of the terms *leadership* and *management* in the literature:

> There is a school of leadership in the literature since 1930 that has been hidden by the obvious confusion and chaos of the literature as it is presented in the books, chapters, and articles. Under the surface, I found a consistent view of leadership in the background assumptions and in the meanings behind the words used in the definitions and models. This school conceptualizes leadership as good management. I will call it the industrial paradigm of leadership. (1991, p. 10)

Rost found that most twentieth-century "leadership" authors were actually expounding about management theory, erroneously using the word *leadership* to describe *good management*. Rost credited James MacGregor Burns as the only author writing before 1990 about a distinctive theory of leadership independent of the industrial paradigm and its "good management" theories. He stated that Burns's work is "extremely important as a transitional statement that has immense possibilities to lead us toward a new school of leadership" (Rost 1991, p. 11). To be consistent with our metaphor, Rost might say that he found that twentieth-century "leadership" writers were rudderless and adrift in the Management Canyons though they believed they were sailing smoothly on the main channel of the Leadership River!

Eventually, water from the Management Canyons makes its way to small streams that experiment with hierarchical and collaborative organizational structures, through the Quality Coastal Range, and finally spills over coastal waterfalls into Chaos Bay and the Sea of Complexity, the subject of our next chapter.

The ninth leadership school, illustrated by Transforming Falls. Now we must turn around and head out of the Management Canyons and back to the main flow of the Leadership River. The river now only retains a modest influence from the Commerce Fork and associated management theories. As a result, water from the Government Fork surfaces. In addition, we find the character of the water also contains influence of uncharted springs from various disciplines including political science, history, theology, education, communication studies and psychology that have been quietly charging the river along its journey. This section of our river system metaphor represents how, since 1978, thanks to historian and political scientist James MacGregor Burns, leadership has been emerging as a unique discipline in the social sciences.

Immediately past the Quality Jetty, the river spills over a high waterfall named Transforming Falls, giving birth to the ninth leadership school: the *transforming leadership* school, first described by James MacGregor Burns in his classic book *Leadership*. Burns offers several similar definitions of leadership, which he summarizes well toward the end of the book when he states, "Leadership is the reciprocal process of mobilizing, by persons with certain motives and values, various economic, political, and other resources in a context of competition and conflict, in order to realize goals independently or mutually held by both leaders and followers" (1978, p. 425).

Thus, for Burns, leadership is fundamentally concerned with changes that must be made in order for a group to realize its collective goals. Management differs from leadership in that often the best management strategy may be stasis. Burns asserts that leadership occurs on a continuum ranging from transactional to transforming leadership (see figure 4.6). Burns's transforming leadership is sometimes labeled "transformational leadership," a term Burns used only twice in his book. While related, the words are not synonyms. *Transformational* leadership makes for great alliteration when it is paired with transactional leadership, but it is the adjective form of a noun and it suggests a state that has already been achieved. *Transforming* leadership, the adjective form of a verb that Burns uses almost all the time, indicates an ongoing process (Couto 1995). Ronald Heifetz (1994), influenced by Burns, developed an important case for using the term *adaptive leadership* instead of *transforming leadership*. More recently there has been discussion about replacing the term *transforming leadership* with the term *charismatic leadership* (Howell 1998), but Burns's term is still the most widely accepted in the literature.

Figure 4.6. Transactional/Transforming Leadership Continuum

Transactional leadership is an exchange between leaders and followers that facilitates the accomplishment of some goal or purpose shared by both parties. Transactional leadership is relatively easy to conduct. Examples include a person donating funds or volunteering time for a cause they support, or a person voting for a politician who represents political and social ideals congruent with the supporter's wishes. After the transactional exchange, parties may or may not engage in future transactions. The transforming end of Burns's leadership continuum is no mere exchange of favors as it is in transactional leadership. Transforming leadership is far more difficult to conduct on a large scale, but it also has great potential to produce significant, lasting change for everyone involved.

The author of this chapter has published a graphic depiction (see figure 4.7) of the combination of Burns's and Heifetz's transforming/adaptive leadership theories (Burns 2008). In this depiction, X^1 represents an honest assessment of where an organization stands with regard to fulfilling its quintessential purpose and values; X^2 represents a vision and ultimate reality of the organization if it were fulfilling its purpose and values in every possible way. If X^2 could be achieved easily through some sort of simple transaction, then there would be no need for adaptive work or transforming leadership. For organizations to move from X^1 to X^2, they must complete more than simple transactions; they must learn to transform or adapt if they are to make progress. The obstacles between X^1 and X^2 provide a variety of transactional and transforming/adaptive challenges for people and their organizations.

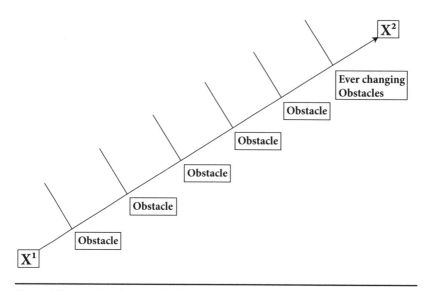

Figure 4.7. Transforming/Adaptive Leadership

Heifetz (1994) suggests that problems, or in this case the obstacles between X^1 and X^2, can be classified into three major categories. Type 1 problems are technical problems with technical solutions (e.g., problem: you are hungry and it is time for dinner; solution: buy food and cook dinner). Type 1 problems fit nicely near the transactional end of Burns's leadership continuum.

Type 2 problems are more difficult. They are problems with technical solutions, but the technical solutions may not be readily available or may require adaptation or transformation before they are employed (e.g., problem: you are hungry, it is time for dinner, but you do not know how to cook; solution: transform/adapt by learning how to cook, and then buy food and cook dinner).

Type 3 problems are not technical problems with technical solutions, they are adaptive problems. The adaptive solutions to Type 3 problems are complicated, often requiring some components to be broken down into technical or adaptive problems with Type 1 or 2 solutions, while other components require adaptive transformation by everyone involved (e.g., problem: you are hungry, it is time for dinner, but in your developing nation, there is no food readily available. Solutions in this case are not clear: Should you accept surplus grain shipments from another country—a short-term transactional fix? Should you transform/adapt to develop a subsistence-oriented self-sustaining agricultural infrastructure—a long-term transforming/adaptive solution? Should you sell your scarce natural resources to an industrial nation so that you have capital to develop a comprehensive agricultural infrastructure—a long-term transforming/adaptive solution?). Type 3 problems are the most difficult obstacles on the journey from X^1 to X^2.

A major leadership challenge and important skill is to identify and classify the type of problem facing the organization and develop solutions appropriate to the problem type. There is a propensity on the part of leaders to offer, and for followers to accept, only simplistic Type 1 or Type 2 solutions for Type 3 problems in order to avoid transforming work altogether. For example, when well-intended organizations and nations try to alleviate global hunger by providing grain as humanitarian aid for hungry people in a developing nation (Type 1 transactional response to a Type 3 adaptive problem), it may actually undermine the developing nation's ability in the long run to develop its own agricultural infrastructure (Moyo 2009).

As organizations grow through transformations that help them overcome obstacles between X^1 and X^2, a fascinating paradox emerges. Organizations live in dynamic environments that foment endless obstacles. As an organization approaches X^2, the ever-changing environment will create new adaptive challenges that must be met or the organization will not survive. The global economic turmoil that began in 2008 provides an illustration of environmental turbulence that requires organizations to continuously monitor the environment and develop real-time adaptive strategies.

Christians understand this paradoxical journey from X^1 to X^2 because they experience it in their personal spiritual lives. For Christians, X^1 represents an honest assessment of how well we are functioning as a Christ follower in all areas of life, and X^2 represents living a life that unveiled reflects the Lord's glory and is fully transformed into his likeness and total glory. This verse suggests that God is at work in transforming believers: "And we, who with unveiled faces all reflect the Lord's glory, *are being transformed into his likeness* with ever-increasing glory, which comes from the Lord, who is the Spirit" (2 Corinthians 3:18 NIV 1984). If X^2 could be easily achieved, Christians would live in this way. Though Christians may aspire to live lives that are transformed into the likeness of Christ at all times, they fail to do so. Growing Christians are on a lifelong personal spiritual journey of sanctification, becoming more Christlike by overcoming obstacles only to find new areas of their lives that also need sanctification. On the journey, Christians may benefit by employing spiritual disciplines and practices that help them overcome obstacles to their growth. However, each Christian's journey is unique, and standardized dogmatic prescriptions or formulas for spiritual growth have only limited benefit. The nature of a Christian's transforming journey requires them to live out their faith daily in response to the Holy Spirit's leading in the unique context of their lives.

Similarly, while some, including Bass and Burns, have attempted to develop standard guidance for navigating the transforming journey for organizations, these standard prescriptions have no more utility than dogmatic spiritual prescriptions for Christians on their spiritual journey. Indeed many of the leadership and management theories we have discussed "upstream" may be usefully employed during some portions of an organization's transforming journey. Like Christians on their sanctifying journey, organizations too must live in their own unique internal and external environmental contexts, employing various leadership and management skills and theories in response to those ever-changing contexts. In the next chapter we will discuss in greater detail how organizations can become effectively attuned to the critical demands of their ever-changing environment.

For organizations as well as individuals, Burns's transforming journey from X^1 to X^2 has another significant component. Burns says that transforming leadership occurs when leaders and followers "raise one another to higher levels of motivation and morality" (1978, p. 20). When Burns introduced his theory, scholars like Bernard Bass took little issue with the idea that transforming leadership helped people in organizations to raise one another to higher levels of motivation. Burns's requirement for moral elevation, however, raised important questions and immense criticism. In the postmodern world, scholars have argued that *there is no standard* upon which to base Burns's moral requirement. Therefore, they reason, transforming leadership must be amoral. For these scholars, the journey from *any* X^1 to *any* X^2 is transforming leadership.

However noble the motivation for this postmodern egalitarian argument may be, it is laden with problems, especially for those who want to conduct Christian leadership. For example, Hitler orchestrated a major transformation of Germany and in this transformation, Germany moved from *an* X^1 to *a horrific* X^2. Germany's transformation was immoral no matter whose postmodern moral standard is employed (save that of a dedicated Nazi). Even the most relativistic postmodern leadership scholar has difficulty equating Hitler's despotism with the transforming leadership of the likes of Mother Teresa, Abraham Lincoln, Desmond Tutu or Martin Luther King Jr. Leadership is far too noble a term to assign to the actions of history's tyrants and their toadies.

Transforming leadership represents the essence of human growth as individuals and organizations overcome obstacles and change for the better journeying toward X^2. Moral transformation is the soul of the transforming theory of leadership. Even so, the question of the critics looms: What standard will judge the morality of transforming leadership? For this we turn to special revelation.

The fifth contributing influence and the tenth leadership school, illustrated by Servant Lake. Servant Lake establishes a standard for moral elevation that Burns requires for transforming leadership. The source of Servant Lake is a refreshing artesian spring of living water that has traveled for miles and centuries through an underground aquifer that originates from the bottom of Lake Logos where our journey began.

While Christ is the model and ideal for servant leadership, the term itself was coined in the management literature in the 1970s by Robert Greenleaf (1977). Greenleaf was inspired by Herman Hesse's *Journey to the East*. In this story a company of men set out on a journey with their servant Leo. As long as Leo was with the group, serving them in practical and spiritual ways, the group made progress. When Leo unexpectedly left, the group fell apart. Later it is discovered that Leo was actually the head of the Order that sponsored the original journey. In discussing who a servant leader might be, Greenleaf writes:

The servant-leader *is* servant first—as Leo was portrayed. It begins with the natural feeling that one wants to serve, to serve *first*. Then conscious choice brings one to aspire to lead. That person is sharply different from one who is *leader* first, perhaps because of the need to assuage an unusual power drive or to acquire material possessions. . . . The leader-first and the servant-first are two extreme types. . . . The difference manifests itself in the care taken by the servant-first to make sure that other people's highest priority needs are being served. The best test, and difficult to administer, is this: . . . Do they, *while being served*, become healthier, wiser, freer, more autonomous, more likely themselves to become servants? (pp. 13-14)

Christians have far more than Hesse's fictional Leo and Greenleaf's humanistic altruism to inspire them to be servant leaders. Christ is the supreme example, and Christian saints too numerous to count are inspiring examples because they have also taken up the servant leader vocation for the last two thousand years. The uniting of the cornerstone Christian concept of servant leadership with the emerging transforming leadership school describes in no uncertain terms what the heart and soul of *Christian leadership* has always been about, but service is only one component of Christian leadership.

THE END OF THE RIVER—A CHRISTIAN LEADERSHIP THEORY

In 1970, Jay E. Adams published a book for Christian counselors in which he developed an explicitly Christian theory of counseling he called Nouthetic Confrontation. "Nouthetic" is a transliteration of the Greek noun *nouthesia* and the Greek verb *noutheteō*. These Greek words do not translate directly into English, but their use in the New Testament implies two important characteristics. The first is that people and communities make spiritual progress by clearly recognizing, learning about and persistently confronting obstacles in their path (Colossians 3:16). The second is that overcoming the obstacle is for the benefit of an individual or community (1 Corinthians 4:14). Adams's transliterated term *nouthetic* provides an apt description of the transforming leadership process described by Burns. In addition, Christian moral principles provide substance and direction for transforming servant leadership. The moral question raised in Burns's transforming theory is answered through the special revelation that emerges from biblical moral principles. Christian leadership is concerned with the transforming journey of organizations and individuals, raising them not just morally (as Burns posits), but moving them toward their sanctified purpose.

While a biblical standard for the moral component of transforming leadership might be readily accepted by Christian readers, for our theory to have utility in secular institutions as well as for those who conduct leadership and who are not Christians, the moral elevation controversy must be addressed further. For most twenty-first-century North Americans, a declaration of the existence of a Christian absolute moral standard sounds judgmental, narrow-minded and bigoted. A case must be made that Christ's moral principles can serve as an absolute moral standard applicable to *all people everywhere.*

North Americans and Europeans (and countless others around the world) live in societies heavily influenced by postmodernism. Postmodern critics argue that the imposition of the Christian metanarrative is precisely why so many injustices have been perpetuated throughout history by many who claimed to follow Christ. These critics have a valid point. History has no shortage of examples of individuals, groups and nations claiming the authority of Christ as they have committed hegemony and all manner of heinous offenses. Partially as a reaction to these historic abuses, and also because of a host of philosophical, economic, social, political and scientific paradigms that have steadily gained traction over the last century, postmodernism rejects metanarratives and the claims to moral absolutes such narratives generate.

While the rejection of metanarratives solves the problem of moral hegemony by nefarious regimes, it opens up the equally troubling problem of moral relativism. If there are no absolute moral standards, then there is no basis for determining if something is right or wrong. There is no standard upon which someone could legitimately condemn the behavior of Hitler. If there are no moral absolutes, the morality of Nazism is just as valid as any morality generated by any other worldview. Following the logical progression of moral relativism generated by postmodernism leads to nihilism, where there is no meaning and no purpose—everything just "is."

With nihilism there is absolutely no need for transforming leadership! X^2 is meaningless. Why even go there? Nietzsche's notion of leadership is fairly simple, and it takes us upstream to the Power Tributary. He suggested that since there is no meaning or ultimate purpose for anything, it makes sense that a person exercise their "will to power." If there is no meaning, then one might as well devote their life to gaining power over the "herd." This is as logical a destination as any for postmodernism and moral relativism.

Something innate in human beings cries out against the absurdity of moral relativism. What Hitler did was wrong. We know this is true, even if we are unwilling to admit that there is a baseline morality that informs our judgment. Even so, we see this morality in play in far less extreme examples. For instance, when my older brother used to make us milkshakes, he would pour more for him and less for me. I knew that wasn't fair. When he drank his down to make the level in our two glasses the same, and then told me that everything was equal, I still knew that something was amiss. If everything just "is," then why do we innately *know* when some things are not *fair*?

Christian leadership liberates us from the relativism quagmire. C. S. Lewis, in *The Abolition of Man*, presents a crosscultural study (general revelation) identifying moral absolutes he labels the *Tao*. By identifying these examples of universal and crossculturally accepted moral precepts, Lewis raises the probability that moral absolutes exist and, even more troubling for postmodernism, the possibility of the existence of a universal God who generated the moral absolutes. Over the decades, nihilists and postmodern philosophers have not been able to generate compelling arguments against Lewis's position.

It seems the only arguments against Christian moral standards are the abuses generated from the aberrations of those standards we find all too often in history. Poor behavior does not invalidate the legitimacy of moral standards. Indeed these very standards allow us to judge the immoral behavior of some who have called themselves Christians over the centuries.

The living water from Lake Logos that bubbles into Servant Lake sorts out the moral turmoil generated by Burns's transforming leadership theory. Biblical standards provide a foundation upon which the transforming moral improvements can be based. While Christians and non-Christians alike may engage one another in debates about worldview and doctrinal practices, biblical standards supersede these dogmatic conflicts and inform agreement about major moral principles. Biblical standards like stewardship, integrity, love and human dignity are crosscultural moral absolutes any person on the planet can endorse no matter what they believe or don't believe about God.

The Leadership River is now fully developed. We can now establish a preliminary definition of Christian leadership: *Christian leadership facilitates the transforming and sanctifying journey of individuals and organizations from X^1 to X^2 in both material and spiritual ways.* Drawing from the varied influences upstream, the river's true character, Christian leadership is evident as it flows into the Sea of Complexity. In the next chapter, we will see how Christian leadership functions in the chaotic organizational climate of the twenty-first century.

REFERENCES

Adams, J. E. 1970. *Competent to Counsel.* Grand Rapids: Baker.

Blake, R. R., and J. S. Mouton. 1964. *The Managerial Grid.* Houston: Gulf Publishing.

Boone, L. E., and D. D. Bowen. 1987. *The Great Writings in Management and Organizational Behavior.* New York: Random House.

Burns, J. M. 1978. *Leadership.* New York: Harper & Row.

Burns, J. S. 2000. "A River Runs Through It: A Metaphor for Teaching Leadership Theory." *Journal of Leadership Studies* 7 (3): 41-55.

———. 2008. "Leadership for the Common Good." In G. S. McGovern, *Leadership and Service,* pp. 201-24. Dubuque, IA: Kendall/Hunt.

Couto, A. 1995. "Social Capital and Transforming Leadership." 12th Scientific Meeting of the A. K. Rice Institute, *Leadership as Legacy: Transformation at the Turn of the Millennium.* Washington, DC.

Deming, W. E. 1986. *Out of the Crisis.* Cambridge, MA: Center for Advanced Engineering Study.

French, J. P. R., Jr., and B. Raven. 1960. "The Bases of Social Power." In D. Cartwright, *Group Dynamics,* pp. 607-23. New York: Harper & Row.

Greenleaf, R. K. 1977. *Servant Leadership.* New York: Paulist Press.

Heifetz, R. M. 1994. *Leadership Without Easy Answers.* Cambridge, MA: Belknap Press of Harvard University.

Hersey, P., and K. Blanchard. 1988. *Management of Organizational Behavior.* Englewood Cliffs, NJ: Prentice-Hall.

Howell, J. M. 1998. *Organizational Contexts, Charismatic and Exchange Leadership.* Unpublished position paper, Kellogg Leadership Studies Project.

Lewis, C. S. 1955a. *The Abolition of Man.* New York: Macmillan.

———. 1955b. *Surprised by Joy.* Orlando: Harcourt Brace & Company.

Moyo, D. 2009. *Dead Aid: Why Aid Is Not Working and How There Is a Better Way for Africa.* New York: Farrar, Straus & Giroux.

Peters, T. J., and R. H. Waterman Jr. 1982. *In Search of Excellence.* New York: Harper & Row.

Rodin, R. S. 2010. *The Steward Leader*. Downers Grove, IL: IVP Academic.

Rost, J. C. 1991. *Leadership for the Twenty-First Century*. New York: Praeger.

Stogdill, R. M. 1948. "Personal Factors Associated with Leadership: A Survey of the Literature." *Journal of Psychology* 25: 35-71.

Vroom, V. H., and A. G. Jago. 1988. *The New Leadership: Managing Participation in Organizations*. Englewood Cliffs, NJ: Prentice Hall.

FOR FURTHER READING

Barker, J. (director). 1990. *The Business of Paradigms* [Motion Picture].

Buber, M. 1958. *I and Thou*. Translated by R. G. Smith. New York: Charles Scribner's and Sons.

Burns, J. S. 2002. "Chaos Theory and Leadership Studies: Sailing Uncharted Seas." *Journal of Leadership and Organizational Studies* 9 (2):42-48.

Drucker, P. 1989. *The New Realities*. New York: Harper & Row.

Gleick, J. 1987. *Chaos: Making a New Science*. New York: Penguin.

Kaufman, S. A. 1995. *At Home in the Universe*. Oxford: Oxford University Press.

Lewis, C. S. 1960. *Miracles*. New York: Macmillan.

Marion, R. 2008. "Complexity Theory for Organizations and Organizational Leadership." In *Complexity Leadership Part 1: Conceptual Foundations*, edited by M. Uhl-Bien and R. Marion. Charlotte, NC: Information Age Publishing.

Peters, T. 1987. *Thriving on Chaos*. New York: Excel.

Senge, P. 1990. *The Fifth Discipline: The Art and Practice of the Learning Organization*. New York: Doubleday.

Stacey, R. D. 1996. *Complexity and Creativity in Organizations*. San Francisco: Berrett-Koehler.

———. 2000. *Complexity and Management: Fad or Radical Challenge to Systems Thinking?* London: Routledge.

———. 2001. *Complex Responsive Processes in Organizations: Learning and Knowledge Creation*. London: Routledge.

Wheatley, M. J. 2006. *Leadership and the New Science: Discovering Order in a Chaotic World*, 3rd ed. San Francisco: Berrett-Koehler.

5

CHRISTIAN LEADERSHIP ON THE SEA OF COMPLEXITY

John S. (Jack) Burns

—◊◊◊—

Immediately Jesus made the disciples get into the boat and go on ahead of him to the other side, while he dismissed the crowd. After he had dismissed them, he went up on a mountainside by himself to pray. When evening came, he was there alone, but the boat was already a considerable distance from land, buffeted by the waves because the wind was against it. During the fourth watch of the night Jesus went out to them, walking on the lake. When the disciples saw him walking on the lake, they were terrified. "It's a ghost," they said, and cried out in fear. But Jesus immediately said to them: "Take courage! It is I. Don't be afraid." "Lord, if it's you," Peter replied, "tell me to come to you on the water." "Come," he said. Then Peter got down out of the boat, walked on the water and came toward Jesus. But when he saw the wind, he was afraid and, beginning to sink, cried out, "Lord, save me!" Immediately Jesus reached out his hand and caught him. "You of little faith," he said, "why did you doubt?"

MATTHEW 14:22-31 (NIV 1984)

SAILING INTO TWENTY-FIRST-CENTURY CHRISTIAN LEADERSHIP

In the previous chapter, we concluded with an understanding of transforming servant leadership as the basis for a Christian leadership theory grounded in both theological and theory-based insights. The theological foundation for Christian leadership that we developed in the first three chapters highlights Christ's example as a servant and our response as believers. We understand that we are citizens of heaven sent to be ambassadors for Christ. We are called to steward the gifts God has given us to bring him glory and advance his kingdom work.

The theoretical basis for Christian leadership is heavily influenced by James MacGregor Burns's (1978) ideas about transforming leadership. We described Burns's transforming leadership theory as a journey from X^1 to X^2 where X^2 represents the purpose and values of organizations or individuals, and X^1 represents an honest assessment of where they are today with regard to absolutely fulfilling the purpose and values. Between X^1 and X^2 there are numerous obstacles that can be overcome only after individuals and organizations engage in ongoing adaptations or transformations. Burns also required transforming leadership to be morally elevating, and Christian leadership embraces biblical moral principles that are also universally and crossculturally accepted (e.g., honesty, justice and love).

We ended our journey on the Leadership River with this preliminary definition: Christian leadership facilitates the transforming and sanctifying journey of individuals and organizations from X^1 to X^2 in both material and spiritual ways. However, our journey is not over because the many currents of the Leadership River system make their way into Chaos Bay bordering the Sea of Complexity. Now we must set sail on the Sea of Complexity, where we find how new discoveries grounded in the physical and biological sciences mix with the principles of Christian leadership to form a dynamic understanding of the organizational and environmental contexts in which Christian leadership is conducted in the twenty-first century.

At this point a reader might wonder why we are going to look at physics and biology in our study of leadership. As this chapter unfolds it will become clear that for centuries, particularly since the Enlightenment, these "hard" sciences have been influencing social science, philosophy and even theology. Over the centuries, the profound but often unacknowledged influence of science has also informed our past and present understanding of Christian leadership.

The next few pages of this chapter will summarize a vast and growing literature in both the hard sciences and the social sciences in what has been called the "new science." We will learn how the "machine paradigm" about organizations (from the "old science") is undergoing a paradigm shift. We will find out that organizations are organic and that they live in a complex web with other organic agents. Our discussion of the new science will lay the critical foundation of theory that will inform our description of deeper, richer ways to think about Christian leadership. In this chapter we will not include the technical scientific discussions that usually accompany the investigation of these topics. That level of detail is beyond the scope of this book. This summary of the new sciences will provide sufficient background for the theoretical foundation we are laying. For those who want to dig deeper, the lists of references and further reading material at the end of the chapter provide resources for further investigation.

Throughout history, there have been many fascinating explanations for natural phenomena. For example, Aristotle developed an explanation for gravity. He said that the universe was made up of a group of concentric spheres. The Earth sphere at the center was surrounded by the sphere of water, which was surrounded by the sphere of air, which was surrounded by the sphere of fire, and finally, encircling all the others, was the sphere of the heavens. Aristotle also believed that all matter was composed of four basic elements: earth, water, air and fire. Aristotle explained gravity by suggesting that if an object contained more of one element than another; it would seek to move to its appropriate sphere (Barnes 1984). Thus, a rock falls "down" because it contains more of the element Earth—it simply seeks to be more completely enfolded by its appropriate sphere. For centuries, Aristotle's ideas shaped philosophical, metaphysical and scientific worldview assumptions, and they were more or less unquestioned until Sir Isaac Newton's equations blew Aristotle's spheres out of the sky.

Newton, a seventeenth-century mathematician and physicist, developed the equations of motion that helped to lay the foundation of scientific advances for centuries (Cajori 1960). Newton's work helped to establish the long-standing paradigm of the "mechanical universe," a universe that is analogous to a giant clock that is ticking away through eternity. Influenced by Newton, scientists believed that the universe could be understood through reductionism, the process of breaking the universe into its most basic parts in order to understand how everything works. The primary aim of science was to discover the deep laws that govern how the clock operated and, if possible, control it or accurately predict how it would work in the future.

Even in the face of the power and reliability of the mechanical universe paradigm, scientists knew that some of the phenomena they were interested in, like the geometry of a cloud, had obvious nonlinear, nonmechanical characteristics that defied mathematical modeling. For more than a century now, the hard sciences have abandoned the mechanical universe paradigm and have been exploring new ideas in quantum physics, chaos and complexity.

It can be argued that since the age of Enlightenment, the "authorized" assumptions about the nature of the universe have been described through the epistemological and metaphysical paradigms of the hard sciences. These paradigms define the "playing field" where *all* disciplines are expected to perform if they are to be considered credible. The result is that in Western worldviews, social scientists, not to mention philosophers and theologians, must acknowledge the primacy of the paradigms influenced by the empirical nature of science. This has created interdisciplinary tension because the empirically based mechanical paradigm assumptions "required" to explore human behavior and beliefs has often proved to be insufficient. Given the age-old tension between the hard sciences and other disciplines, it is somewhat ironic that today emerging new-science paradigms are far more compatible with "unauthorized" paradigms held by many social scientists, philosophers and theologians.

THE NEW SCIENCES: QUANTUM MECHANICS, CHAOS THEORY AND COMPLEXITY SCIENCE

Quantum physics. The aim of seeking to understand the mechanical universe through a lens of scientific reductionism was to find the basic building blocks of the universe. Quantum mechanics is the study of the structure and interactions of elementary particles of matter. Early in the twentieth century, physicists discovered that the "laws" that govern macroscopic objects, the larger parts of the machine, do not function in the same way at the quantum level, with the smallest parts of the machine. These quantum explorations blew the Newtonian mechanical assumptions out of the air just as surely as Newtonian discoveries shattered Aristotle's heavenly spheres.

Indeed quantum scientists do not describe the universe as a fact-based reality, a machine built with understandable parts working together in predictable ways. Instead, the universe is described as a series of interconnected probabilities. These scientists recognize that even if the universe functions in some deep deterministic way, the mechanism functions beyond the predictive capacity of humanity and out of range of human control. Thus, Newton's old and still highly functional equations float on deep and largely unknown laws of a quantum, not mechanical, universe.

As we take up our journey on the Sea of Complexity, we find that organizations also can no longer be considered as machines built component by component and then reliably and predictably "run" by talented managers. Instead, we find that organizations themselves are agents in the quantum world where they are understood best as organisms that reside within a complex web of internal and external relationships with myriad other agents.

Chaos theory. Scientists have long recognized that Newtonian math never worked well with obviously turbulent phenomena like smokestack emissions, waterfalls and weather systems. No math has ever existed to calculate the continuously changing geometry of a cloud, or to predict the path of a molecule of water within it. The universe abounds with nonlinear physical phenomena for which precise Newtonian equations are impossible.

Chaos is an unfortunate name for the theory in physics that gained traction during the last third of the twentieth century. *Chaos* implies randomness, yet chaos equations in physics do not reveal randomness but instead yield complex patterns. The precise development of these patterns defies prediction by any known means. In chaos theory, a strange attractor functions to shape the emerging pattern of the system. In physics, strange attractors and patterns of chaos can be illustrated in what physicists call phase space, a tool used to turn calculations into pictures. A given point in phase space represents the complete state of knowledge, as determined by a calculation, about a system's behavior at a single instant. At the next instant (new calculation), a new point is generated. It is possible to construct a map of the generation of discrete points over time as calculations track how a dynamic system operates around its strange attractor (Gleick 1987; Stacey 1996). The computer pictures of fern-like or bug-shaped or other beautiful chaotic systems in phase space represent the mathematical construction of patterns that develop around strange attractors.

These discoveries began when, in 1961, a theoretical meteorologist named Edward Lorenz was trying to develop a model for long-range weather prediction. He accidentally developed the initial equations that described the Lorenz attractor (see figure 5.1), and subsequently chaos theory.

For organizational theorists, the emergent chaotic patterns of organizations and the "strange attractor" that defines these patterns are of particular

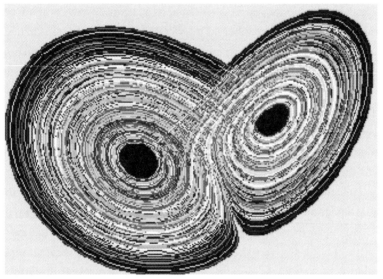

Figure 5.1. Lorenz Attractor
Each point represents the value of the calculations of three variables at an instant in time in phase space. As the values of the nonlinear calculations change over time, the locations of points change, never having a single point intersect with another point. In the Lorenz attractor, trajectories are bound to an orbit around two strange attractors infinitely creating a pattern that defies prediction about where a particular point will be at a specific future time. (Image by Roger Grace.)

interest. Some have proposed that the strange attractor for organizations is its purpose and values (X^2) (Burns 2002; Wheatley 2006). Thus, for organizations, *any behavior that appears to be supportive of the organization's purpose and values is potentially legitimate behavior*, even if the behavior was not predictable, planned, desired or controlled and appears to be far from the organization's most recent expression of authorized behavior.

Complexity theory. Complexity theory, the third component of the new science, is also at variance with the mechanical paradigm of the universe.

Again, from this theory we learn that organizations, instead of being mechanical, are organic, can learn and can self-organize to accomplish the transforming adaptations required to navigate through the obstacles on their journey from X^1 toward X^2.

Complexity theory emerged from the biological sciences. Complexity theorists have identified large gaps in Darwin's mechanical ideas about evolution that are incapable of being filled by random mutations over vast amounts of time. These scientists propose that order, such as it exists, emerged through self-organization instead of exclusively through Darwin's random chance mutations. This means that before Darwin's natural selection set up shop, at a deeper level in the rich chaotic soup of basic matter, ordered structures emerged. For these biologists, humans were not the result of accidental Darwinian mutation, but instead were expected in the universe! One of these biologists, Stuart Kauffman, writes:

> The vast mystery of biology is that life should have emerged at all, that the order we see should have come to pass. A theory of emergence would account for the creation of the stunning order outside our windows as a natural expression of some underlying laws. It would tell us if we are at home in the universe, expected in it, rather than present despite overwhelming odds.
>
> . . . Life, in this view, is an emergent phenomenon arising as the molecular diversity of a prebiotic chemical system increases beyond a threshold of complexity. If true, then life is not located in the property of any single molecule— in the details—but is a collective property of systems of interacting molecules. Life, in this view, emerged whole and has always remained whole. Life, in this view, is not to be located in its parts, but in the collective emergent properties of the whole they create. Although life as an emergent phenomenon may be profound, its fundamental holism and emergence are not at all mysterious. . . . The collective system is alive. Its parts are just chemicals. (1995, pp. 23-24)

Like the quantum and chaos physicists, these complexity scientists readily admit that the deep laws at work are beyond reductionist scientific explanations. Chemical reactions occur; patterns emerge; something creative, something novel and not deterministic happens. As a complexity theorist, Kauffman (most likely unintentionally) is throwing options into the biological paradigm that may in fact be compatible with the Christian understanding of creation. The concept of order emerging from the chaos arising "as the molecular diversity of a prebiotic chemical system increases beyond a threshold of complexity" seems to resonate with the biblical account of creation: "In the beginning God created the heavens and the earth. Now the earth was formless and empty, darkness was over the surface of the deep, and the Spirit of God was hovering over the waters. . . . Then the LORD God formed a man from the dust of the ground and breathed into his nostrils the breath of life, and the man became a living being" (Genesis 1:1-2; 2:7). Perhaps the deep laws Kauffman and others at the Santa Fe Institute have been uncovering are what Thomas Aquinas described as the character of the Creator being evident in the creation.

THE NEW SCIENCE PARADIGM APPLIED TO ORGANIZATIONS LIVING IN THE SEA OF COMPLEXITY

So how does the new science relate to leaders and their organizations? Robert Marion (2008) has identified three important dynamics at work in complex systems that inform how leaders and organizations are able to adapt to environmental demands through complexity theory's principle of self-organization.

First, systems are able to self-organize and create order even without input from external sources. Dynamic patterns of interaction among organizational agents can influence the potential for self-generation. These dynamic patterns may be more important for the creation of organizational operating structure than the actions of leaders or others external to the organization! For example, most organizations establish policies and procedures (high-task orientation) that describe how things are supposed to be done. Often people will quietly "violate" those policies and procedures because they have learned more efficient ways to do the work. At best they feel it is cumbersome or unnecessary to update the policies and procedures manual to reflect actual practice, and at worst, if they are found out, they hope they have such a track record of success that they will not be punished for breaking the rules.

Second, Marion suggests that order can be created by casting off (dissipating) energy instead of consuming it. This "violation" of the second law of thermodynamics is a revolutionary way to look at the relationship between energy and order. Instead of creating order by pumping energy into a system to hold it together, systems often push out energy to relieve the tension constrained by firm structures. This allows a different order to emerge that requires less energy. For example, most organizations use a great deal of energy to establish and enforce resource allocation policies and procedures. In times of turbulence (crisis) these policies and procedures can become cumbersome. Energy that sustains them is often removed—cutting through the red tape—so that new structures may emerge to expedite the acquisition and distribution of resources to more efficiently deal with the crisis.

The third dynamic Marion observes is that in organizations, linear predictions (long-range strategic plans) aimed at controlling the nature of organizational structures and outcomes over time are not possible. Functional structures develop somewhat randomly, are usually dynamic and emerge from complex interactions. In other words, stuff happens! In the long run, structures (and long-range plans written in stone) will prove to be ineffective at dealing with emergent unpredicted environmental demands. Sticking to the plan can prove to be fatal for an organization.

Both quantum physics and complexity theory teach that organizations paradoxically exist as independent entities and as part of a dynamic interconnected environmental web. What happens in the environmental web is at least as influential as what happens in the organization's internal web of relationships. Indeed, the initial emergence of the organization itself is a function of a web of interactions between innumerable agents and systems. It is not possible to identify a "first agent" or system because the interactions and relationships descend to the quantum level. From a Christian perspective, the theoretical "first" or causal quantum interaction is folded into the mystery of God's creative activity.

Physicists and biologists working in complexity science are focusing a great deal of their research on the dynamic connections of matter. Similarly, social scientists are beginning to explore the dynamic connections of agents and systems within and between the organizational web. The key element in all of these relational connections is *information*, which is the lifeblood of organizations and, indeed, the lifeblood of the entire web!

Information and meaning. Information and meaning go together. First published in 1923, Martin Buber (1958), in his classic book *I and Thou*, suggested that meaning is gained when humans come into relationship with one another and genuine information is shared between them. Thus, when information is shared and interpreted among agents, meaning is developed. But what is information, and how is it that information enlivens and develops meaning in an organization? To begin to answer this question, it is useful to discuss what information is not. Information is not a "thing" or an entity, though it is often treated as such in the mechanical paradigm of organizations. Relegating information to the status of some kind of thing disregards its dynamic, resilient and invisible nature. For a moment, think about a childhood memory, like your first day of school. That memory is information that has been retained even though every cell in your body that experienced that first day of school has died and been replaced several times.

Information is much more than memories. Some physicists like John Archibald Wheeler suggest that information is a principal component of reality. Wheatley wondered,

> What if physicist John Archibald Wheeler is right? What if information is the basic ingredient of the universe? This is not a universe of things, but a universe of the "no-thing" of information. And this information is organized by a second invisible element, meaning. If the universe organizes through these invisible forces, then we must contemplate new processes for working with them. Information and meaning-making do not obey the classical laws of physics that govern matter. As energetic forces, they move and act differently—they can travel with great speed anywhere in the universal web and appear suddenly as potent influences that surprise us. In the West, we didn't grow up learning about non-material forces. But this has become a critical curriculum. We must learn how to work with life in all its dimensions, seen and unseen. (2006, pp. 165-66)

When guided by mechanical assumptions about organizations, the non-material nature of information is often ignored and treated as another piece of the machine. Managers try to control and constrain information when they view it as a commodity. "Everybody needs information to do their work. We are so needy of this resource that if we cannot get the real thing, we make it up. When rumors proliferate and gossip gets out of hand, it is always a sign that people lack the genuine article—honest, meaningful information" (Wheatley 2006, p. 99). Communication problems are usually ranked as a major issue in organizations and relationships. "Communication problems" is code for information problems. Double-loop learning can help resolve information problems and allow us to accept its nonmaterial nature.

Single-loop and double-loop learning. Ralph Stacey (1996) has described how single-loop and double-loop learning impact systems. Organizational systems are made up of agents that function in relationship with each other. These agents develop dominant and recessive schemas (rules) that govern their interactions, and thus their ability to share information and make meaning. Stacey calls the collection of agents using sanctioned dominant schemas to fulfill a system's primary mission the *legitimate system*. The legitimate system is engaged in single-loop learning when it evaluates how effectively agents employ their dominant schemas. Negative feedback (punishment) reinforces conformity with the authorized schemas. In this way, the legitimate system is intently focused on internal performance, insulating itself from what it considers extraneous distractions from the external environment (see figure 5.2).

D R = Agent's Dominant and Recessive Schema

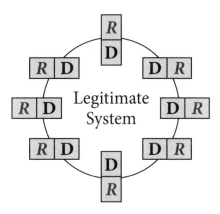

Figure 5.2. Model of Single-Loop Learning
Single-loop learning occurs when the agents employ their dominant schemas as the legitimate system performs its primary function. Agents who employ recessive schemas or perform dominant schemas in less than satisfactory ways are corrected through negative feedback tactics.

For example, we can describe a flock of sparrows as a legitimate system. Sparrows share dominant schemas that make them proficient at escaping a known threat from the environment, like a cat climbing up their tree. Their dominant schemas tell them to escape the cat by flying off together in a kind of crazy flocking/flying pattern. Their schemas enable them to fly this way without crashing into each other or other predictable environmental threats like branches, power lines and myriad other relatively fixed obstacles in their path. Following their dominant schemas for flying as a mad flock, the birds are focused on information/feedback from each other and are mostly oblivious to sudden or unexpected information from the larger environment. Thus, it is quite possible for a flock to fly right into the engine of a 737 taking off on the runway near their home.

This is an example of the strengths and limits of single-loop learning. As long as the environment does not change too suddenly or unexpectedly, the "fly as a mad flock" dominant schema will continue to be an efficient response to the environment's demands; but if an unexpected demand emerges, the flock may find itself in jeopardy.

Double-loop learning occurs in complex systems. In these systems agents not only maximize their behavior through single-loop learning under "normal" circumstances (e.g., fly as a mad flock), but agents are also able to modify their behavior by employing recessive schemas in response to information they receive from the dynamic environment around them. If sparrows were capable of complex adaptive behavior involving double-loop learning, the birds would still engage in mad-flock behavior based on their dominant schemas. However, they would also be capable of novelty and self-organization by experimenting with recessive schemas.

Through double-loop learning, a flock of sparrows might learn to inhabit trees far away from airport runways because they saw what happened to some hapless friends who flew in front of a 737. Double-loop learning might also help them develop novel schemas where they learn that if they perch in trees where dogs patrol the yard, they do not have problems with cats. The point is that double-loop learning allows the flock to assess an environmental demand, and then to import and exploit novel adaptive behaviors from new combinations of schemas.

Agents not only belong to the organization's legitimate system, but they are also members of shadow systems (Stacey 1996). A shadow system (see figure 5.3) does not necessarily exist in order to carry out the primary task of the organization. Indeed, shadow systems may or may not be coupled with the legitimate system. Agents belong to shadow systems for social, political, economic, spiritual and myriad other reasons.

Growing organizations must develop ways to become nourished by information learned by agents in the shadow systems because the shadow systems provide a different perspective on the environment that may be useful to the legitimate system. Self-organization in response to the influx of dynamic information from shadow systems depends on the system's ability to engage effectively in both single- and double-loop learning.

Emergent creative and adaptive organizational behavior occurs in a zone physicists refer to as the "zone of phase transition." In this zone, through double-loop learning, information emerging from the environment can be accommodated as agents experiment with new combinations of dominant and recessive schemas. By self-organizing around these new schemas, agents

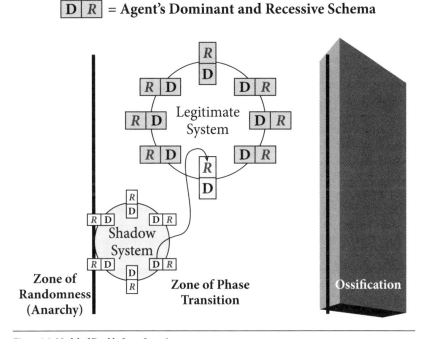

Figure 5.3. Model of Double-Loop Learning
In the zone of phase transition, the strange attractor (the organization's purpose and values) keeps the organization from isolating itself from the environment where it ossifies, or flying into randomness and anarchy. Double-loop learning allows the organization to import and experiment with new recessive schemas that have functioned as dominant schemas in the shadow systems. These experiments allow the organization to adapt to ongoing environmental demands.

have the potential to articulate the organization's purpose and values in creative and novel ways.

Recall from our earlier discussion about chaos that an organization's ultimate purpose and its values (x^2) make up the essence of the strange attractor. The strange attractor serves to filter incoming shadow system schemas. The organization can then use selected schemas to engage in experimental behavior within the legitimate system to see if the new schemas contribute to the organization's purpose and values.

As recessive schemas are swapped with dominant schemas in these experiments, the system will experience some failure. These failures are disconcerting but are rarely fatal, and they provide enhanced opportunities for organizational learning. Thus failure serves as a catalyst for more double-loop learning. Fear of failure typically keeps organizations from creativity. However, as long as the organization remains bound to and has faith in its strange attractor (x^2), it improves its chances of continuously discovering creative, successful ways to adapt to the demands of the environment.

Let's consider the church as the legitimate system and a member named Tom as an agent in the legitimate system. Tom is also a member of numerous shadow systems, including a committee within the church, a denomination-wide committee, his workplace, his family, a recreational sports team, different groups of friends and a civic organization. Most of these shadow systems are not charged with the successful implementation of the church's legitimate system schema. Agents like Tom are free to experiment with schemas in the shadow systems that are not sanctioned by the legitimate system of the church. In the context of the shadow system of Tom's profession, he learned how to develop web-based viral marketing strategies. Double-loop learning in the legitimate system of the church occurs if Tom is allowed to introduce recessive schemas, in this case his desire to develop an experimental viral marketing campaign to supplement the church's outreach ministries.

When any organization encourages experimentation with new schemas and interactions among agents, the system learns to abandon rigid, mechanical-paradigm, control-based tactics associated with negative feedback from single-loop learning (e.g., "We've always done it this way, so we're not going to do this new thing"). Instead, the organization learns to have faith in its purpose and values (x^2) instead of its policies and procedures. This faith in the strange attractor will allow it to exploit the benefits of double-loop learning.

Having faith in the power of the strange attractor to keep the system from imploding or exploding often feels like very poor strategy. Accordingly, the legitimate system's single-loop mechanical response is to become defensive, exerting control strategies that could drive the organization into ossification. Recall the story of Peter walking on the water at the beginning of this chapter. After a few steps, he took his eyes off of Christ, his strange attractor (x^2), and instead, "when he saw the wind, he was afraid" (Matthew 14:30). He looked at the environmental threat, reverted to his old schema, and that is when he began to sink like a rock!

Ossification. Exclusive single-loop mechanical strategies shut down enriched double-loop learning as the organization relies on learning only through "authorized" information channels (e.g., a supervisor's information gathered exclusively from former employees' exit interviews). As a result, potentially vital information emerging from the environment is dismissed as irrelevant (e.g., information a former employee shares with former colleagues who are teammates on her recreational softball team). Through negative feedback, the legitimate system actually defends itself against what it considers disruptive information from the environment. If organizations expend enough resources and energy, they can erect a barrier between the legitimate system and environment that cannot be breached. Behind such a barrier, stability reigns. In fact, the organization may cease importing vital information from the environment, and over time it will ossify, meaning it will transform from a living, growing organism to something as rigid and unchanging as a skeleton. Many organizations have indeed been managed to death! (See figure 5.4.)

Joel Barker (1990), in his classic video *The Business of Paradigms*, explains how the Swiss watch manufacturers missed a paradigm shift. This can also be described as how the Swiss managed their industry into ossification. Until 1968, the Swiss had dominated watch making for more than a century. Their legitimate system was governed by dominant schemas that said great watches had highly engineered mechanical components, and the Swiss could build mainsprings, gears and all of the other components of watches better than anyone in the world. Some enterprising Swiss watchmakers invented the quartz movement watch (shadow system activity), but because it didn't follow legitimate system schemas, the idea was rejected. Meanwhile, Seiko and Texas Instruments obtained the rights for the quartz movement

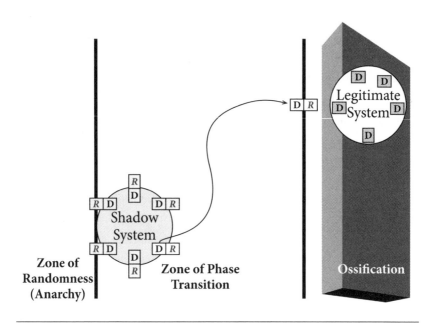

Figure 5.4. Model of Ossification/Organizational Death
Ossification occurs as the legitimate system isoltates itself from turbulence in the environment. Because of rigid single-loop learning and negative feedback, agents are barred from importing schemas from shadow systems and can only employ the organization's dominant schemas.

electronic watch from the Swiss and turned the whole industry away from mechanical watches. It might also be fair to wonder if too many Christian organizations, by doggedly sticking to entrenched schemas that govern how ministry "should" be done, are on a path to ossification.

Some organizations have long recognized how the dominant schemas of the legitimate system can stifle institutional learning, creativity and emergent organizational growth. Years before Stacey was writing about shadow systems, the Minnesota Mining and Manufacturing Corporation (3M) realized the need for gaining access to information through conduits not officially recognized by the corporation. For decades, scientists at 3M have been encouraged to ignore rigid institutional structures in order to "bootleg" resources for entrepreneurial projects. These shadow system projects encourage creative emergence of novel ideas and products. Bootlegging has provided the company with many innovations over the years.

One legendary example is of a 3M employee (legitimate system agent) who was also a member of a church choir (shadow system agent). He found that bookmarks kept falling out of his hymnal as he shuffled from song to song during worship services. He teamed up to form a bootleg experiment with another 3M scientist who had developed an inferior but nonetheless interesting adhesive—it didn't stick things together very well, but it also didn't tear paper apart when it was removed. The result was the development of the perfect bookmark for a church hymnal: Post-it notes!

Zone of randomness (anarchy). Often organizations recognize the hazards of imploding into ossification, and they will not expend the energy or resources to erect impermeable barriers against the environment. Organizations also face the danger of exploding into completely random behavior where anarchy reigns (see figure 5.5).

When a sinking ship takes on more water than its bilge pumps can handle, the crew and passengers must abandon ship. Then survival is no longer a function of the legitimate system of the ship, but depends on each individual's effort. Sometimes the external environment is extremely volatile and information can overwhelm the legitimate system's ability to handle it. Information overload can sink the legitimate system, causing agents to abandon it and to navigate independently through the turbulent environment.

Organizations can explode into anarchy when they import schemas too rapidly or import irrelevant schemas. Examples might include becoming addicted to meaningless novelty occurring in the environment (e.g., constantly adopting the latest changes in technology or marketing buzzwords), or having a culture of conflict avoidance and thus implementing the obviously self-serving and organizationally irrelevant schemas of politically powerful agents. To prevent such an explosion into randomness and anarchy, the legitimate system must develop ways to identify and pace its response to essential information as well as ways to identify and ignore irrelevant information. Thus the strange attractor can filter irrelevant information.

Managers must develop strategies for modulating the provocation importing new schemas will create. Every organization will handle change differently, and the pace of change will depend on the organization's environmental context. A youth ministry will have to be geared up to handle rapid change and will have to develop structures to accommodate that kind of turbulence. A monastery can afford to be far less responsive to environmental pressures.

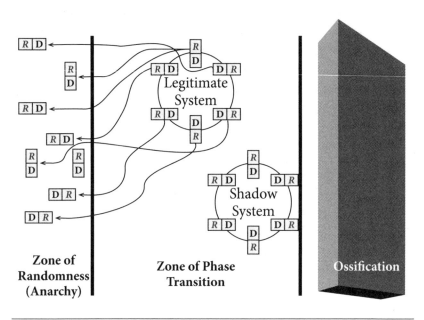

Figure 5.5. Model of the Zone of Randomness (Anarchy)
In the zone of randomness, the legitimate system ceases to be an organization. Agents become "free" agents, independently navigating through the environment without regard to the purpose or values of the former legitimate system.

Change can jeopardize the organization's purpose and values (X^2). Imagine a vibrant church that triples its membership over a five-year span. This kind of growth could actually destroy the church! The sheer number of new members could overwhelm the purpose and values held by the initial group that made up the church because each of these new members will bring myriad schemas from shadow systems into the church. This is not an argument against church growth; it is an argument for constantly teaching and reinforcing the strange attractor to the membership of the church. New members must be taught (and old members reminded) about the purpose and values of the church. Indeed the strange attractor of the church is strengthened when every member understands and embraces the enduring purpose and values of the church. If members of the church, or agents of any organization, are not committed to the organization's purpose and values (X^2), then there is no strange attractor to hold the organization together. When the strange attractor ceases to exist, or is significantly weakened, then the organization loses its unifying identity. Division, infighting, political power plays and other factional bickering are characteristics of organizations with a weak or nonexistent X^2.

DEFINING CHRISTIAN LEADERSHIP IN THE SEA OF CHAOS

In the previous chapter we established a preliminary definition of Christian leadership: Christian leadership facilitates the transforming and sanctifying journey of individuals and organizations from X^1 to X^2 in both material and spiritual ways. In the new science paradigm, conducting leadership looks very different from leadership in the mechanical paradigm. Leadership theorists are just beginning to explore the Sea of Complexity and all that this emerging paradigm can teach us about conducting leadership in twenty-first-century organizations. From our early explorations we have learned that organizations are not mechanical, but are living, interconnected organisms that have a purpose in God's kingdom. We know that organizations need to be nurtured with information so that they can learn and grow by adapting and transforming. Christian leadership pairs this deep knowledge about the dynamic nature of organizations with our own growing and deepening personal faith that informs everyday behavior, including how we live as knowledgeable and faithful "agents" in our organizations.

When we combine the theological foundation for Christian leadership from chapters 1 through 3 with the theoretical foundation we have laid in chapters 4 and 5, we have a robust description of Christian leadership:

> Christian leadership is conducted by servant leaders and followers during the ongoing redemptive and transforming/adaptive journey of an organization from X^1 (an honest assessment of its current status) to X^2 (its God-ordained purpose and values). Organizations learn, self-organize and emerge in a

paradox of stability and instability in a zone of phase transition, where faith in the organization's X^2 acts as a strange attractor that keeps the organization from imploding or exploding. Nonetheless, there is a dynamic tension between the tendency of organizations to ossify through control-based strategies that cut off information from the environment or to explode into randomness and anarchy by being overrun by irrelevant information from the environment. Christian leadership recognizes that information is the lifeblood of the organization, and relevant information must be imported from the environment and allowed to circulate freely into, within and out of the organization.

Christian leadership is conducted in light of truths derived from general and special revelation. Christians embrace organizational collaborative community modeled by the community of the Trinity. Christians in relationship with Jesus rely on Scripture, their community, prayer and the guidance of the Holy Spirit as they conduct leadership. Through information-rich relationships, Christians steward their gifts and resources to facilitate the process of growing the organization ever closer to its x^2. No matter what their role in organizations, Christians honor, and by faith entrust, the organization to its God-ordained purpose and values, its x^2.

In this description, leadership is not reduced to the "leadership" behavior of a leader or team of "top" people. Leadership is conducted throughout the organization, through all agents. Joseph Rost (1991) talked about how this kind of nonhierarchical collaborative form of leadership would be necessary in the twenty-first century. Leadership is conducted as a collaborative, nonhierarchical activity because in dynamic systems, all agents have potential access to vital information from the environment.

Though leadership is behavior that is broadly conducted, it is specific in function. First, the organization will not engage in transforming behavior unless a culture develops where all agents are encouraged to routinely revisit and affirm their support for the God-ordained purpose and values (x^2) of the organization. Second, conducting leadership requires a continuous flow and assessment of environmental information as it relates to X^2. Third, all agents are responsible for forwarding information about adaptive schemas from the shadow systems that provide opportunities for the legitimate system to learn, adapt and overcome environmental obstacles. Fourth, organizations must consistently engage in creative experimental behavior in order to test the efficacy of new schemas.

As an organization goes through this transforming/adaptive process, paradoxically X^2 becomes clearer and clearly unattainable! It is clearer because it is viewed from multiple environmental perspectives over time, but though there is significant adaptive progress toward it, it remains unattainable as clarity only reveals new emerging obstacles and the need for even more adaptive work. This ongoing activity allows an organization to lift its collective vision from the distractions of the mundane to discover its enduring essential purpose (Wheatley 2006). This clarity of ultimate purpose and values frees the organization to become creative as it responds to environmental challenges.

Christians understand the paradox of the ever-clearer and always elusive X^2 from their own spiritual journeys. After an initial experience with Christ, a Christian convert is often faced with major initial lifestyle changes, and from their initial perspective that is their X^2. Those lifestyle changes accomplished, the goal of Christ is at once clearer and obstructed by emerging and heretofore unacknowledged issues the believer needs to now address. Christians call this the process of sanctification. Sanctification is never fully achieved in this life, though it remains a lifelong mission for Christians.

What we have learned about leadership and organizations from the new science is not foreign to Christians. Christian metaphysics and epistemology are not limited by the material world. Many Christians conducting leadership have often intuitively rejected mechanistic practices when it comes to leadership in Christian organizations. Christians understand that their organizations are enlivened by their members and by God. Machine-paradigm management strategies have had and will continue to have a place in many functional areas of Christian organizations (e.g., accounting/business office functions). Recognizing and celebrating the living and unseen spiritual nature of organizations and the exciting dynamic environment in which our organizations live is empowering. Christians and Christian organizations have been emerging by learning, adapting and self-organizing for more than two thousand years. Christian leadership recognizes that this dynamic process must continue for our organizations to thrive and become fully responsive to the challenges of kingdom work in the twenty-first century.

REFERENCES

Aquinas, T. 1947. *Summa Theologica of St. Thomas Aquinas*. Volume 1. Translated by Fathers of the English Dominican Province. New York: Benziger Brothers Inc.

Barker, J., director. 1990. *The Business of Paradigms* [Motion Picture].

Barnes, J., ed. 1984. *Complete Works of Aristotle*. Princeton, NJ: Princeton University Press.

Buber, M. 1958. *I and Thou*. Translated by R. G. Smith. New York: Charles Scribner's and Sons.

Burns, J. M. 1978. *Leadership*. New York: Harper & Row.

Burns, J. S. 2002. "Chaos Theory and Leadership Studies: Sailing Uncharted Seas." *Journal of Leadership and Organizational Studies*, 9 (2): 42-48.

Cajori, F. 1960. *Sir Isaac Newton's Mathematical Principles of Natural Philosophy and His System of the World*. Berkeley CA: University of California Press.

Gleick, J. 1987. *Chaos: Making a New Science*. New York: Penguin.

Kauffman, S. A. 1995. *At Home in the Universe*. Oxford: Oxford University Press.

Marion, R. 2008. "Complexity Theory for Organizations and Organizational Leadership." In *Complexity Leadership Part 1: Conceptual Foundations*, edited by M. Uhl-Bien and R. Marion. Charlotte, NC: Information Age Publishing.

Rost, J. C. 1991. *Leadership for the Twenty-First Century*. New York: Praeger.

Stacey, R. D. 1996. *Complexity and Creativity in Organizations*. San Francisco: Berrett-Koehler.

Wheatley, M. J. 2006. *Leadership and the New Science: Discovering Order in a Chaotic World*, 3rd ed. San Francisco: Berrett-Koehler.

FOR FURTHER READING

Burns, J. S. 2000. "A River Runs Through It: A Metaphor for Teaching Leadership Theory." *Journal of Leadership Studies* 7 (3): 41-55.

Drucker, P. 1989. *The New Realities*. New York: Harper & Row.

Greenleaf, R. K. 1977. *Servant Leadership*. New York: Paulist Press.

Heifetz, R. M. 1994. *Leadership Without Easy Answers*. Cambridge, MA: Belknap Press of Harvard University.

Lewis, C. S. 1960. *Miracles*. New York: Macmillan.

Peters, T. 1987. *Thriving on Chaos*. New York: Excel.

Senge, P. 1990. *The Fifth Discipline: The Art and Practice of the Learning Organization*. New York: Doubleday.

Stacey, R. D. 2000. *Complexity and Management: Fad or Radical Challenge to Systems Thinking?* London: Routledge.

———. 2001. *Complex Responsive Processes in Organizations: Learning and Knowledge Creation*. London: Routledge.

KEY SKILLS *and* PRACTICES *in* CHRISTIAN LEADERSHIP

6

COMMUNICATION IN
THE IMAGE OF GOD

Ronald K. Pyle

—ᵕᵕᵕ—

INTRODUCTION: A THEOCENTRIC PERSPECTIVE

Communication is among the most important experiences in all of life. Through sending and receiving messages, our world takes on meaning, relationships are built, identities are established and goals are formed. Communication scholar John Stewart, with coauthors Zediker and Witteborn, has suggested that the quality of one's existence is directly related to the quality of the communicative relationships experienced (2005, p. 70). Communication is foundational to leadership in families, small groups, churches and organizations. Because the quality of all those group experiences is directly related to the quality of our communication, it makes sense for us to understand and apply the best of what we know about human communication. By God's grace, it is our hope in this chapter to enhance the quality of your personal and group life by providing a description of some of the key principles of communication that are important as we lead.

In this chapter we offer a theocentric perspective of human communication that places God at the center of our understanding of communication and asks, "What does our understanding of God have to do with communication?" The foundational conviction driving this chapter is that communication itself is made in God's image. In his helpful book about preaching, John Stott offers the following insight: "The essential secret [to preaching] is not mastering certain techniques but being mastered by certain convictions" (1982, p. 92). The approach Stott suggests we take toward preaching is equally true of our understanding of communication. There are important skills to be discussed in this chapter, and we hope you find them useful. But prior to the question of *how* to communicate is the question of *what it is* to communicate.

DEFINING AND DESCRIBING COMMUNICATION

While many different definitions of communication exist, most agree on the foundational descriptors in this definition: *Communication is the complex, contextualized, collaborative process of verbal and nonverbal meaning-making* (modified from Stewart 2009, p. 22). In the section that follows we will consider each of these foundational descriptors and how they contribute to a theocentric perspective on communication.

Communication is complex. God is complex. In the mystery of God's own tripartite person, in the stunning diversity of creation and in the intricate unfolding of God's activity in human history, God's complexity is demonstrated. Being made in God's image, our communication is also complex. It's a miracle that human beings make sense out of one another at all. Add our cultural, social, physical, gendered, ethnic and personal differences, and the miracle is even more profound. The process of communication can be described physically, mentally, socially and even spiritually, but after all of that, mystery remains. One of the tasks of communication is to embrace rather than try to solve the complexity of communication. Remaining mindful of this complexity, we will be less likely to assume that the messages we send and receive represent, with complete fidelity, the meanings intended.

Communication is contextual. God creates and acts into contexts. Out of nothing, God created the first physical and relational contexts. In Eden, unadulterated relational intimacy, temptation and brokenness all emerge as part of creation's context. From that moment forward, all communication is bounded by various contexts. In John 10, Jesus encounters people who do not believe, and he flatly says to them, "You do not believe because you are not my sheep" (John 10:26). In chapter 11, just a few verses later, Jesus weeps with Mary and Martha because their brother Lazarus has died. In each situation, the relational context creates a different communication from Jesus.

All communication occurs in settings that include physical, relational, cultural and gendered, and psychological contexts. Each of these aspects of context warrants further explanation.

Physical context. "Natural aspects" of the physical context are composed of elements that affect how we relate, but over which we have no control. Time of day and amount of sunlight are examples of natural aspects. Since these elements are out of our control, we can't do much to change them. However depressed we find our group's energy level at 4 p.m. on a dark and gloomy February afternoon, there is not much we can do to change the weather. What we can change is our awareness of the natural aspects of the physical context. Other aspects of the physical context are called "designed" aspects. These elements are present in the physical context and controlled by human beings. Examples of designed elements include seating arrangements, use of media such as visual art and music, and dress. The same afternoon meeting described above might be improved by wise use of lighting and by engaging modes of presentation once the meeting has begun. Because the physical context is usually a dominant part of the first experience we have with others, it is remarkably powerful in establishing an initial impression. It is easy to imagine how differences in office decor can send varied messages. The designed elements in some offices communicate cold professionalism while other offices might be perceived as less formal, but perhaps less professional as well.

Relational context. In his pioneering work on relationships, social psychologist William Schutz (1958) claimed that all of us experience three fundamental relational needs. The first is the need for inclusion, to feel that we belong. Whether it comes in families, churches, workplaces or social settings, if people are unsure about whether they are accepted they are likely to either distance themselves to protect against more social pain or to immerse themselves in groups and risk losing a sense of their individuality. People who are healthy in terms of inclusion can be a productive part of a group and can also be alone without assuming they are unacceptable.

The second relational need is the need for affection, to give and receive love. People who remain unsure about whether they are loved will tend to insulate themselves by maintaining surface-level relationships or they will try to become everyone's best friend, assuming that all relationships must be close. Healthy individuals can give and receive verbal and nonverbal expressions of love. They can also maintain more socially distant relationships when that is appropriate.

The third need is related to control and the desire to give and receive influence. If people believe they lack the ability to influence others, they will tend to either give up trying to influence, isolating themselves, or they will seek to control situations, thus demonstrating their ability to influence. Healthy individuals can exercise influence when it is appropriate to do so, and they can also be led by others when that is appropriate.

Knowing these relational needs may help leaders become more aware of the needs of those we lead. For example, those of us who give leadership to ministry groups may notice a volunteer leader who seems relationally engaged in direct conversation with us but distant and withdrawn when they are in groups with other leaders. In such a situation, it may be wise for us to gently probe the extent to which this volunteer believes they are included. Knowledge of the relational needs may also help us understand our own responses to situations. For example, when we find it hard to delegate, we could reflect on our need to influence and remember that we don't need to control all events in order to know we have influence.

Cultural and gendered context. Culture is generally defined as the sum total of ways of living built up by a group of human beings and transmitted from one generation to another. Culture affects all of the ways we make meaning. Culture informs our understanding of the meanings of words and nonverbal cues (such as gestures). Culture also affects our assumptions about relationships by telling us what it means to be a man or a woman, what counts as virtuous or immoral behavior, what constitutes success, and virtually every other meaning we make. For example, a person from an individualist culture (where individual rights and goals take precedence over group needs) might celebrate when the food bank for which they volunteer leaves their previous affiliation to start their own entity. To the individualist, the increased fiscal and procedural autonomy are cause for rejoicing. Meanwhile, a person from a collectivist culture (where group needs take precedence over individual rights and goals) may observe the same situation and mourn the absence of loyalty to the parent organization.

Culture also affects ways of dealing with conflict. Let's say, for example, that two people volunteer for the same nonprofit organization and have a difference of opinion about how to maximize organizational impact. The first person's culture mandates that conflicts be faced directly and that each individual's goals get powerfully articulated. The second person's culture mandates that organizational harmony is far more important than individual preference and that the appropriate response to conflict is to accommodate the other. For each person, culture provides an assumed nature of reality.

The sex and gender of the people communicating constitutes an important part of context. One of the first questions asked of a new birth is the sex of the child. From the first moments of a child's life, sex and gender (not synonymous terms) supply important context affecting communication. "Sex" relates to the biological differences we typically refer to with the terms *female* and *male*. "Gender" relates to the cultural constructs involving social roles, behaviors and expectations we typically refer to with the terms *feminine* and *masculine*. It isn't the objective of this chapter to venture into the difficult question about whether observable differences between women and men are the product of nature or nurture or some combination thereof. Our purpose as it relates to this discussion is simply to underscore the fact that gender has a tremendous influence on how we make meaning in our communicative encounters.

Many of us never stop to consider that our assumptions about "the way things are" grow out of cultural and gendered contexts. The best way to learn about the cultural and gendered assumptions of another is to listen and ask good questions. We all have our own cultural and gendered assumptions. Our leadership is enhanced when we become more aware of those assumptions. Particular attention should be given to how our assumptions about culture and gender affect others in our organizations. The male supervisor, for example, who sprinkles staff meetings with stereotypic athletic metaphors about sports, may unwittingly be sending messages of exclusion to male and female coworkers who have not enjoyed similar athletic experiences.

Psychological context. Psychological context refers to the inner aspects of ourselves that we bring into all of our communication events. Self-concept is the collection of objective and subjective beliefs and attitudes built up over all the years of our life. *Beliefs* involve information we have about ourselves. Some information we embrace about ourselves is objective, such as our age or height. But much of the information we hold about ourselves is subjective, which doesn't make the information any less real. An example of a subjective belief is when a strained relationship with a member of the leadership team leaves us feeling inadequate as a supervisor. While the subjective belief that we are "inadequate" may or may not be objectively true, it constitutes a belief we might hold. *Attitudes* are positive or negative feelings. In the present example, we may feel insecure as a parent. The beliefs and attitudes we hold about ourselves come from the families in which we were raised, from our cultures, from the comments others make to and about us, and from our own internal reflection on our experiences. Leaders are wise to respect the influence we have in shaping our own and others' self-concepts.

Author Parker Palmer notes that "while inner work is a deeply personal matter, it is not necessarily a private matter" (1994, p. 38). Leaders work out their self-concepts as they cast, in Palmer's words, either light or shadows on those whom they influence. Casting light involves the behaviors leaders enact that invite transparency and openness. By casting light, leaders invite themselves and others into true relational contact. In 1 John 1:7 the Scripture affirms, "But if we walk in the light, as he is in the light, we have fellowship with one another." True fellowship comes when we dare to step into the light.

Palmer describes some of the common "shadows" in which leaders hide (1994, pp. 19-40). He points first to the shadow of insecurity about identity. Some leaders confuse their function (e.g., boss or accountant) for their identity. Palmer asserts, "Identity does not depend on titles, or degrees, or function. It depends only on the simple fact that I am a child of God, valued and treasured for what I am" (p. 34).

The second shadow is a kind of functional atheism—the belief that ultimate responsibility for everything rests with us and our ability to control things. The functional atheist group leader is the one who, regardless of whether they have a confessed belief in God's sovereignty, doesn't really trust God's work and God's timing. As a result, they micromanage many aspects of the group's life, including how a group communicates and what a group communicates about in an effort to control how events turn out.

A third shadow is fear. When leaders fear the chaos of life, or when they fear the death of a plan, a dream or an agenda, they cast a shadow and invite those around them to hide in the shadow of fear as well. My colleagues in biblical studies remind me that the single most frequent command in the

New Testament is "do not be afraid." In true faith there is freedom from fear.

The references to Palmer's (1994) work remind us of how self-concept can also be shaped by our faith commitments. The fact that much of our self-concept is subjective does not mean there is no objective reality about us. Those of us who follow Jesus Christ can affirm that we are loved and accepted (an objective reality) even if subjectively we may not feel that way at the moment. This is why Christians must be in a healthy community with other believers, because the language and truth from this means of special revelation greatly shape our identity in Christ and facilitate our sanctification.

What makes communication appropriate or inappropriate, helpful or detrimental in a given situation almost never depends solely on the communication itself, but on the context in which the communication is performed. For example, how close we stand to another person depends not on a universal principle, but on contextual variables such as the physical setting (a crowded elevator vs. an empty bus), the nature of our relationship (a stranger vs. a spouse) and the cultural context. Maintaining an awareness of the powerful role of context can help us become more conscious of how meanings have been constructed.

Communication is collaborative. To collaborate literally means to "co-labor." God is collaborative. God collaborates with God's own person, as in creation when he said, "Let us make mankind in our image" (Genesis 1:26). In ways still shrouded in mystery, God's triune person collaborates—each person of the Trinity with the others.

God also collaborates with human beings. Even though God is completely autonomous and sufficient without human beings, God dignifies humans by collaborating with us. When God called Moses, for example, the calling that resulted was constructed between God and Moses. God initiated and Moses responded. Both were laboring to produce the calling.

The fact that communication is collaborative means that communication is not something that one person *does to* another. Some people mistakenly think of communication as it is illustrated in figure 6.1.

This model of communication, sometimes called an "action" view of communication, assumes that the message goes from one person to another unobstructed so that the message received is identical to the message that was sent. It also assumes that the receiver is passive. It doesn't take a very careful examination to realize that communication doesn't function in this fashion. The problem is that many of us behave as if it does. The project leader may be operating with an action view of communication when sitting in on a presentation, making no comments, then believing that "everyone knows" that silence means approval. The truth is that sending a message (with or without words) is not the same thing as communicating. In order for communication to occur, meaning must be shared.

Figure 6.1. Action View of Communication

Others, seeking to express a cause/effect view of communication, think about communication as it is illustrated in figure 6.2. While this diagram does succeed in capturing the fact that both parties in the process of communication are active, it fails in several other ways. The primary problem with this model rests in the assumption that communication is sequential, with a message happening first and then a response (feedback).

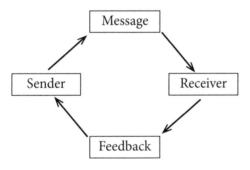

Figure 6.2. Sequential View of Communication

When we believe that communication is sequential, we fall too easily into a mistaken focus on fault and blame. In the tightly controlled conditions of a chemistry lab, cause and effect may make sense (chemical A causes an explosion when mixed with chemical B). In the complex world of human relationships, however, cause and effect will not adequately describe the communication. For example, when two normally compatible group members argue, what was the "cause"? Was it the impatience of the one? Was it the stubbornness of the other? Was it the most recent interaction the two experienced? Was it stress from home being transported to the group? Their communication could have been "caused" by these or a thousand additional factors; it is almost impossible to say for sure.

Our forward progress relationally is halted when we devote time and energy to trying to deduce the cause of a communicative outcome. There may be a time to try to sort out how our relationships end up where they do, but regardless of how a relationship got to its current position, the more important question is, "What can we do now to help bring health to the relationship?"

To reflect a theocentric understanding of communication and to more accurately represent human communication, we offer the model of communication illustrated in figure 6.3. This model begins with the assumption that God's grace precedes any communication and surrounds the communication process. God's grace is supremely evident in the person and work of Jesus. In his letter to the Colossians, Paul says of Jesus, "He is before all things, and in him all things hold together" (Col 1:17). If it is true that "all things" are held together in Jesus, that includes communication. In this view, communication is neither an accident of nature nor a creation of human action; it is a gift from the God who holds everything together. Because all things are held together by Jesus, God's grace envelopes human communication in ways of which we can be conscious and in ways of which we are not conscious.

In this model, context penetrates everything (see our discussion of context above). The model also shows the effect of "noise," which is anything that has the ability to disrupt the sending and receiving of messages. Noise may be literal external sound (like a loud car engine) that makes communicating difficult. Noise can also be internal distractions, such as our unfinished errands, a relationship that needs to be reconciled or our own insecurity. The model shows that both people are sending and receiving messages at the same time. For example, in a small group meeting all group members send messages (with and without words) all the time. While only one person may be speaking at a given time, all persons are sending messages with the ways they sit, use their face and eyes, and gesture. Communication is simultaneous rather than sequential.

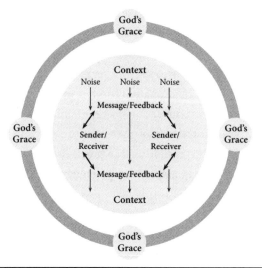

Figure 6.3. Transactional Model of Communication

To further explain the simultaneous and creative nature of communication, some scholars describe communication as "dialogic." "Dialogue" is composed of two Greek roots. The term *logos* is remarkably flexible and can mean, among other things, "logic" or "word," but the essence of *logos* rests in the concept of "meaning." Theorist David Bohm (1996) points out that *dia* means "through" (it does not mean "two"). As a result, to call communication "dialogic" is to reinforce the notion that communication involves meaning that is created through all of the persons involved. Bohm asserts, "The picture or image that this derivation [for the term *dialogue*] suggests is of a stream of meaning flowing among and through us and between us. This will make possible a flow of meaning in the whole group, out of which may emerge some new understanding. . . . And this shared meaning is the 'glue' or 'cement' that holds people and societies together" (p. 6).

The bidirectionality of the arrows is meant to show that everyone is affected by their own and by others' messages. We have tremendous potential to help or to harm others with our communication. We have a similar potential to help or to harm ourselves. When we send messages of grace and acceptance, we receive our own grace in return. When we send messages of harsh criticism and judgment, the toxicity of those messages splashes back to contaminate us. Galatians 6:7 reminds us that we reap what we sow.

By seeing communication as "dialogic," we can remember that the meaning of our messages is neither fixed nor completely dependent on what we were trying to communicate. Meaning is made between the persons involved. Imagine that the chair of the missions committee at a church attempts to build morale by having a dinner party for the committee members. The meaning of the party is dependent both on the messages sent (the invitation, the conversations at the party, etc.) and the messages received (how committee members made sense of the event). To one committee member, the meaning of the party was uplifting and encouraging; to another, the meaning of the party was a giant waste of time. We are wise to check the meanings that are created (see the discussion of "perception-checking" below). Checking meanings can be done relatively simply by asking and listening.

Communication involves verbal and nonverbal meaning-making. The prologue to the Gospel of John says, "In the beginning was the Word [*logos*], and the Word was with God, and the Word was God" (John 1:1). The word *logos* has multiple meanings—"meaning," "logic," "argument" and "word," among others. In John 1:14, John tells us that the *logos* is also a Person: "The Word became flesh, and dwelt among us, and we saw His glory, glory as of the only begotten from the Father, full of grace and truth" (NASB). Time and space here don't allow for a complete exploration of the *logos*. The point is simply that God is the original Creator of meaning. When we use words to create meaning, we function in the image of God. Our challenging calling as ambassadors of Christ is to reflect Jesus in the meanings we create. Meaning is made both verbally and nonverbally.

Verbal meaning-making. The word *verbal* means "by word." People sometimes confuse *verbal* (by word) with *oral* (by mouth). Thus, in conducting an evaluation, a supervisor might tell a coworker, "You will receive feedback in writing and verbally," when the supervisor means that feedback will be given using both written and oral modes. If the feedback is in the form of words, the communication is verbal whether the words are sent orally or in writing.

Verbal expressions are sometimes symbolic representations. A symbol is something that stands for or represents something else. This happens when words are used to stand for things and experiences. For example, we use words like *computer* and *car* to stand for objects in our world. We also use words to stand for abstractions and experiences, like "inspiring" or "frustrating."

One especially powerful type of symbolic representation happens through the process of naming. Philosophers remind us that naming brings a world into consciousness. Once we have a name, the object of our consideration is brought to our awareness in a way that it wasn't before. From the beginning of creation, God named. For example, God called the light "day" and the darkness "night." Being made in God's image, Adam was given the awesome privilege of naming the animals God had created (Genesis 2:19). Naming bestows not just a label but an identity as well. We name too. Sometimes we name others (or ourselves) in ways that honor and encourage, by naming another "significant" or "competent." Sometimes we name in ways that distort our God-given value, such as when we name someone "worthless."

But verbal expression is more than the symbolic representation of things and experiences. Verbal expression can also create actions. For example, when I sit at the lunch table and say to my coworker, "Will you please pass the water?" I am not so much representing as I am creating an action that we call a "request." As we grow up in a given culture, we learn how to perform the actions that are important in that culture. Sharing meaning around the actions we create helps us define those actions.

For example, imagine that a support staff person has made errors on several documents and the supervisor believes it is necessary to have a meeting to clarify expectations about accuracy. That conversation between the supervisor and the support staff person could be defined as the action of "encouraging" or as the action of "reprimanding." If these two people are going to share meanings, they will need to have a common understanding of the communication action that was created between them. One can imagine the confusion if the supervisor defined the exchange with the support staff person as "a friendly encouragement to do excellent work," while the support staff person defined the exchange as "being reprimanded." The identities people assume and the behaviors that coincide with those identities vary greatly between "encouraging" and "reprimanding." When people share an understanding of their identities and the collaborative actions they create, whole groups (families, ministries, organizations, etc.) can share a common vision. The best way to arrive at shared and productive definitions and visions is to talk about the identities, actions and meanings being created.

Another important verbal expression is the narrative. Communication scholar Walter Fisher defines narration as "symbolic actions—words and/or deeds—that have sequence and meaning for those who live, create, or interpret them" (1987, p. 58). Fisher regards storytelling as the essence of human nature. Whether you want to go that far or not, stories have exceptional power to establish individual and group identity. In interpersonal relationships, families, churches and virtually every other human gathering, stories are told and the stories we embrace serve to define us and our relationships. At the university where I teach, relationships between students and faculty are a high priority at least in part because stories about such relationships are consistently lifted up as praiseworthy.

As we endeavor to be faithful stewards in our God-given spheres of influence, we would be wise to recognize how our words impact the people God has blessed us to be around. We can also investigate how the stories we tell and repeat create individual and group identity.

Nonverbal meaning-making. Nonverbal means "not by word" and involves all of the ways that meaning is made without words. Communication scholars estimate that about 65 to 70 percent of the meaning created between people occurs primarily through the nonverbal realm. Some of the nonverbal displays that help us construct meaning include facial expressions, eye behaviors (including eye contact or lack of it and sustained eye gaze), body movement and gestures, touch, vocal behaviors (including the rate and pitch of a voice, inflection, volume, accents and articulation), smell, use of physical space (including distances between persons), silence, appearance, use and meaning of time (for example, how important it is to be "on time" to a meeting), and artifacts (objects and visual elements such as color and shape). Below are some of the functions that are fulfilled by nonverbal behaviors or combinations of behaviors.

- Identity: Nonverbal behaviors help to establish and maintain identities. This is one of the reasons that most people use appearance, artifacts (such as clothing), tone of voice and facial expression to create a "professional" image when interviewing for a job.

- Expression of emotion: Most of the time, nonverbal behaviors (such as facial expression, tone of voice and touch) are superior to verbal behaviors in expressing emotion.

- Defining relationships: We send messages of acceptance or contempt, liking or disinterest through behaviors such as eye behavior, touch, space, silence and facial expression.

- Interpreting verbal messages: Behaviors such as tone of voice, facial expression, eye behavior and body movement are all used to help others know how to make sense of the verbal messages we send. For example, the words "nice going" could be a compliment or a criticism depending on the nonverbal behaviors accompanying the words.

As we send and receive nonverbal messages, it is important to remember that the verbal and the nonverbal aspects of communication are usually blended. For example, whenever words are communicated by mouth, there are also nonverbal elements involved. Remember also that culture and context are always part of the interpretive process. For instance, direct eye contact may mean "interest and engagement" in one culture while meaning "disrespect and challenge to authority" in another culture. Both verbal and nonverbal forms of communication involve perception and interpretation so it will be helpful to remember that others may not be receiving the messages we think we are sending. Generally, when the verbal message and the nonverbal message contradict each other, people will tend to believe the nonverbal message.

Sending clear verbal and nonverbal messages. Communication authors McKay, Davis and Fanning (2009, pp. 35-58) provide some helpful hints for sending clear messages:

1. *Don't ask a question when you need to make a statement.* What sounds like a question—"Don't you think that was a good movie?"—is really a statement, "I think that was a good movie." The supervisor who says, "How much did that last mailing cost?" may actually be making the statement, "I'm not comfortable with the amount of money spent on the mailing."

2. *Keep your messages congruent.* Congruence is present when the content of the message, the tone of voice, and the facial and body displays all match. Communicating orally to your spouse that you want to hear about their day and then sending nonverbal messages that show you are distracted, bored and disinterested creates obvious incongruence.

3. *Be clear about your wants and feelings.* Expecting others to somehow know our unexpressed desires is unfair to them and frustrating for us. If, for example, you want to have a quiet evening at home with the family, say so. Sometimes we drop subtle hints or display certain nonverbal behaviors hoping the other will intuit our wishes. When those wishes go noticed, we punish our relationship partners for not fulfilling the desire we failed to express.

4. *Distinguish between observations and judgments.* For example, "We haven't seen a treasurer's report for three months" is an observation; "Our treasurer has been irresponsible" is a judgment. In most instances, observations will call forward less defensiveness than judgments.

In addition to these suggestions, we can enhance clarity by checking our perceptions. We are constantly in the process of interpreting the verbal and nonverbal messages people send. The problem is that we may not interpret accurately. When we encounter an ambiguous message, one of the most helpful moves we can make is to check our perceptions.

Suppose you lead a small group and that a member who is usually quite outgoing and talkative comes to a group dinner. On this occasion she greets nobody and sits quietly at the table. Her small group is left unclear about the meaning of her behavior. A gentle perception check (which may be best done privately) begins with stating an observation. In this case, one could say, "You've been quiet this evening." The next part of a perception check is to offer a couple of possible interpretations: "Maybe you're not feeling well, maybe something is on your mind, or maybe there is something I don't know about." By ending this part of the perception check with "maybe there is something I don't know about," you open the range of possible explanations. The final part of the perception check is to ask for clarification. You could say, "What's up?" or "Is there anything we should talk about?"

Because the nonverbal realm is often riddled with ambiguity, we can help others make sense of our nonverbal behaviors by adding verbal messages of explanation. In the example in the preceding paragraph, the quiet group member could have pulled you aside and said, "I had a really hard day at work and need a little time to be quiet." Her verbal message helps the rest of the group interpret her nonverbal behavior.

Listening as meaning-making. Listening employs both verbal and non-verbal meaning-making to produce the single most Christlike communication event that humans experience. As people who seek to follow Christ, we have the privilege of listening to God and listening to each other. In fact, listening to God and to others is a primary way that we live the two greatest commandments: to love God with our whole selves and to love one another (Matthew 22:37-40). For two millennia the Christian church has developed practices, traditions and literature facilitating the ability to listen to God. The vastness of these efforts makes them impossible to catalog here. As important as it is to listen to God, the focus of this chapter is on listening to one another.

Unfortunately, listening is not always done effectively. One impediment to listening is the belief that listening is natural. It isn't. Listening is not synonymous with hearing. Hearing is a physiological process of receiving sound. Listening involves more. Listening includes attending, comprehending and responding to messages. Another hindrance to listening is the rate at which most messages come to us. Most human beings can understand verbal messages that come to us at up to 600 words per minute. A listening gap is created because most people speak verbal messages at about 120 words per minute. If the "gap time" is filled with appropriate processing, the listening is likely to be more effective; if the gap time is filled with noise, listening is probably going to be less effective.

As mentioned earlier, the noise that hinders listening can be either external or internal. External noise refers to environmental distractions such as loud traffic, televisions or music that make listening difficult. Internal noise comes from inside us and includes distractions such as unfinished tasks, defensiveness and insecurities. Noise can become involved in other listening problems, such as what Vangelisti, Knapp and Daly (1990) call "conversational narcissism." Conversational narcissists turn listening into an opportunity to talk about themselves.

Sometimes selfishness isn't the primary problem. Some of us want to help others by offering advice. Listening difficulties arise when we formulate and rehearse our responses while we could be listening to the other. Cloud and Townsend (2003) remind us that listening is not the same as waiting for your turn to talk. Suppose a friend who teaches in a college ministry expresses frustration, saying, "The college students don't seem to want to talk with me. They come to the meeting, walk past me and sit immediately in a group. I don't feel like a very good teacher." In this case, it isn't listening to simply reply, "No, you're a good teacher." Such a comment, while well intentioned, is simply waiting your turn to offer an opinion. Real listening requires that we do or say something that demonstrates that we have actually understood, or at least tried to understand, the other's message. Instead of disagreeing with the friend about his or her effectiveness as a teacher, one could respond by saying, "It hurts to want connection with a student who isn't very responsive."

True listening is harder than some skilled communicators make it seem. Authentic listening is difficult because it requires us to empty ourselves of our agendas and insecurities enough to receive another. Earlier we described listening as "Christlike" because in listening we lay ourselves aside in service to another. Christ's self-denial is described in Philippians 2:3-7:

> Do nothing out of selfish ambition or vain conceit, but in humility consider others better than yourselves. Each of you should look not only to your own interests, but also to the interests of others. Your attitude should be the same as that of Christ Jesus: Who, being in very nature God, did not consider equality with God something to be grasped, but made himself nothing, taking the very nature of a servant, being made in human likeness. (NIV 1984)

The best listeners value others, become another's servant and deny one's self-interest. The holy road to authentic, meaningful human relationships is paved with the bricks of selfless service. True listening is a rich experience for both parties. The listener gets to participate in the growth of another; the one being listened to receives one of the most dignifying and encouraging experiences of life. True listening leaves us feeling valuable and significant. A few of the key skills in effective listening are discussed below.

Humility and empathy. The foundations of authentic listening are found in the twin virtues of humility and empathy. Humility invites us to have a sane estimation of ourselves. True humility recognizes that we do not possess unobstructed access to all truth and that, as Paul asserted, we see "in a mirror, dimly" (1 Corinthians 13:12 NRSV). With our own limitations in mind, we may be more likely to embrace listening as a way to serve others and grow personally. Without humility, we have little motivation to listen because we may not believe we have much to learn from the other.

Likewise, empathy has profound implications for listening. Empathy is the ability to understand another's thoughts and feelings. Empathy is one of the most crucial elements in effective listening and communication in general. It allows us to create messages that make sense to others and to respond appropriately to the messages sent by others. Without empathy, listening too easily becomes a self-centered act in which we listen only for our own benefit and communicate to satisfy our own needs only. As we grow in humility and empathy, those inner qualities can produce outward behaviors important in the listening process.

Attending. Attending is an important initial step in effective listening. This is where we demonstrate, with our bodies and our words, our availability and focus upon the other person. We can do this by creating a physical context free of distractions. When we turn the TV off, shut down our iPod, put down the newspaper and put away our cell phones, we declare the value of the other as worthy of our full attention. We can also demonstrate availability by facing the other and making appropriate eye contact. The degree of eye contact deemed appropriate can vary with culture and context, but generally eye contact should be sustained about 70 percent of the time.

Inviting depth. Once the conversation has begun, it may be appropriate to invite the other to talk about their ideas and feelings. This can be enabled by issuing a direct invitation such as, "Can you tell me a little more about _____?" Another way to invite people to communicate is to use open-ended questions, which call for responses that go beyond single words or short phrases. Asking, "Did you have a good day at school?" is closed and likely results in "yes," "no" or minimal responses. Saying, "Tell me about what you learned in history today" invites a more developed response. One caution about open and closed questions: there are no guarantees. You can frame the most beautiful open question and have it met with a closed response. Human free will being what it is, we don't control the degree to which people will participate in the conversation. As one who cares about communication, your job is to *invite* a healthy conversation.

Clarifying questions. As the conversation continues, you will need to interpret and respond to the messages sent by others. At this point, the listening objective is to make clear meaning between you and the other. Asking clarifying questions can help. Clarifying questions sound like this: "Earlier you said you are facing troubles; what kind of 'troubles' are you facing?"

Clarifying through paraphrasing. Another meaning making tool is the paraphrase. The purpose of a paraphrase is to establish clarity about thoughts and feelings. A badly done paraphrase can thoroughly ruin a communication opportunity. If a friend says, "I feel sad," a sure-fire recipe for communicative disaster is to enact a badly done paraphrase like this: "So, what I hear you saying is that you feel sad." Since the word *sad* was relatively clear, a paraphrase was unnecessary. A well-done paraphrase consists of four parts: (1) It is a restatement, not a question; (2) It restates the other's meaning rather than simply repeating their words; (3) It is given in your own words; and (4) It comes with a "verification check," which is an opportunity to check the accuracy of your paraphrase. A verification check is expressed with a question like, "Is that it?"

Suppose a coworker vents to you, saying, "I've had it with this place! They keep piling on the work and expect me to do tasks I haven't been trained to do." In this situation the speaker is obviously frustrated with the amount of work and lack of training. Still, the listener may be unclear about the degree to which the speaker may feel insecure. A paraphrase could sound like this: "You seem frustrated and perhaps unsure about how to complete the work you've been given, is that it?" From here the speaker can confirm the paraphrase or further clarify the source of the frustration.

Humans Express God-Given Creativity in Communication

God is unique. One of the ways that God's uniqueness is evident is that God creates out of nothing. Being made in God's image, we have something of the capacity to create. We create out of what God has given us. This creativity is displayed in various ways—musically, visually, dramatically—and through communication. Indeed human communication is the fundamental building block out of which everything meaningful in our world is created. Above we explored some of the ways that meaning is created through verbal and nonverbal behaviors, and through listening. Here are three more specific created realities that are of particular importance to leaders.

Communication creates identities. Every single communication experience involves identities—our own and those of others. Earlier in the chapter we described "self-concept." A self-concept is not given at birth; it is created through communication. From our earliest childhood, we interact verbally and nonverbally with family and society. Those interactions help to create what is called a "reflected appraisal," which is what I think you think about me. When we sit at the family dinner table and begin talking about our day, the responses of others (or lack of responses) contribute to a self-concept that may be one of significance and value or the opposite.

I once was seated on an airplane with a woman whom I had never met and her daughter, who seemed to be about ten years old. As the woman told me about her family, she identified her daughter as an "oops baby," meaning that the pregnancy that produced the daughter was unplanned. I found myself wondering what it was like to live with the reflected appraisal of being an "oops"—a mistake. Another way identities are created is through social comparison. As we grow up and have more social interaction with peers, we begin to compare ourselves and ask, "Am I superior or inferior to them? Am I alike or different from them?" While comparison is rarely helpful to a self-concept, it is a common experience.

Just as others contribute to our self-concepts, the verbal and nonverbal messages we send also contribute to others' reflected appraisals and self-concept development. The moment someone walks into our homes, churches or places of business, we send messages that contribute to their reflected appraisal of the interaction. Are they greeted with warmth and enthusiasm, or are they ignored? Are they listened to with interest, or are they dismissed as insignificant? We have the God-given creative potential to affect the reflected appraisal (to various degrees) of all the people in our spheres of influence. Such an opportunity ought to bring us humbly to our knees, praying that by God's grace our influence will be positive.

At this point I want to offer two comments. First, awareness is the initial step toward health. When we become aware of our power to affect others, we should pray that we walk with wisdom. Second, there is grace. If we have sent messages that deny the worth and significance of others, we can make moves to heal past hurts and help construct a more positive future. Further, if we are the one whose sense of self has been damaged by the words and actions of others, we don't need to be imprisoned by language that distorts our God-given identity as revealed by the truth of Scripture.

Communication creates relationships. Because of the power of communication to affect those around us, human beings live in a state of connectedness with each other. In communication, the question isn't whether we will be connected to others; the question is always *how* we will be connected. Connectedness is part of God's design in creation. In the creation narrative, God fashioned Eve to live in relationship with Adam. When blessed with the gift of relationship, Adam declares, "This is now bone of my bones, and flesh of my flesh" (Genesis 2:23). When we all realize that we are "of the same stuff," calloused indifference isn't a legitimate option.

The nature of the relationships between us is created through communication. The words we use and the nonverbal behaviors in which we engage announce the nature of our relationships. Communication scholars Watzlawick, Beavin and Jackson (1967) provided the foundational description of relationships as generally being "symmetrical" or "complementary." Symmetrical relationships are based on similarity and equality, while complementary relationships are based on difference and inequality. All communication sends relational messages. If a supervisor calls a staff meeting and requires all staff members to be there, the communication is complementary. The communication has defined the relationships as unequal (rightly or wrongly). Likewise, a supervisor who invites and listens respectfully to staff suggestions is doing a more symmetrical communication act. All of us who conduct leadership of any kind are wise to maintain awareness about the relational implications of our communicative actions.

Communication creates communal cultures. Previously we discussed culture as part of the context enveloping communication. Our earlier point was that culture affects communication. Our point here is that culture itself is created in communication. Communication theorists tend to describe culture as systems of shared meaning that are created by communication (Griffin 2009). Communication scholar Ernest Bormann (1983) directs us to two questions as culture is developed. One question relates to the key communication activities through which groups make sense of themselves. The second question relates to the sense members of a group make of their communication experiences. Communication creates the "taken for granted" reality of all groups. Family, church, organizations and all other group cultures are created through the communication process. The process of the creation of a group culture may be represented in diagrammatic form as illustrated in figure 6.4.

The center rectangle in the model of organizational communication (figure 6.4) represents "double interacts." Double interacts are placed in the center of the model because, as theorist Karl Weick (1979) described in his seminal work on organizational communication, double interacts are the core of all communication actions. Double interacts are especially significant because they hold tremendous power to shape the nature of the group.

In organizational communication, we find acts, interacts and double interacts. Weick defines *acts* as statements or behaviors done by one person.

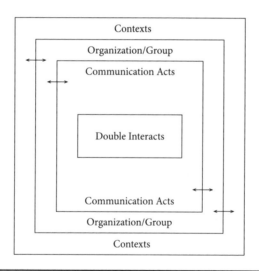

Figure 6.4. A Model of Organizational Communication

For example, an act is when an office supervisor says, "I want staff members to tell me their ideas for how to improve the office." An *interact* is an act followed by a response. An example of an interact is when a particular office staff person comes to the supervisor with an idea. The most crucial communication decision comes next: a *double interact* is an interact followed by an adjustment or response by the first person. If the supervisor chooses to receive the suggestion gracefully, that double interact will tend to produce collaboration and investment since the staff person is likely to feel valued.

A very different double interact occurs if the supervisor responds to the staff member's suggestion with a reprimand. The reprimand double interact is likely to produce mistrust and passivity among the staff since offering suggestions (even though invited to do so) resulted in punishment. For good or for ill, the nature of the organization is shaped by the kind of double interacts that are enacted, especially those that are repeated.

In figure 6.4, note the bidirectionality of influences. The contexts that affect organizations and groups are themselves affected by those groups. Consider that a neighborhood church is affected by the contexts in which it exists. Ethnicities, socioeconomics and neighborhood norms, for example, will all affect how the church functions as the church in that neighborhood. Simultaneously, the neighborhood cultural context is affected by the presence of the neighborhood church. For example, when vacation Bible school reaches out to the children in the neighborhood and when the church food bank provides meals, we see the church affecting the culture.

There is also a bidirectional relationship between the group and communication acts. The group affects the communication acts by establishing group norms. Suppose that you conduct leadership for a group that provides life-skills training for troubled teens. In those training sessions there may be a norm that disclosure is very open and public. As a result, the weekly meetings are punctuated by updates on dating life, work life and home life. Those same group norms are created through communication acts. If open and honest sharing gets rewarded with attention and affirmation, a norm in favor of open sharing is developed. In communication, we create the norms that simultaneously shape our communication acts.

Because all groups (whether they are families, service groups, businesses or other organizations) are created out of communication acts, it may be helpful to describe some of those specific acts. Griffin (2009) summarizes the suggestion of ethnographers of communication that if we want to understand group culture, we should pay attention to stories, rites, rituals, rules for sociality and organizational politics.

Stories. Corporate stories communicate group ideology and policy. For example, when you go to church, listen to the stories that get told about the church's mission, values and commitments. Personal stories are stories we tell about ourselves that often display how we see ourselves, or sometimes how we would like to be seen. Collegial stories are stories we tell about others in the group. Such stories also tend to reveal perceptions of the identities and roles of others in the group. In general, when listening to stories, listen for characters (who are the heroes and the villains?), the actions (which behaviors get praised and which denounced?), the settings (the site of the action may affect the meaning of the action) and the goals of the actions (the overall purposes).

Rites. Rites are often elaborate planned activities that are usually carried out in a public setting. Rites typically indicate an important point in the life of a group or parts of the group. For example, a rite of enhancement, such as an awards ceremony or appreciation dinner, indicates what a group values.

Rituals. Rituals are familiar, repeated routines. They differ from rites in that rituals are not always elaborate or public. Rituals may inform our understanding of the group by drawing our attention to actions that have become a repeated part of the group culture. Rituals may be organizational (involving the entire group) such as a company Christmas party or a family reunion, or social (involving only parts of the group) such as the informal evening walks parents may take or lunch outings certain support staff enjoy together.

Rules for sociality. Behavioral rules (usually unstated) tell people in the group how to handle social experiences such as joking, criticism and conflict. Rules for sociality may produce positive or negative outcomes. In a particular office situation, for example, an unspoken rule for sociality may be, "If someone criticizes your ideas, don't take it personally." In a particular family, an unhealthy rule for sociality could be, "Ignore the conflict you have with another family member, pretend it doesn't exist and never talk directly with them about it."

Organizational politics. Patterns of influence and power in a group make up the organizational politics. The person with designated power (a title or position, for example) is not always the person with actual power. The people with real power in groups are usually those to whom people come for advice, opinions and help.

By understanding the various communication actions above, we can better identify and modify the communication through which our groups are created.

Conclusion: Stewardship of the Gift of Communication

By this point, at least some readers may be overwhelmed with the scope and importance of communication. Such a response is sane. Communication is incredibly broad, complex and powerful. Communication is also one of the most significant gifts God has given us. Rather than causing you to be overwhelmed and thereby paralyzed, our hope is that this chapter has helped to identify and explain some of the processes of communication.

As you endeavor to live into some of the communication truths described in this chapter, consider a biblical perspective from Paul's first letter to the Corinthian church. In 1 Corinthians 4:1-2, Paul writes, "So then, men ought to regard us as servants of Christ and as those entrusted with the secret things of God. Now it is required that those who have been given a trust must prove faithful" (NIV 1984).

This passage describes two important aspects of how Paul thought about himself and how we can think about ourselves. First, he stated his desire that we should be as "servants of Christ." Communication is a gift designed to serve Christ, and by Christ's command, to serve one another. Second, he called himself one "entrusted with the secret things of God." Some biblical translations use words such as *trustee* or *steward*. Readers may want to examine Scott Rodin's book *The Steward Leader* (2010) for an expanded treatment of what it means to see the leader as one entrusted with the Master's concerns until the Master returns.

Until Christ returns, we who call ourselves followers of Christ are to take care of the "mysteries of God." Those mysteries are many, and we consider the mystery of human communication to be included. Paul finishes this verse by reminding us that trustees must prove faithful. Here is the standard for your use of communication: You are not being commanded to be dynamic, powerful or persuasive—the results of your use of communication are God's business. You are required to be faithful. To be faithful is to live, with the grace that God gives you, into the truth insofar as you know it. God will help each of us sort out what faithfulness looks like. May we all be patient and gracious to ourselves and others in all of our communication acts.

References

Bohm, D. 1996. *On Dialogue*. Edited by L. Nichol. London: Routledge.

Bormann, E. 1983. "Symbolic Convergence: Organizational Communication and Culture." In *Communication and Organizations: An Interpretive Approach*, edited by L. Putnam and M. Pacanowski, pp. 99-122. Beverly Hills: Sage.

Cloud, H., and J. Townsend. 2003. *Making Small Groups Work*. Grand Rapids: Zondervan.

Fisher, W. 1987. *Human Communication as Narration: Toward a Philosophy of Reason, Value, and Action*. Columbia: University of South Carolina.

Griffin, E. 2009. "Cultural Approach to Organizations." In *A First Look at Communication Theory*, 7th ed., pp. 250-60. Boston: McGraw-Hill.

McKay, M., M. Davis and P. Fanning. 2009. *Messages: The Communication Skills Book*. Oakland: New Harbinger.

Palmer, P. 1994. "Leading from Within: Out of the Shadows, into Light." In *Spirit at Work: Discovering the Spirituality in Leadership*, edited by J. Conger, pp. 19-40. San Francisco: Jossey-Bass.

Rodin, R. S. 2010. *The Steward Leader*. Downers Grove, IL: InterVarsity Press.

Schutz, W. C. 1958. *FIRO: A Three-Dimensional Theory of Interpersonal Behavior*. New York: Holt, Rinehart and Winston.

Stewart, J., ed. 2009. *Bridges, Not Walls*, 10th ed. Boston: McGraw-Hill.

Stewart, J., K. Zediker and S. Witteborn. 2005. *Together: Communicating Interpersonally*, 6th ed. Los Angeles: Roxbury.

Stott, J. 1982. *Between Two Worlds*. Grand Rapids: Eerdmans.

Vangelisti, A., M. Knapp and J. Daly. 1990. "Conversational Narcissism." *Communication Monographs*, 57: 251-74.

Watzlawick, P., J. Beavin and D. Jackson. 1967. *Pragmatics of Human Communication*. New York: W.W. Norton.

Weick, K. 1979. *The Social Psychology of Organizing*, 2nd ed. Reading, MA: Addison-Wesley.

7

CONFLICT AND NEGOTIATION

John S. (Jack) Burns

—◆◆◆—

When we get serious about the Christian life
we eventually end up in a place and among people
decidedly uncongenial to what we had expected. That place
and people is often called a church. It's hard to get over the
disappointment that God, having made an exception in
my case, doesn't call nice people to repentance.

EUGENE PETERSON, *LEAP OVER A WALL*

INTRODUCTION

Conflict and negotiating ways to resolve conflict between human beings is
the topic of countless books, workshops and courses. There is a whole army
of consultants, mediators and other professional negotiators trained to in-
tervene in every conceivable situation. It would be impossible to condense
all of this information and present it in a chapter of a book. Indeed, this topic
deserves far deeper investigation than what we are able to offer here. Our
purpose in this chapter is to focus on a Christian perspective of conflict and
its resolution.

Conflict is inevitable among people and in organizations—yes, even
among Christians and in Christian organizations. The quotation above
comes from a chapter about the refuge Philistine city named Ziklag that was

given to David and his band of followers. After years of struggle in the wilderness, David anticipated he would find an Eden-like experience for him and his people in Ziklag. But Ziklag was not Eden! Using the conflicts and struggles David had in Ziklag as an archetype, Eugene Peterson comments about every church with which he has ever been involved:

> I've never been anything but disappointed: every one turns out to be biblical, through and through: murmerers, complainers, the faithless, the inconstant, those plagued with doubt and riddled with sin, boring moralizers, glamorous secularizers. . . . In sixty-three years I've worshipped and worked in . . . eleven Christian congregations. They've all fit the basic profile of Ziklag. I was pastor to one of these companies for thirty years and thought I could beat the odds and organize something more along the lines of Eden, or better yet New Jerusalem. But sinners kept breaking and entering and insisting on baptism, defeating all my utopian fantasies. (1997, pp. 101, 234)

All of us are "biblical" through and through. We are biblical in our personal relationships and we are biblical in our organizations, no matter how sanctified their purpose. As a result, we do a very biblical thing: we have conflict. In this chapter, we will posit a biblical purpose for conflict, examine when Christians might choose to engage in or avoid conflict, and explore how Christians can negotiate principled resolutions to conflicts.

SOMETIMES CONFLICT SHOULD BE AVOIDED

The purpose for Christians to engage in conflict should be for *restoration and reconciliation* between people (Wittwer, 2010). When restoration and reconciliation are the purpose for conflict, we do not engage in the conflict to defeat the other party, but to enhance our potential for relationship and spiritual fellowship. In Luke 17:3-4 we read, "If your brother or sister sins against you, rebuke them; and if they repent, forgive them. Even if they sin against you seven times in a day and seven times come back to you saying 'I repent,' you must forgive them." Conflict occurs because sin shrouds our relationships. In this passage Christ teaches that there will be times when it is necessary to choose to be in conflict with others in order to confront the sin in the relationship. However, Christ lays out the purpose of the conflict: restoration and reconciliation. In this same passage Christ also teaches that a party may be very aware of their sin, and the appropriate response is not to rebuke, but to offer ongoing forgiveness. Thus sometimes, even when we are in the right, conflict may only exacerbate the problem. It can be wrong to engage conflict because we can achieve the goal of restoration and reconciliation through forgiveness.

Christians know about the need for and the power of forgiveness, because this is exactly what Christians expect from God. We certainly do not want a conflict with God. Instead, we want restoration and reconciliation through his forgiveness. Sometimes we overlook God's teaching about the contagious nature of forgiveness—how we are obliged to forgive others in response to the forgiveness we have received. Indeed, how many of us have taken seriously the part of the Lord's Prayer that says, "And forgive us our debts [sins], as we also have forgiven our debtors [those who have sinned against us]" (Matthew 6:12). We dare not ignore this scary passage! We are asking God to forgive us in exactly the same way as we are willing to forgive other people! We want to end our conflict with God so that we can be restored and reconciled through his complete forgiveness. Are we willing to forgive in the same way so that we can experience restored and reconciled relationships with each other?

Besides opening the door for relationship restoration and reconciliation, a life-changing benefit also accrues when we offer forgiveness. When we forgive others we weed out bitterness in our lives. Bitterness can take hold and choke the life out of relationships. "Make every effort to live in peace with everyone and to be holy; without holiness no one will see the Lord. See to it that no one falls short of the grace of God and that no bitter root grows up to cause trouble and defile many" (Hebrews 12:14-15).

Bitterness spreads by a root that has the potential to overtake our entire character. Go to a retirement home and look around. You will see some people who have terrible physical, social and/or economic challenges. Despite all of this, they radiate joy. You will also see people who seem to have everything together with regard to health and potential for social connections, and they have no worries about finances. Yet some of these people are bitter and awful to be around. If you take the time to hear the stories of these people, the former live at peace (often Christian-based) with their circumstances and the life they have lived. The sour folks will be more than happy to tell you stories with well-rehearsed details about an injustice they suffered

long, long ago. They have let a bitter root about this injustice grow until it
has entangled every part of their life and it reaches out to strangle their relationships with everyone. In Ephesians Paul advises, "Get rid of all bitterness, rage and anger, brawling and slander, along with every form of
malice. Be kind and compassionate to one another, forgiving each other, just
as in Christ God forgave you" (Ephesians 4:31-32).

Sometimes the right and righteous thing to do when it comes to disputes
with other people, even when we are right, is to avoid conflict and offer
forgiveness instead. Forgiveness can open a path to restoration and reconciliation, and it will destroy the bitter root that would love to grow in the
fertile soil of our self-righteousness.

Our self-righteousness can also be fueled by super-heated emotion. Often
the righteousness of the reasons we generate for conflict is skewed because
our emotions cloud our reasoning. Indeed, when we are angry we can be
willing to fight even when deep down we know we are in the wrong (Wittwer,
2010)! Remember the story of Cain and Abel?

> Now Abel kept flocks, and Cain worked the soil. In the course of time Cain
> brought some of the fruits of the soil as an offering to the Lord. And Abel
> also brought an offering—fat portions from some of the firstborn of his flock.
> The Lord looked with favor on Abel and his offering, but on Cain and his
> offering he did not look with favor. So Cain was very angry, and his face was
> downcast. Then the Lord said to Cain, "Why are you angry? Why is your face
> downcast? If you do what is right, will you not be accepted? But if you do not
> do what is right, sin is crouching at your door; it desires to have you, but you
> must rule over it. (Genesis 4:2-8)

When we are emotionally charged, our motives for conflict may be far
from the God-ordained purpose of restoration and reconciliation. Cain was
angry at his brother and God, and that anger exploded into an irreconcilable
conflict with both. Why was Cain so worked up? He was angry because he
was busted! He tried to cut a corner by offering a sacrifice that was second-
rate, and he got called on it. We are prone to Cain's error as well. When we
feel the emotional heat rising, we must ask ourselves why we are angry. We
must be willing to look beyond our façade of superficial righteousness.
Often we become angry because we too have been busted! Some error of our
ways has been exposed, and at some level we are embarrassed and our pride

has been hurt. Our emotional response is anger toward the one who has exposed us, and we are ready to do battle with everyone and everything that is associated with the exposure. If we find that we are angry and generating a lot of energy to justify or put a positive spin on something we have done, that should be a red flag to warn us to step back and examine our motives for conflict more deeply and honestly.

As I was preparing to write this chapter, I had my own "Cain" moment. For several years we have owned a small lake cabin with fifty precious feet of waterfront. When we first moved in, the property on the north side of ours was owned by absentee heirs to an estate that was tied up in a protracted probate battle. The neglected cabin and its 125 feet of mostly inaccessible waterfront had fallen into woeful disrepair. Where our two properties joined, the neighbor had a six-foot weed- and muck-covered shoreline next to two feet of equally unkempt shoreline on our new property. This combined eight-foot section was the only unused part of our otherwise steep and rocky waterfront that could potentially be developed into a small beach with gentle access to the lake. I decided to reclaim the eight-foot mess by clearing all of the weeds and cleaning the muck from the bottom of the lake. I uncovered a nice sandy beach under all of the muck, and for several years, our use of this vast improvement on the border of the properties went unnoticed by the absentee owners. Even when the property eventually changed hands and turned into an occasional summer rental, the new property owner had no issues with the children of his infrequent tenants and our children sharing the beach I had developed.

Then the property changed hands again. The new owner is a neighbor on the other side of the rental who bought it to expand his own extensive waterfront holdings. Over the years, I have had enough conversations with this neighbor for me to know that he likes dogs, fishing and quiet solitude. He is also quite territorial and does not want people trespassing on his property. At first, he continued to occasionally rent the cabin to the same tenants as the previous property owner, and last summer our children once again played with tenants' children on the "common" beach that I continued to maintain. After a few months, I received a terse email from my neighbor, the gist of which was a demand for me to keep our children off of his beach.

My immediate reaction? I was angry. Over the years I had put a lot of effort into developing and maintaining the little beach. Our children have great memories from all the years they have played there. Where did the new owner come off making such a stink about his six feet of waterfront that he cannot even see from his cabin?

I was Cain! I was busted! I was the trespasser. I had no right to develop the beach in the first place, and our children had no right to play on the neighboring property. My "biblical" nature allowed me to feed my anger by dreaming up any number of retaliatory measures aimed at my curmudgeon neighbor. Sin was indeed "crouching at my door" in all of those thoughts.

I knew what happened to Cain and was determined not to let this conflict escalate. Besides that, I was about to author a chapter on Christian conflict resolution! My choice, the right choice, was to choose not to engage in any kind of conflict with my neighbor. I have quietly rearranged my two feet of the old beach shoreline so that there is no temptation for our children to go and play where they have played for years. Instead, we decided to move our boat dock and develop an even larger and more user-friendly beach where the dock used to be. (We didn't even know this potential beach was going to waste under the old dock location, until we started to think about creative ways to solve this conflict.)

In his recent book *The Steward Leader*, Scott Rodin develops a theology of Christian stewardship. Christian stewards understand that the life they have is a gift, and that gift is to be stewarded to advance the kingdom of God. Rodin posits that God's grace not only restores and reconciles us with God through Christ, but grace allows us to be reconciled in our relationships with other people:

> With the Great Commission, the Great Commandment now calls us back to love one another and to take care of our neighbor. We've been called to the ministry of reconciliation, peacemaking and servanthood. We are able to love our neighbor properly because we can now love ourselves as God's beloved— and redeemed—creation. By redeeming our relationship to God, Jesus calls us into this right relationship with our neighbor. The enmity and strife that was evidenced immediately in Eden, that was confirmed just as immediately by Cain and that now characterizes so much of our nation and our world was also assumed by Christ. His "becoming flesh" meant his assumption of this discord. His death for the sins of the world meant his overcoming this strife.

His resurrection meant that we can now participate in this work of reconciliation. He has taken back our brokenness, assumed it, redeemed it and now calls us to himself to be children in his kingdom, where we are empowered to live in right relationships with our neighbor. Relationships are gifts bought with a precious price and returned to us to be stewarded with obedience and joy. (p. 46)

As Christians, we have to ask ourselves why we are bracing for a fight. Why are we angry? Is the purpose of this conflict to restore and reconcile, to be good stewards of the gift of grace God has given us so that we can love our neighbors properly? When we are in the wrong, getting into a conflict or not extracting ourselves from a conflict already engaged is very wrong indeed.

Sometimes Conflict Is Righteous and Necessary

Some Christians have severe reservations about ever engaging in conflict. Some of those reservations may be based on unrealistic expectations regarding how Christian organizations and the people in them should function and/or misunderstanding of the benefits of healthy conflict. Gangel and Canine (1992) have identified seven misconceptions about conflict in Christian organizations:

1. *Conflict is abnormal.* Some people seek to completely rid relationships of all struggle. They consider it improper, if not deviant, to expect conflict to be part of the human experience. . . . Unfortunately, life does not agree with this viewpoint.

2. *Conflict and disagreement are the same.* Here we face a problem of intensity. Severe conflict can and does occur where little disagreement exists. At the ideological level two armies may do battle (conflict), but the individual soldiers do not find themselves in disagreement at all. . . . On the other hand, "disagreement" may be a cop-out when the conflict is far more serious. It may not be a simple misunderstanding but rather a momentous clash of values between two equally influential groups. To call this a simple disagreement understates and minimizes the importance of the issues involved.

3. *Conflict is pathological.* Some believers view conflict as evidence that people are frustrated, psychologically maladjusted, or neurotic in their behavior. From this viewpoint conflict becomes a disease which must be cured.

4. *Conflict must be reduced or avoided.* When a person views conflict from

only a negative perspective, it is a short step to making it imperative to subdue conflict at all costs.

5. *Conflict is a personality problem.* This excuse frequently appears so that the conflict cannot be probed to any significant depth. All personalities have problems with other personalities at some point in time. Conflict usually involves much more than the "smoke screen" of the personality problem.

6. *Conflict is linked only with anger.* No one would deny that conflict often carries strong emotional messages with it. At times conflict conveys a faulty concept when we link it *only* with anger. People can engage in strong conflict with others and not demonstrate anger.

7. *Conflict is the admission of failure.* Here we face a misguided understanding of conflict. Conflict management may call for an admission of failure, but to be occupied in the conflict process does not guarantee either success or failure. The tacit message sent by this misconception implies conflict is always bad and wrong for God's child. The option of working through conflict and becoming stronger from it seems foreign to this false view of conflict. (pp. 129-31)

Conflict may be necessary when forgiveness or other actions are ineffective at getting the restoration and reconciliation process going. The key here is being certain that godly objectives are driving the need to engage in conflict. James MacGregor Burns (1978), in his landmark book *Leadership*, suggests that transforming leadership only becomes possible when followers have the ability to choose between competing (conflicting) transforming alternatives. Burns was not writing from a Christian perspective, but restoration and reconciliation often require the kind of moral transformation Burns describes in his book. Irving Janis (1972) wrote about how, by avoiding constructive conflict, groups can lapse into groupthink and make horrible decisions. In healthy conflict, the parties have the ability to develop open agreements that allow them to be reconciled and restored with each other, merging their individual interests with the larger organizational agenda. When communication lines remain robust, conflict can help people in the organization more clearly understand issues that may be a threat to the interests that satisfy the organization's purpose and values (Gangel and Canine 1992).

While there are excellent and righteous reasons for organizations to not only tolerate conflict but also encourage it, conflict can also become destructive. It can destroy relationships as well as organizations, especially as communication lines break down (Gangel and Canine 1992). History is replete with stories of conflicts gone awry, leaving horrific destruction in their wake. One does not have to look far to find examples of friendships, marriages, families, churches, businesses, governments, nations and everything in the gaps on this list where conflict has been destructive. No wonder some Christians view conflict avoidance as the righteous way to navigate difficult straits in relationships and organizations. Nonetheless, Christians will and should become engaged in conflict in order to bring about reconciliation with disputing parties. The next section of this chapter will forward a model for Christians to employ when they engage in conflict.

PRINCIPLED CHRISTIAN CONFLICT NEGOTIATION

In the previous section we explored how there is often a choice regarding whether or not we should initiate a conflict. Often, however, the conflict is not a matter of choice because it is woven into the fabric of many human interactions. For example, a retailer and a customer are naturally in "conflict" over the price of merchandise. One wants to spend as little as possible, and the other wants to charge as much as possible. At other times, we are unavoidably drawn into a conflict by others. A manager reprimands you for your unit's poor productivity and quality because he or she does not realize that it is your coworker who has been slacking off. As a result, you find yourself in a conflict with both your manager and your coworker.

The genesis of the conflict is irrelevant. Unresolved or poorly engaged conflicts have the potential to destroy relationships and organizations. People often mistakenly resort to conflict management strategies that can only yield win/lose or lose/lose "solutions." These dysfunctional conflict coping strategies include:

1. Minimizing substantive issues and trying to ignore the existence of the conflict (lose/lose)

2. Acquiescing or developing a compromise that gives the appearance of resolution without dealing substantively with the fundamental interests of the parties (lose/lose)

3. Putting the conflict on some sort of hiatus until a party feels that they have stockpiled enough power or other resources to prevail over their opponent's position (win/lose)

4. Employing slash-and-burn strategies designed to make the other party suffer even if they "win" (lose/lose)

5. Developing a pattern of ongoing conflict and domination over another party over both trivial and substantive issues to keep them in a submissive position in the relationship (win/lose)

These dysfunctional win/lose or lose/lose "resolutions" only provide temporary peace, and in time conflict usually reemerges (often in a different form) because the deep relational and other interests of the parties have not been satisfied. We can learn how to negotiate to forge win/win outcomes that satisfy the interests of all parties. We can learn how to negotiate a principled resolution that is consistent with the restoration and reconciliation objectives of Christian conflict. While this process is difficult, it is not impossible.

Scott Rodin (2010) reminds us that stewards are not the owners of anything given to them by the master. As Christian stewards we recognize we are charged with taking care of the Master's "things," including our very lives and everything that touches our lives: our families, our relationships with people, the organizations to which we belong, our environment, our jobs, our various gifts and skills, our economic circumstances—all these and more—everything! The Master has not given us these things to own. Instead, the Master has called us to steward the Master's things for the *Master's purposes*. Rodin challenges us to reflect about how the Christian's vocation of steward should motivate us to be in relationship, fellowship and community both with God and with all of his creation. The heart of the Master is quite clear as John recorded Jesus' description of the purpose of his life on Earth: "For I have come down from heaven not to do my will but to do the will of him who sent me. And this is the will of him who sent me, that I shall lose none of all those he has given me, but raise them up at the last day" (John 6:38-39). Jesus himself lived as a steward, taking care of the people created by God.

Stewardship has deep implications for us as we engage in principled Christian conflict resolution. We cannot negotiate as "owners" looking out for our selfish interests! As stewards, when we are in a conflict, we must represent the true owner, the Master. We must represent and reflect the Master's heart. Jesus' heart was to lose none of those he had been given. We must make every effort to negotiate in such a way that none are lost, but that all parties are restored and reconciled. The Christian purpose of conflict and negotiation is both freeing and binding: it frees us from the need to behave like owners by only looking out for ourselves, and it binds us to represent the Master in all we say and do.

The concept of principled Christian conflict negotiation we have developed for this chapter draws its methodology largely from the work of Roger Fisher, William Ury and Bruce Patton (1991) and their classic book on negotiation called *Getting to Yes*. In their book, these Harvard scholars developed a four-step method for negotiation that can be summarized under the following general headings: (1) separate the people from the problem; (2) focus on interests, not positions; (3) invent options for mutual gain; and (4) insist on using objective criteria. Their negotiation methodology, though not explicitly Christian, is consistent with and facilitates the Christian purpose of conflict: to restore and reconcile.

THE FIRST STEP OF PRINCIPLED CHRISTIAN CONFLICT NEGOTIATION: SEPARATE THE PEOPLE FROM THE PROBLEM

Prenegotiation is the crucial first *technical* step to take before we enter into a negotiation. The actual first and ongoing practice we must take in negotiation in the prenegotiation step and throughout the process is to be in prayer about the conflict and its negotiation. We must recognize that every conflict, large or small, is an overt foray onto a spiritual battlefield. Unfortunately, our natural inclinations and instincts with regard to conflict and negotiation have not been shaped by God, but by our fallen nature. Beginning with the prenegotiation step, we need to bathe the process in prayer every step of the way. Conflict is an area where the evil one can thrive, but it also can be an opportunity for God to triumph gloriously.

Besides prayer there are five technical processes associated with the prenegotiation step: (1) identify the problem; (2) determine all of the important stakeholders; (3) identify the key interests associated with the conflict; (4) determine if there are "easy" issues that could be negotiated and resolved successfully before dealing with the more difficult problems; and (5) explore the options available that satisfy as many of our interests as possible if we decide not to negotiate, or if the negotiation meets an impasse.

Identify the problem and the purpose for the negotiation. The first thing to do when entering a negotiation is to spell out the restoration and reconciliation goal of the conflict. This step helps to remind us of what we really want to do as stewards of this relationship. Further, it helps the other party understand our purpose, even if they do not share that purpose with us. When this purpose is revisited during the negotiation, it can become a means to enhance trust between the parties.

When we are in a conflict, all kinds of issues vie for recognition and can masquerade as the essential problem or cause of the conflict. Our understanding of the problem is based on our perceptions, and our perceptions may or may not be based on objective reality. Our perceptions are bolstered by the various "facts" we assemble and give priority to regarding the problem. Fisher, Ury and Patton explain, "As useful as looking for objective reality can be, it is ultimately the reality as each side sees it that constitutes the problem in a negotiation and opens the way to a solution" (1991, p. 23).

We also tend to think of issues in their immediate context, not recognizing that most problems and our perceptions of them are a product of a long line of antecedent issues and the personalities of those involved. Spangle and Isenhart explain:

> Few problems are problems of the moment. Generally, they have roots in the history of the relationship. . . . Past relationships and problems become the ghosts for current realities and frequently affect negotiations within families, between environmental groups and industries, and between management and employees. . . . In many ways, organizations resemble families. For example, both contexts possess histories that cast shadows over current discussions. In both settings, the personalities of members influence group dynamics. (2003, pp. 27, 277)

Because "biblical" human beings are involved in conflicts and the negotiation of conflicts, our tendency is to look for someone to blame! Deep understanding of the problem must not become a quest for fixing blame, even when blame appears to be justifiable. When we assign blame to a person, it then becomes very easy for us to believe that the person *is* the problem. Linking the problem to a person is something we learn early and practice often. We see evidence of this behavior everywhere, ranging from a squabble between children in preschool ("Sidney is the 'problem' because Sidney does not share toys with me") to international conflicts ("Saddam was the 'problem' in Iraq because Saddam was a megalomaniac and tyrant"). When people are identified as *the problem*, then we believe the solution to the problem is simple: get rid of the people ("Sidney should be put in time-out or expelled from school"; "Saddam should be hunted down and killed"). Focusing our energy on developing strategies for eliminating the people distracts us from looking at and resolving the actual issues and interests that constitute the entire problem.

No doubt people do contribute to problems, but Fisher, Ury and Patton (1991) suggest in negotiation we work hard to decouple the problem from the people associated with it. When this decoupling occurs, it becomes possible to thoroughly analyze the problem, and when necessary become very tough on the underlying issues that contribute to the problem. Being tough on the underlying issues means we do not have to be tough on the people who are associated with the problem! Our goal to restore and reconcile relationships becomes possible because people and their dignity can be preserved in the negotiation process. They have an opportunity to change their behavior because the underlying issues can be exposed and addressed.

Deep understanding of a problem means that we must step away from our carefully constructed and often biased perception of reality in order to look at the problem from all points of view. This means we will have to listen to how others perceive the problem. People on both sides of the table will have to accept responsibility for their contributions to the problem. This is easier to do when everyone recognizes that problems usually are far more complex and go far deeper than the offensive behavior that may have been perpetrated by the participants.

There are many reasons we may not want to decouple the people from the problem and dig into a deep understanding of the problem. First, the person with whom we are having conflict may be a thoroughly disgusting person! This is one of the hard problems for Christians in negotiation. We have to go back (possibly reluctantly) to the biblical purpose of the negotiation: restoration and reconciliation. As stewards representing the heart of the Master who died not only for us, but also for this disgusting opponent of ours, we need to pray about finding the path to separate the problem from the person so that we can both develop a deep understanding about the problem and get the negotiation on a path toward restoration and reconciliation for everyone involved.

During the summer of 2010, the Gulf Coast of the United States was under siege from one of the worst oil disasters in history. People spent a lot of energy looking for someone or some organization to blame for the explosion and the resulting gushing flow of oil into the gulf, resulting in horrific environmental, economic and social problems. While people, organizations and institutions have contributed to the initial failure, explosion and the many other resulting problems, fixing blame on a person, group of people, organizations or institutions will not help us understand the problem so that we can prevent it in the future. Fixing blame, finding a scapegoat, only serves as a distraction to the central issue: developing an understanding about what went wrong, what works well to clean up the mess and, in light of this understanding, how we should proceed in the future. The immediate reaction in 2010 of fixing blame, firing people, extracting financial penalties and fines from companies, suing everyone in sight, developing politically charged regulations and myriad other distracting kinds of behaviors have done little to develop our deep understanding of this colossal problem.

Sometimes we may fear that if we develop a deep understanding of the problem, and even more our opponent's perceptions of the problem, that we must then agree with our opponent. Thorough understanding does not equate with agreement. Indeed, one can understand deeply and thoroughly disagree. Deep understanding might also reveal that we have it wrong and that our perception of the problem is wrong! At times Christians dig deep trenches around their perceptions and positions because they have decided theological truth is at stake in the dispute. Christians should not be afraid of discovering capital-T Truth, regardless of the source of the discovery. All Truth is God's. Perhaps it is important to be reminded of the story of Balaam. Balaam's donkey knew and acted on Truth that Balaam was unable to see (Numbers 22:21-33). If God can reveal Truth to and through a donkey, he can certainly reveal Truth to and through the other party in our conflict!

Determine all the important stakeholders in the negotiation. Often a conflict affects far more than the obvious disputants. Other parties may also have interests associated with the conflict. Deep understanding of the problem and its eventual successful negotiation may depend on input and buy-in from these stakeholders. This is a kind of two-edged sword. On one hand, the more parties at the table participating in the negotiation, the more likely that rich information about the underlying issues that contribute to the problem will be understood and a resolution will have broad-based buy-in. On the other hand, each additional party added to a negotiation complicates and can confound the context of communication and perceptions, and add additional time and logistical considerations to the negotiation.

Organizations with multiple stakeholders will have to consider a variety of contextual issues in the prenegotiation step. Organizational structures provide the "playing field" and cultural norms that must be addressed in the negotiation process. Spangle and Isenhart discuss how structure "regulates social interaction by supporting norms that determine *who* is authorized to talk to whom and *about what*" (2003, p. 279). Organizational structure often works to insulate the organization from environmental turbulence. Negotiations can produce turbulence that can be disturbing to the organization, and the structural barriers to effective resolution must be acknowledged and, if possible, neutralized in the prenegotiation step.

Finally, when multiple stakeholders are involved in the negotiation, *the process* of the negotiation must be made clear during prenegotiation. Stakeholders must agree to the process, and it is important to remind parties of the process as well as the status of the negotiation within the process as the negotiation plays out.

Identify key interests. Interests give shape and definition to the problem. The most powerful interests are those that are associated with our fundamental needs as human beings. Think of the various stages of Maslow's hierarchy (subsistence, safety, social, esteem, autonomy, self-actualization). Each of those sets of needs can be associated with various interests we hold. Fisher, Ury and Patton (1991) call our basic needs the bedrock concerns upon which people anchor their interests.

During the prenegotiation step it is very important for us to suppress our desire to develop positions or respond to the other side's stated or anticipated positions. Instead we should clearly identify our interests. Interests can be exposed as we uncover the needs that form the foundation of the positions we are tempted to take. As we examine our interests, we need to affirm that they are linked with our desire to represent the Master and forge opportunities for restoration and reconciliation. We should also try to understand what interests the other party might hold. This process may reveal interests we share. Spending time in the prenegotiation step recognizing and affirming all parties' interests will facilitate a principled negotiation, especially as we move into the second and third steps of the negotiation process.

Determine if there are easy issues. Communicating with adversaries is never easy, and communication is essential for a successful negotiation. The opportunity for meaningful communication improves when there is greater trust between the parties. In the prenegotiation step we may have a chance to build trust and improve communication by settling easy issues that affirm our purpose to restore and reconcile relationships.

Sometimes we get so fired up about the negotiation over the difficult issues on the table that we overlook issues that are not controversial or particularly problematic. After all, those "side issues" are not the ones that are driving us into conflict and a negotiation. During the prenegotiation step it is important to recognize those easy issues and move quickly to resolve them before taking on the tougher ones. Breaking the ice in this way can enhance the relationships that will be tested on the more difficult problems. Even if negotiation over the tougher issues is not successful, at least these easy issues will have been resolved and that success may open the door for future discussions revisiting the tough problems. If easy issues are ignored or put to the side to be considered at a later date, and the negotiation on the tough issues breaks down, the easy issues are not likely to be addressed at all.

Explore the Best Alternative to a Negotiated Agreement (BATNA). The final prenegotiation technical process is to understand what the best-case scenario would be with regard to satisfying our interests if we decide to either not negotiate in the first place or to walk away from the negotiation if it meets an impasse. Not all conflicts can be successfully negotiated. As Christians we need to look for ways to continue in as good a relationship as possible with the other party even if we are not able to negotiate a resolution to a dispute. Can we agree to disagree and remain in dialogue? Are there other ways our interests or significant chunks of our interests can be satisfied if we don't negotiate?

Fisher, Ury and Patton (1991), who invented the term *BATNA*, suggest that your BATNA becomes a standard by which any negotiated agreement will be measured. A firmly developed BATNA gives clear definition to this standard. Fisher, Ury and Patton suggest three components for developing your BATNA. First, they suggest you make a list of things you will do if an agreement cannot be reached. Taking the time to make a list of things you might be able to do can help you think creatively about how you might satisfy your interests both through and without negotiated settlement of the conflict. The second component needed for developing a BATNA is to work over the list you developed in the first BATNA component and develop the best ideas into working alternatives that are no longer ideas but actions you know you could initiate if negotiations break down. Finally, the third component for developing a BATNA is to review the alternatives from component two and select the best alternative. Once again, the clearer this best alternative becomes, the better equipped you are to judge the potential outcome of a negotiation.

When I began negotiating for a position as a faculty member at a Christian university, I believed God was calling me to develop a Leadership Studies program in the context of the Christian university similar to the program I had successfully developed in the context of a secular state university. The negotiation for this faculty position was quite complicated—I was bargaining as an "accommodated spouse" because the Christian institution was ready to offer my wife a position as a vice president. The culture of the Christian university had no tradition of spousal accommodation for dual-career families. Indeed we were told stories of people who had been hired from dual-career families in the past and one spouse had to be willing to give up their career so that the other could follow their calling to the institution. Worse yet, the institution did not offer a single course in my discipline area! Hiring me to teach in a program that did not yet exist seemed to be an impossible barrier, and in the initial negotiations, this was made very clear. The university's BATNA was also quite clear: reopen the search for a vice president and find a candidate that did not have spousal baggage!

My wife and I both had very strong BATNAs in that we had terrific (and higher paying) positions at our current university, we were members of a strong Christian community in the small town where the university was located, and we had opportunities to continue our decades-long evangelistic and discipleship ministry in the secular environment of the state university. As we negotiated with the Christian university, we communicated openly and honestly about our BATNAs as well as our sense of calling to our new positions (even to a program that did not yet exist!). Over the course of a few weeks of negotiation, all parties discovered ways to meet all of our interests that were superior to each of our BATNAs.

THE SECOND STEP IN PRINCIPLED CHRISTIAN CONFLICT NEGOTIATION: FOCUS ON INTERESTS

When we have decoupled the problem from the people and we have developed a deep understanding of the problem, our interests associated with the problem can become even clearer. In addition, when we develop a deep understanding of the nature of the problem, our opponent's interests can also take on shape and meaning. For Christians engaged in conflict resolution, these interests are often sanctified interests that allow all parties to grow closer in their relationship with God and each other so that all concerned can more creatively and effectively do kingdom work. This second step, focusing on interests, is the one where a great deal of progress can be made in the negotiation. Fisher, Ury and Patton explain that "interests motivate people; they are the silent movers behind the hubbub of positions. Your position is something you have decided upon. Your interests are what cause you to decide" (1991, pp. 40-41).

We cannot forge real solutions to problems when disputants lock onto intractable positions. Positions are usually premature and often don't lead to a resolution of conflict. Positions also throw a fog over the negotiation so that the real problem and interests that define the problem become obscured or relegated to the sideline. People tend to haggle over positions and end up with a compromise. The very nature of a compromise is that both parties must lose something associated with their position. Further, when a compromise is reached over a position, for the most part neither party's interests are substantively met. When energy is focused on disputes over positions, we are no longer engaged in the process of understanding the problem, all parties' interests around the problem, and conducting a meaningful negotiation about the problem. There are four key advantages to discovering parties' interests.

First, when we focus on interests and not on positions, we are likely to discover that we share interests with our opponent! For instance, when I buy a car, I have an interest in and am willing to pay a fair price for a car that is safe, reliable and has the options I need. The car dealer with whom I trade has an interest in selling safe, reliable, appropriately equipped cars because the reputation and profitability of the dealership is bolstered when they sell high-quality products to satisfied customers.

Second, besides shared interests, we may discover that we have complementary interests. When I purchase a new car it is in my interest that the car dealer makes enough profit that they stay in business. If the dealership goes out of business because they have lost too much money on the sales of cars, I will not have a place to go for warranty service and to purchase other cars in the future. The dealer has an interest in making a profit, but the dealer also has an interest in me being a satisfied consumer because I have been dealt with fairly. If I am satisfied, I am likely to let friends and family know about the great purchasing experience I had when I bought my shiny new car, and I'm also likely to return to the dealer when I need to purchase my next car.

Third, we may find interests that are benign to one party though they are deeply held by the other. On one hand, I may have no interest in taking the minimal time required to fill out a survey from a car manufacturer about a dealership, because I do not care about the relationship the dealer has with the manufacturer. On the other hand, these kinds of surveys are an important interest to the dealer because car manufacturers grant special status to highly rated dealerships. This special status and the incentives that accompany the status can improve employee morale, manufacturer marketing support and public perception of the dealership.

Finally, we may discover those interests that are clearly in conflict between the parties. When I trade in my old car I have an interest in unloading the old car and getting as much equity out of it as possible, and I don't want to go through the hassle of selling it myself. The dealership has an interest in paying as little as possible for my clunker so they can either wholesale it or sell it off their lot for a reasonable profit and still ensure that their reputation isn't damaged by unloading this lemon on another customer.

My first career in higher education was as a student life professional at a major state university. I was responsible for the student life program in the forty or so fraternities and sororities affiliated with the university. I had just finished reading the first edition of *Getting to Yes* when I found myself in a sticky conflict. In that book, Fisher, Ury and Patton (1991) suggested that even if you are the only person in conflict using their ideas, it may be possible to turn a position-driven negotiation into a principled negotiation. I had nothing to lose and everything to gain by using their ideas. It worked! The success hinged on focusing on interests instead of positions.

The conflict started when a fraternity's "pledges" (new students who wanted to join the fraternity) were in a quandary about how to secure the decorations for what they were told needed to be a lavish pledge dance they would put together for the fraternity members and their guests. With no meaningful budget to purchase the materials they needed in order to decorate for the dance, the group decided to pursue alternative ways of procuring decorations.

Initially, the pledges made a few midnight excursions to an unguarded construction site and carted off scrap lumber. Over time, their trips yielded materials that were not scrap. Soon they bypassed the construction site altogether and burglarized a lumber yard and a garden store. Eventually they accumulated a massive amount of pilfered supplies with which to decorate for their dance. The Saturday morning of the event, some of the pledges were in the process of building an elaborate plywood tunnel from the sidewalk up to the front door of the fraternity. Others were inside the fraternity erecting a stage, and dozens of potted plants and trees were waiting to be attractively placed around the finished project. A police officer drove by, saw the materials, compared it to his list of stolen merchandise, and by the end of the morning the entire pledge class was under arrest.

This was a public relations nightmare for the university (not to mention the fraternity). The president of the university was on an extended trip out of the country, and the introverted and incredibly busy provost—who was not normally charged with dealing with student issues, their parents or the media—was fielding all sorts of calls from the press, legislators and shocked parents. Everyone wanted to know what the university had "done" to these young men in the three short months they had been in the university's care, why the university allowed this corrupt organization on its campus and what the university was going to do about this situation.

In this tense atmosphere, as the university official in charge of the fraternities, I was called to a meeting with key cabinet members of the university administration. I was joined by two students, the president of the felonious fraternity and the interfraternity council president. The university had already locked onto several negotiating positions, including closing down the fraternity and expelling all of the pledges. My head may have been on the block as well.

This tense meeting began and the university officials jumped all over the fraternity president, who quietly took all of their blows and apologized profusely when given the chance. Once that was over, the officials started going through a process of refining how they would implement their positions of throwing the fraternity off campus and bouncing the students out of school. That is when I started my *Getting to Yes* experiment.

I asked the vice president for student life if one of our key interests and part of the student life philosophy was that in response to the mistakes we knew students would make, we would do what we could do as a university to help students learn and grow from their errant behavior. Of course I knew the answer was yes. Once that was admitted, I began to ask a series of questions of all those gathered around the table that played on that and other deeply held institutional interests. As a result, an interest-driven question emerged: If we throw all of these students out of school, how will we be able to continue to work with them so that we know they learn the kinds of lessons from this that we hope they will learn?

Once we shifted our focus to interests instead of the university's draconian positions, the entire tone of the meeting changed. We began to negotiate a principled resolution to the conflict. As a result of that negotiation, no one was kicked out of school. While all sorts of educational sanctions were placed on the fraternity and the individual students, the whole episode became one where individual students, the felonious fraternity, the fraternities and sororities in general, and the university all were able to grow because we were able to satisfy many of our interests in the negotiation.

While this incident and negotiation took place in about as secular a context as there is, the Christian purpose of conflict—to facilitate restoration and reconciliation—became possible because we were able to forge a principled resolution. Years later my son-in-law was working as a teacher at a Christian high school in western Washington. He introduced me to the athletic director of the high school, who surprised me when he said that he already knew who I was. He saw my puzzled look and, embarrassed, he admitted that he had been one of those errant pledges who was able to learn a very important life lesson. We never know how God will use conflict to bring into play his sanctified interests even as he works for parties to become restored and reconciled; we dare not lose sight of this goal.

THE THIRD STEP IN PRINCIPLED CHRISTIAN CONFLICT NEGOTIATION: EXPLORE IDEAS TO MEET INTERESTS

This third step is where it becomes possible to leave positions far behind and begin to think outside the box in order to generate creative ideas that will satisfy as many interests as possible. If the first and second steps have been done well, this step becomes a highly energized and exciting step for all parities. When the disputing parties enter this phase, an opportunity opens up for them to work together in ways they would have never thought possible. Generating lots of creative ideas is the key to making this step work. Christians who prayerfully walk through this step may find God helping them find incredibly creative ways to satisfy the sanctified interests of the disputants.

During this step, I like to do a brainstorming technique in order to get broad input and lots of different ideas. First, we identify an interest or cluster of interests that we want to work on. Next, everyone is instructed to independently write an unedited and unfiltered list of ideas they have about how to meet the mutually shared interests. This free-writing session should run for a minimum of five minutes, but could easily go ten to twenty minutes depending on the topic. The facilitator should not be fearful of silence or inactivity, as people may need time to collect their thoughts as they continue adding to their lists. When Christians are participating in this activity, it is a great practice to enter into it with prayer, inviting God to inspire the brainstorming.

Once everyone has had sufficient time to think about and write down their ideas, the next step is to begin to share all of the ideas. I start at one end of the room and have the first person share the first item on their list. I write a brief but descriptive summary of the idea on a whiteboard and then move to the second person whose turn it is to share their first idea. We continue around the room getting summaries of everyone's first ideas on the board. Then we repeat the process getting everyone's second ideas. No judgment or evaluation of ideas is allowed at this point as the board becomes crowded with lots of ideas. The sharing continues one person at a time, one idea at a time, around and around the room until every item from every person's list is up on the board. As we go down peoples' lists, they will see that some ideas are shared among members of the group. This brainstorming technique ensures that everyone's ideas get heard, and it gets everyone into the habit of talking and contributing, which is essential for the next part of this process.

After all the ideas are on the board, it is time to discuss them. Great options to satisfy all parties' interests are often found through God's inspiration as well as creative thinking outside the bounds of normal policies and procedures. The goal now is to develop a prioritized list of the options that appear to satisfy the greatest number and the most important interests of all parties. Strict evaluation of the options isn't necessary at this point, although illegal, immoral and obviously unethical ideas can be immediately erased. In addition, some ideas may be so far-fetched that they would be impossible to implement under any conceivable circumstances, and they too can be erased if they cannot be grounded in some sort of pragmatic reality. Some ideas are going to emerge as novel and creative, and will of necessity generate a lot of conversation. Other ideas might spring from these discussions, and those ideas should be incorporated into the mix of possible options.

In this exciting step the group may not even notice that energy is being channeled away from competition between the parties and onto mutually generated and explored ideas that have potential for meeting various interests. It is important to move forward on the options that will address at least some of the interests. It may be that no options are generated for some interests, and those may remain unmet. These interests can be revisited later, or relegated to BATNA status.

Even when parties are dealing with benign or competing interests, it may be possible to find options that are satisfactory for both parties. According to

Fisher, Ury and Patton, it is easiest to agree on options for benign or competing interests when parties find that options are "of low cost to you and high
benefit to them, and vice versa" (1991, p. 76). Developing options that satisfy
benign or competing interests can pave the way for ensuring an ongoing relationship between parties and successful negotiations in the future. Recall the
example above where a car purchaser has little interest in taking the time to
fill out a dealership's customer satisfaction survey, but the dealership can
derive great benefits from the manufacturer based on the survey results of a
customer they know has had a good experience. This represents a low-cost
way for the customer to help meet the keen interests of the dealership.

The Fourth Step in Principled Christian Conflict
Negotiation: Determine the Best Option(s) and
Develop an Agreement

In this final step of the negotiation, we choose the best ideas we came up
with in step three and we develop an agreement to implement them. Recall
that the third step requires creativity and free-flowing conversation with
minimal criticism or evaluation. In the fourth step, these creative options
must be evaluated. This is where creativity meets accountability. In this step,
an objective standard is introduced into the process. The first standard any
option must meet is that the Christian purpose of conflict, to restore and
reconcile, must be supported by the option and the subsequent agreement.
Examples of subsequent standards that may be employed include biblical
authority, mission statements, fiscal realities, denominational doctrines or
dogma, codes of ethics, independent appraisal or review, and compliance
with essential policies. The objective standards employed must be recognized by all parties as appropriate and fair for evaluating options. If options
generated in step three do not meet the established standards, then the ideas
must be refined before they become a part of an agreement.

Summary

In this chapter we have examined first the purpose of Christian conflict—to
restore and reconcile people with whom we have conflict. When conflict is
a choice, Christians must ask themselves hard questions regarding whether
the restoration and reconciliation process can be best accomplished with or

without conflict. Christians must examine their own motivations for conflict and remove themselves from conflicts where their motivations and purposes are not consistent with Christian principles.

Some conflict is unavoidable, but conflict done well can facilitate restoration and reconciliation. There are various scenarios that play into dysfunctional win/lose or lose/lose conflict "resolution" that resolves little in the long run. Drawing heavily from Fisher, Ury and Patton (1991), we have offered a four-step model of principled Christian conflict resolution. The four steps are:

1. *Separate the people from the problem* during several prenegotiation stages including prayer, deep exploration and understanding of the problem, determination of all the important stakeholders, identification of the key interests associated with the conflict, determination and resolution of easy issues between the parties, and exploration and identification of a BATNA.

2. *Focus on interests*, which helps keep parties from prematurely developing positions that do little or nothing to satisfy parties' interests.

3. *Explore ideas that will meet as many interests as possible.* During this step parties look for creative options that will facilitate win/win solutions that satisfy parties' interests, not superficial positions.

4. *Determine the best options and develop an agreement.* The creative options developed in step three must first and foremost move parties toward restoration and reconciliation. Then they are prioritized based on mutually shared objective standards. Options that do not meet these standards must be modified or discarded.

We are indeed all "biblical" individuals who live in "biblical" relationships in "biblical" organizations and institutions. As stewards representing the will and desires of the Master, we are called to advance the noble Christian purpose of conflict, to restore and reconcile relationships. In this way we can participate in conflict to help build God's kingdom instead of tearing it down. No wonder Jesus told people at the Sermon on the Mount, "Blessed are the peacemakers" (Matthew 5:9). Principled Christian conflict resolution can bring peace.

REFERENCES

Burns, J. M. 1978. *Leadership.* New York: Harper & Row.

Fisher, R., W. Ury and B. Patton. 1991. *Getting to Yes.* New York: Penguin.

Gangel, K. O., and S. L. Canine. 1992. *Communication and Conflict Management in Churches and Christian Organizations.* Nashville: Broadman.

Janis, I. L. 1972. *Victims of Groupthink: A Psychological Study of Foreign-Policy Decisions and Fiascos.* Boston: Houghton Mifflin.

Peterson, E. H. 1997. *Leap over a Wall: Earthly Spirituality for Everyday Christians.* New York: HarperCollins.

Rodin, R. S. 2010. *The Steward Leader.* Downers Grove, IL: InterVarsity Press.

Spangle, M. L., and M. W. Isenhart. 2003. *Negotiation: Communication for Diverse Settings.* Thousand Oaks, CA: Sage.

Wittwer, J. 2010. *Making Peace with Others.* Performance at Life Center Foursquare Church, Spokane, WA, June 6.

FOR FURTHER READING

Kellett, P. M., and D. G. Dalton. 2001. *Managing Conflict in a Negotiated World.* Thousand Oaks, CA: Sage.

8

Decision Making

Becoming an Expert of the Process

John R. Shoup and Chris McHorney

—ɯ—

So give your servant a discerning heart to govern your people
and to distinguish between right and wrong. For who
is able to govern this great people of yours?

1 Kings 3:9

If any of you lacks wisdom, you should ask God,
who gives generously to all without finding
fault, and it will be given to you.

James 1:5

A Leader's Primary Activity Is Making Decisions

One way to recognize the leader of any group is to identify who people go
to for a decision. While the formal leader of a group will have the legitimate
and final authority to establish the what, who, when, how and even why of
all possible scenarios under his or her charge, people often seek out the informal leader for the real wisdom. Regardless of who is sought out for
guidance, the process of making a decision is complicated. The premise of
this chapter is that the more consequential the decision, the more the leader

needs to be an expert on the processes guiding the decision. This chapter is designed to equip decision makers with the knowledge and skills necessary to enhance their decision making and overcome the common processes that unknowingly bias decisions toward unanticipated and undesirable outcomes. This chapter provides a synthesis of various principles from both general and special revelation to help decision makers execute wise and ethical judgments that will increase the probability of successful outcomes.

WE ARE NOT BY NATURE GOOD AT MAKING CRITICAL DECISIONS

The complexity of the human brain reveals that we are "fearfully and wonderfully made" (Psalm 139:14). The brain contains 86 to 100 billion neurons, which allow for 60 to 100 trillion connections (Sousa 2006). Our brain is poised to give a fight-or-flight response within nanoseconds to an unannounced stimuli. Our brain is continuously filtering information—such as sensations from the clothes on our skin, ambient noises and smells, and random thoughts—so as to allow us to focus on what is deemed relevant. We are able to compartmentalize anxiety and emotions in order to concentrate on the present. For the average adult, the brain can read 300, listen to 450 and speak up to 180 words per minute and instantaneously construct meaning and generate insights from a string of symbols that make communication possible (Ley and Chang 2008).

While the brain can process information and make inferences at tremendous rates, it has at least two limitations when it comes to making decisions. First, the brain is self-referencing. When it comes to making inferences and judgments, the brain relies on itself to make sense of the data. As a result, biases, expectations, experiences and values knowingly and unknowingly shape perceptions. The second limitation is axiomatic to the first. Given that the brain can only rely on what it knows at the conscious and unconscious level, any and all knowledge is bounded. The brain is incapable of omniscience. Imagine how easy making a decision would be if we were all-knowing. Every decision is only as good as the information and knowledge on hand at the time of the decision. When it comes to making decisions, it is important to recognize that the data we are using is incomplete and potentially distorted.

Based upon extensive research from cognitive psychology, Avolio and

Gardner conclude that "humans are inherently flawed and biased information processers" (2005, p. 317). The prophet Jeremiah recognized a similar phenomenon when he recorded that the "heart is deceitful" (Jeremiah 17:9). As a result, it is not surprising "that half the decisions made in business and related organizations fail" (Nutt 2002, p. 3). Part of the solution to making better decisions is to understand the nature of discernment.

The Nature of Decision Making

Borrowing from the work of Ackoff (1989), a first step on becoming an expert in the decision-making process is to appreciate the nature of wisdom, knowledge and information. While good decision making is predicated on having the right information at the right time, the challenge is recognizing what information is relevant and accurate. By the time a decision is made, the content has gone through various levels of interpretation. Why don't we hear people reporting, "I left the wisdom or knowledge you wanted on your desk"? Rather, we typically say, "I left the information you wanted on your desk" (Blair 2002, p. 1020). The differences suggest that there is a soft but important hierarchy of understanding when it comes to making decisions (see figure 8.1).

When making a judgment call, the first point of contact with reality is with

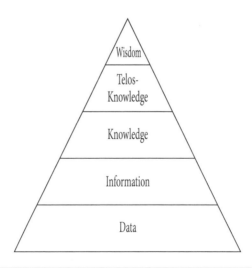

Figure 8.1. Levels of Understanding
(Modified from Ackoff's (1989) hierarchy of types of content of the human mind.)

the *data*, which are bits of facts. Once the mind organizes the data into a cohesive frame, it takes on the form of *information*, a stream of data that has been patterned for a particular purpose. *Knowledge* is formed once the information is organized around a narrative. Along the way, the knowledge takes on additional meaning to justify a course of action or compel a decision. Philosopher Gayne Anacker (2013, personal communication) identifies this phase as *telos-knowledge*, which is a goal-directed knowledge that goes beyond routine categorization or the observation of patterns. Instead, it is knowledge that is applied toward the achievement of goals, ends or purposes (this is what the Greek word *telos* means). Telos-knowledge is really the combining of specific knowledge with the goals, ends or purposes of the decision maker, a complex that supports prudent and rational decisions. Telos-knowledge is both fact- and value-laden, evident by the fact that people with the same information and knowledge often render different judgments (e.g., partisan policies). The highest level of understanding is *wisdom*, which acknowledges that while there are multiple valid judgments, some are more relevant and insightful than others. Wisdom discerns which series of truths or patterns are more important than others (e.g., when does the need of the group outweigh the need of the individual, or when does mercy triumph over judgment?). Wisdom, and its close cousin creativity, will be further developed in this chapter as one of the ultimate goals of good decision making.

Let us use the census as an example to illustrate the hierarchy of understanding. The census gives us data in the form of population numbers. The data is organized into percentages, which yield information on various population distributions (e.g., the percentage of females to males, or the age and ethnic distribution of the United States). While information is useful, it becomes meaningful when a knowledge claim is generated. The information from a previous census is analyzed with current census information to identify trends and patterns. For example, researchers at the University of North Carolina at Chapel Hill (2011) identified six demographic trends that will transform the United States. One such trend is the "graying of America." There was a 15.1 percent increase in the number of people who are sixty-five years or older between the 2000 and 2010 census. If the knowledge is persuasive, it leads to telos-knowledge, which prompts decision makers to implement adaptive policies.

The "silver tsunami" has such significant implications for the labor market, social security and health care that companies and government agencies would be prudent to develop plans to mitigate and capitalize on the shifting demographics. For example, for the shrewd entrepreneur, geriatrics is in for a boom period of growth. At the same time, sustaining social security benefits with the influx of the anticipated retirement wave of eligible recipients seems tenuous. As a result, people may be prudent to plan alternative retirement strategies that are not solely dependent on social security. While there are multiple story lines revealed in the census data and a variety of applications (e.g., plan long term for good health and financial security), there is an additional level of understanding that emerges in the form of wisdom, which is echoed in Psalm 90:12:

> Teach us to number our days,
>> that we may gain a heart of wisdom.

Counting our days reveals that life is short relative to eternity, so we should align our priorities with the kingdom of God (Matthew 7:24-27).

The purpose of the above discussion is to reinforce the notion that knowledge management and decision making are interpretive and subjective acts. As a result, there are unfortunately variables that interfere and bias judgments. Not only are data, information and knowledge filtered by the time they get to the decision maker, but each decision maker also has his or her own filters that lead to distortions and biases about the nature of reality. This is all the more reason to be an expert on what is informing consequential decisions as they unfold.

COMMON KNOWLEDGE DISTORTION AND BIASES

One only has to engage different optical illusions to understand that the mind is easily tricked. The Star Wars ride at Disneyland provides a wonderful example. On this ride, the mind is fooled into thinking it is traveling at light speed to a distant planet, even though the body attached to that mind hasn't moved a horizontal foot. At the risk of oversimplifying a complex process, at the start of such rides the motion simulator provides a sudden jolt that is cleverly woven into the plot. The initial joggle disturbs the fluid in the inner ear, creating some disequilibrium. The body primarily relies on the fluid in the inner ear for balance and orientation. Once the fluid in the inner ear is disturbed, the body compensates by overrelying on the other senses for orientation. The mind is now dependent on what the eyes witness on the screen in front of them. The motion simulator provides continual swaying action to prevent the fluid in the inner ear from returning to its normal state. As a result, the mind is tricked into perceiving fast and far travel when in reality the ride never left the building.

Not only is our mind tricked to perceive things that are not there, but it also likes to make up information when there are gaps in understanding. Why is it that when someone cuts us off on the freeway, a typical response toward the other driver is less than flattering, yet our explanation is more forgiving when we commit the same offense? The reason that we are less gracious toward other drivers is because we do not know why we were cut off, so we fundamentally attribute some type of error to the driver's character (e.g., that person must be rude!). When we cut someone off, we tend to know the reason (e.g., I can't be late to pick up my daughter). This is an example of the "fundamental attribution error"—the tendency to overestimate the internal factors and minimize the external factors when explaining the behavior of others. The mind abhors gaps in information. As a result, it will find the best-fitting explanation to fill in the gaps, even if it means making inferences when information is absent.

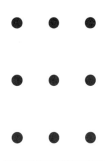

Just as the mind naturally does not allow for gaps in understanding, it is also constrained to limit perceptions to existing patterns or expectations. To illustrate briefly how the brain works when processing data, take a few minutes to see if you can connect the nine dots in figure 8.2 by drawing four lines without lifting your pencil from the paper.

Interestingly enough, most people struggle to recognize that the only way to solve the problem is to go outside the box, as illustrated in figure 8.3. Gestalt

Figure 8.2.

psychology reveals that the mind uses patterns to make sense of data. The parts only make sense in relation to the whole. This explains why most people start with the border when working on jigsaw puzzles. The outside provides a frame of reference for the myriad other pieces. In this exercise, the nine dots form an outline for a box and establish an artificial perceptual boundary that forces minds to think of a solution limited to the box (or pre-established patterns).

For most, it is physiologically difficult to think outside the box. We like to interpret data consistent with our expectations and patterns. A classic example is when Harry Warner of Warner Brothers observed in 1927, "Who the hell wants to hear actors talk?" Learning to think outside the box is one means to wise and creative thinking that is addressed later in this chapter.

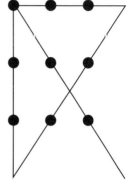

Figure 8.3.

INTERFERENCE WITH DECISION MAKING

The brain is not only prone to distort and make up information; it also has difficulty seeing alternative explanations. These are but a few examples that reveal limitations of the brain that are at the root of some common failings in reasoning. Researchers have identified well over fifty flaws that interfere with good decision making (Bazerman and Moore 2009; Hallinan 2009; Janis 1982; Kahneman, Slovic and Tversky 1982; Lehrer 2009; Nisbett and Ross 1980; Nutt 2002; Pfeffer 2007). The human tendency is to overutilize simple inferential strategies at the expense of more formal processes. Effective decision makers not only evaluate the information germane to the decision, but also audit the decision-making process as it unfolds. Below are eight of the more common fatal decision-making flaws identified within the literature, and respective tips on how to avoid them.[1]

Flaw 1: Lack of active listening. What is the number-one skill for effective decision making? What is the one skill that has a disproportionate effect on making the right decision? What is the one silver bullet, the nonnegotiable, to improve one's ability to make good decisions?

The answer is active listening. James 1:19 encourages us to "be quick to listen, slow to speak and slow to become angry." One needs to listen well in order to get all the data before reaching a conclusion (e.g., being slow to speak and become angry—ultimate acts of reaching a conclusion). Blanchard

---

[1]Flaws 3-6, 8 are modified from Bazerman and Moore (2009) and Bazerman (2006.)

(2006) documents that according to 1,400 executives, failure to listen is one of the most common leadership mistakes. Hearing is not the same thing as listening. Lee and Hatesohl report that while "listening is the communication skill most of us use most frequently . . . studies also confirm that most of us are poor and inefficient listeners" (2012, p. 1). Interestingly enough, we take classes in school to learn how to write and speak well, but we don't have standard classes on how to listen well.

Active listening is very much an intentional and labor-intensive skill. It involves attending to the communication to understand the meaning(s) of the message. Listening for meaning is at the heart of the skilled listener. Strategically, a whole chapter in this book is devoted to effective listening and communication (chapter 6).

Those who listen well make two things happen for the right information to emerge at the right time. First, active listening helps ensure that the knowledge is rightly interpreted. Second, it keeps the knowledge in the information pipeline flowing. People are willing to share information if they know they are heard. When people conclude, "What is the use, my boss does not listen," the information pipeline dries up and the leader ends up flying partially blind when it comes to making decisions. Good listeners create feedback-rich environments, which is critical if leaders are going to have access to relevant knowledge to make informed decisions.

The solution to the first flaw in decision making is to talk less and listen more, the type of active listening described in chapter 6. The book of Proverbs values listening over speaking, repeatedly admonishing the wise to hear and listen (e.g., "turn your ear to my words" in Proverbs 4:20). Proverbs 18:13 reminds us that "To answer before listening—that is folly and shame." And according to Proverbs 17:28, "Even fools are thought wise if they keep silent."

Flaw 2: Inattentional blindness. Imagine you are watching a group of people standing in a circle, half of whom are wearing white shirts and the other half are wearing black shirts. You are asked to count the number of times the basketball is passed between those wearing white shirts. Sounds like an easy task. About thirty seconds into the experiment, a woman walks through the circle carrying an umbrella and is visible for about four seconds. What percentage of people noticed the unexpected event?

Since the original experiment by Neisser and Becklen in 1975, there have been various iterations of the study, including one version that had a lady dressed up as a gorilla in lieu of the lady with the umbrella. For the most part, approximately 50 percent missed the unexpected event. The percentage went up as the assigned tasks got harder (Simons and Chabris, 1999). The inability to recognize unanticipated events when engaged in a task is called *inattentional blindness*. Inattentional blindness is often the cause of car accidents when drivers are engaged in other tasks besides driving. Inattentional blindness can also be, albeit not always, the excuse for our inability to recall information "reportedly" shared while we were watching television.

Attending to specific goals and tasks is important, but it can be at the expense of other information relevant to immediate and future decisions. Once we recognize the phenomenon of inattentional blindness, it seems obvious that we can't naturally process everything at once. While we cannot focus on everything, we have to avoid overreliance on what is in focus, lest we conclude all the relevant information is accounted for when that may not be the case. When making decisions, we must avoid overrelying on what is obvious and pay attention to what is not in immediate focus, lest we miss the gorilla in the room. The solution to inattentional blindness is paradoxical: we must pay attention to what we are not noticing.

Flaw 3: Overreliance on available information. Consider the following questions:

1. In 2013, *Fortune* magazine ranked the following ten corporations to be among the five hundred largest United States–based firms according to sales revenue. Which group listed below had the larger total sales volume?

   A. Priceline.com, Office Depot, Toys "R" Us, Time Warner and Staples

   B. Express Scripts Holding, United Technologies, INTL FCStone, AmerisourceBergen and McKesson

2. According to the Center for Disease Control and Prevention, which of the following resulted in more deaths in the United States in 2010?

   A. Homicide and motor vehicle accidents

   B. Diabetes and Alzheimer's disease

For question 1, no company in list A was in the Fortune 100, while all companies in list B were in the Fortune 100 and consequentially had the larger total sales volume. For question 2, the Center for Disease Control and Prevention lists a combined total of 152,565 deaths from diabetes and Alzheimer's disease and 54,220 deaths from homicide and motor vehicle accidents.

Why do you think people might be more likely to select A for both questions when the answer is B? When making inferences we overrely on what is readily available. Option A in question 1 is populated with companies that have greater name recognition, so it is easy to infer that they had larger sales volumes than those companies with lesser name recognition. Items in option B in question 2 do not garner as much news coverage as those in option A.

Overreliance on the availability of information can lead to faulty decisions. A classic example is employee evaluations. You can have a stellar employee who had a rare and minor outburst with a colleague nine months ago. When it comes to the twelve-month evaluation, it is not uncommon for the anomalous event to be listed. Another example is when a trusted colleague makes unsolicited positive comments about a candidate after you narrow your job search to two candidates. It is not uncommon for that unsolicited comment to be a tipping point in the decision without realizing that the random encounter with your colleague had a disproportionate effect on the decision. When exploring partnerships, it can be too easy to align with a company because of name recognition and miss out on a potentially better partnership if the choice was informed with a bit more formal research. Bazerman and Moore describe how one purchasing agent selected a supplier based upon familiarity with the name, without realizing the "salience of the name resulted from recent adverse publicity" (2009, p. 19).

The problem with readily available information is that it is too easy to conclude that just because information is at hand that the unavailable data is nonexistent or irrelevant. The solution, similar to inattentional blindness, is to develop systematic processes for getting relevant information.

Flaw 4: Anchoring effect. You are hiring a computer engineer for your company. The top candidate has four years of experience and good all-around qualifications. Prior to announcing your recommended starting annual salary of $70,000, a colleague suggests $60,000. Do you adjust your initial figure? What if the colleague suggests $90,000?

Most people adjust their initial estimate to come closer to whatever is stated first. The initial statement functions like an anchor to serve as the starting point for future discussion. In the scenario outlined above, if I was thinking $70,000 and someone stated $60,000, I would more than likely conclude that my estimate was too high and therefore compensate by suggesting a number lower than $70,000. If $90,000 was suggested first, I would more likely think my $70,000 was too low and therefore suggest a number higher than $70,000.

The anchoring effect is often evident in budget planning. Imagine you run a large nonprofit organization. What would you project for contributions for the next year based upon gifts from previous years in the scenario outlined in table 8.1? Notice that there has been a 10 percent increase in contributions each year over four years until the current year, which was a 100 percent increase.

Table 8.1.

Year 1	$1.365 million
Year 2	$1.5 million
Year 3	$1.65 million
Year 4	$1.815 million
Current Year	$3.63 million
Next year	?

Many people would treat the 100 percent increase as the new baseline, inadvertently allowing the last number to serve as an anchor or starting point for future projections (maybe a 50 percent projection) instead of relying on the trend from the previous four years (maybe a 10 percent projection). The error is to treat the 100 percent increase as evidence of a new trend versus an anomaly. A friend who worked in the nonprofit world explained that the anchoring effect impacts the budgeting process. They had a unique year in charitable contributions because upon the death of a particular donor a large estate was left to the institution. As a result, the budget for the next year was set unrealistically high as if there would be comparable estates in the subsequent year. The anchoring effect makes it too easy to minimize or ignore baseline or trend data.

Flaw 5: Nonrational escalation of commitment. When or how does a leader decide to change a course of action when the costs overrun the budget and/or project delays threaten the initial return of investment on a well-planned project? Given the chain of events to bring decisions to fruition, it is usually prudent to plan for some delays and unanticipated expenses. At the same time, there are times when it is better to walk away from a decision regardless of the invested costs. As decisions unfold, new information emerges that may suggest the original projections were wrong and a new course of action is necessary. Unfortunately, the new data often is ignored because of the salience of the invested costs. Nutt (2002) documents several business ventures that went amiss and resulted in a greater loss of money in the long run by staying the course with the hope of recovering the initial investment. The flaw of chasing bad money with good money is known as the *nonrational escalation of commitment.*

The nonrational escalation of commitment explains why some people continue to invest in expensive car repairs in lieu of buying a new car. When it comes to sustaining projects, it is too easy to think that there is too much invested to give up. The solution comes from Kenny Rogers in his song "The Gambler." According to Kenny, once you are in the game, "one needs to know when to hold 'em, know when to fold 'em, know when to walk away, know when to run." It is prudent to assess anticipated costs versus benefits based upon newest and most relevant information subsequent to the original decision. Ongoing assessment will help everyone understand if it is necessary to cut your losses by walking away from a project. Exploring the best alternative to a negotiated agreement (BATNA) discussed in chapter 7 allows decision makers to be proactive in knowing relevant benchmarks that signal the need for midcourse corrections.

Flaw 6: Bounded ethicality. When is a lie not a lie? Why is it too easy for some to round up the number when asked by the dental hygienist how many times they floss per week, and round down when a doctor asks for their weight? Is a teenager lying when he reports to his parents that he was at point A and point C, but leaves out point B in the conversation? There is a human tendency, even for the most honest of people, to hedge one's ethics when convenient. In some cases, it is to be self-serving; in other cases, it is because it is far too easy to think certain ethical standards do not apply to us. This flaw is known as *bounded ethicality*.

Bazerman and Tenbrunsel (2011) document that the majority of unethical activities are not the result of bad apples in the bunch, but rather occur as the result of ordinary and predictable psychological processes. As a result, even good people engage in unethical behavior, without their own awareness, on a regular basis. One reason for this is that 75 to 85 percent of us think we are above average and more objective than most, while others are more prone to self-serving and self-deceiving actions (Chugh, Bazerman and Banaji 2005; Bazerman 2011). For example, should a judge recuse himself or herself if he or she is a close friend with one of the claimants? The conflict of interest seems obvious. Yet Supreme Court Justice Antonin Scalia, who hunted with VP Dick Cheney, refused to recuse himself in *Cheney v. U.S. District Court* (2004). Scalia "insisted that his friendship with the VP would not distort his judgment and did not violate the Supreme Court rules on conflict of interest" (Bazerman and Tenbrunsel 2011, p. 19), even though the Supreme Court had in the past reversed decisions of lower courts with similar appearance of conflicts of interest.

Think of the housing bubble when questionable loans were being approved. The system made it easy for loan officers to hedge their protocols when thinking all people are entitled to a home and that the new homeowners would somehow make a payment plan work, even though they were a risk on paper. Such ethical fading makes specious data promising, unduly influencing the decision. People develop different checklists when evaluating a decision framed in business terms than when framed in ethical terms. This is another reason that ethics are often bounded or precluded from the considerations.

There are several solutions to bounded ethicality. One is to hold ourselves to the same standards we would expect of others, even when we think we are not as vulnerable as others to ethical misjudgments. Another is to have a surrogate conscience whom you can confide in to evaluate every decision for ethical considerations. In addition, keeping the "ultimate why" in front of the "what" will help make sure the ethical frame is part of every decision. Finally, be without guile and without any hint of deception.

Flaw 7: Groupthink. Flaws one through six are cognitive biases at the individual level. Decision making gets even more complicated when social

pressures unknowingly and unduly influence the process. Group dynamics
are powerful, evident by the fact that bad company tends to corrupt good
morals (1 Corinthians 15:33) and that relationships tend to revolve around
the lowest common denominator (2 Corinthians 6:14). Janis (1982) documented the power of social influences on decision making and how under
certain conditions there is a tendency to suspend individual judgment in
deference to the group judgment. Small groups may exhibit a behavior
known as *groupthink* that can contribute to poor decision making. Janis
defines groupthink as "a mode of thinking that people engage in when they
are deeply involved in a cohesive in-group, when the members' strivings for
unanimity override their motivation to realistically appraise alternative
courses of action" (p. 9).

Janis (1982) identifies three types of groupthink. Type 1 is the "overestimation of the group," which can lead to an "illusion of invulnerability"
and the belief in the group's inherent morality. Collective rationalization
and stereotyped views of out-groups can be the outcome of the Type 2
symptom—"closed-mindedness." Last, Janis identified "pressures toward
uniformity" as the Type 3 symptom and listed self-censorship, an "illusion
of unanimity," direct pressure on dissenters and self-appointed "mindguards"
as possible consequences (pp. 174-75).

The antecedents for groupthink include: insulation of the group (decision
makers are far removed from those in the trenches and therefore have different perspectives on issues); impartial leadership (overly opinionated
formal leaders making the group ideal-driven versus data-driven); and lack
of systematic protocols for making decisions (vulnerable to various cognitive biases and flaws when securing and evaluating data).

Scholars have identified groupthink as a possible explanation for the poor
decision making that led to disastrous outcomes at the domestic (Challenger
disaster) and international (failed Bay of Pigs invasion) levels. A brief examination of the latter will demonstrate the threat groupthink poses to rational decision making.

The goal of the invasion was the overthrow of the Communist regime of
Fidel Castro by the invasion of Cuba by US–backed Cuban exiles. Not only
did the Cuban exiles fail to remove Castro from power, but the Cuban army
captured or killed most of the members of the invading force within three

days. In fact, Cuba was able to trade about 1,200 captured rebels for $53 million in medicine and food. Despite a highly qualified advisory group, which included Secretary of State Dean Rusk, Secretary of Defense Robert McNamara and Attorney General Robert Kennedy, the process that led to the decision to back the invasion provided evidence of several symptoms of groupthink (Janis 1982, pp. 14-15, 27):

1. Type 1 symptom: overestimation of the group. The group definitely had an *illusion of invulnerability*. They assumed American B-26 bombers could render the Cuban air force ineffective. Unfortunately, the B-26 bombers were obsolete and the Cuban air force had relatively modern aircraft. As a result of the disparity, the Cuban air force shot down half of the B-26 bombers. Thus, freighters containing supplies and ammunition for the exiles were unable to land as planned. In addition, the Cuban air force was able to bomb the Cuban exiles (p. 21).

2. Type 2 symptom: close-mindedness. The group definitely had a *stereotyped view of out-groups*. The group viewed the Cuban military as "ready to defect" and Castro as a weak "hysteric" leader (p. 36).

3. Type 3 symptom: pressures toward uniformity. Attorney General Robert Kennedy and Secretary of State Dean Rusk served as *self-appointed "mindguards"* for the group. For example, Kennedy, speaking to Arthur Schlesinger Jr. before the invasion, said, "You may be right or you may be wrong, but the President has made his mind up. Don't push him any further. Now is the time for everyone to help him all they can" (pp. 40-41).

Janis (1982) identifies several solutions to minimizing the impact of groupthink. The primary solutions involve appointing a critic in the group and even rotating this role among different group members over time. The appointed critic will challenge assumptions and methods, and facilitate a forum for others to express their concerns. The second solution is "the leaders in an organization's hierarchy, when assigning a policy-planning mission to a group, should be impartial instead of stating preferences and expectations at the outset" (p. 263). Idea-driven groups tend to see only what they expect to see, while data-driven groups tend to see more. A third solution is to hold a meeting after the initial decision to see if the group would reach the same decision again. An immediate objection to the third solution may be, "Who has time for another meeting?" While true, a premise of this chapter is that the more consequential the decision, the more thorough the decision-making process should be.

Flaw 8: Hindsight bias. The eighth flaw is added to reveal how biases can lead to unjustified grumbling. Why is it so easy to second-guess the decisions of others? Think of the following scenarios and suggest how such incredulity is explained.

- You are riding in an unfamiliar area and come to a fork in the road. You follow your spouse's suggestion to go left. After fifteen minutes of driving, it is clear you are lost. You blurt out, "I knew we should have taken the other way."

- As an avid football fan, you wonder why your team executed that play to lose the game.

- Your boss makes a personnel choice that only after a few weeks leaves people wondering how on earth he could have made that decision.

Hindsight evaluates decisions after the results have been manifested, therefore it is 20/20. It is a bias when the decision is unfairly evaluated to conclude that other alternatives were equally available or valid and would have led to more desirable outcomes. Figures 8.4, 8.5 and 8.6 illustrate why the hindsight bias happens. In figure 8.5, a decision emerges in the

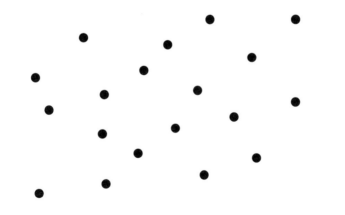

Figure 8.4.

context of various options and contingencies, represented by the dots. Decisions, represented by the lines, unfold in response to emerging con-

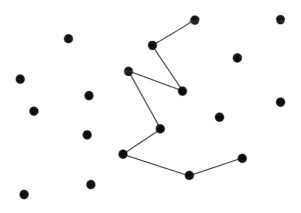

Figure 8.5.

tingencies that both constrain or optimize choices in real time. Figure 8.6 illustrates that after the fact, people do not have access to the various options and contingencies influencing the decision, but only see the decision line. It is misleading to conclude that the outcome of the decision was obvious up front because the line of reasoning appears linear in hindsight. Rather, it is key to recognize the dynamic nature of decision making and acknowledge the many variables that influence how a decision emerges.

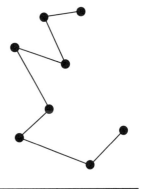

Figure 8.6.

While there are times to critique decisions after the fact, giving decision makers the benefit of the doubt can prevent inappropriate and unfair criticism.

Solutions to the eight flaws. The eight flaws are representative of the typical sources of interference when it comes to making judgment calls. They are provided to illustrate how easily and unknowingly our reasoning can be compromised. The simplicity of the flaws makes the solutions equally simple.

1. Engage in active listening.

2. Pay attention to unanticipated events, including evaluation of unintended consequences.

3. Develop systematic data-gathering and decision-making processes.

4. Appropriately anchor and frame conversations.

5. Know when to hold, fold and walk away.

6. Keep it ethical.

7. Appoint a critic.

8. Give the benefit of the doubt.

WHAT ABOUT EMOTIONS AND INSTINCT?

At the risk of contradicting the need to implement more rational and systematic processes to increase the probability of good decisions, there is a place for intuition and emotions. Contrary to folklore—that the best decisions are purely logical—there are times to trust one's emotions and instinct. Collins (2005) draws attention to various sayings, such as "Go with your gut," "Follow your intuition" and "Trust your feelings, Luke," to raise the question on the relationship between logic and emotion when making a decision. Consistent with Gladwell (2005), Burton (2008) and Lehrer (2009), there is a time to trust one's gut, though some hunches are better educated than others. There is a place for emotions when making decisions. Emotions provide the evaluative filter to recognize what is and is not important, and our emotions actually help make us rational (Damasio 1994).

People can make faulty decisions when they are not careful enough in the process (going solely with the gut) or when they are too careful (going solely with the mind). So it is now a judgment call on what type of judgment call to make when rendering a decision—when to listen to the mind or to the heart. Regardless, one of the take-away action items from this chapter is this: the more consequential the decision, the more important it is to be an expert on how the decision emerges or unfolds. Whether more cerebral or heartfelt, the decision-making process will be unique to each decision, so it has to preclude a formulaic response for all decisions.

DECISION-MAKING INSIGHTS FROM SCRIPTURE

The insights outlined above are those found in general revelation. There are additional strategies and principles from special revelation that are extremely helpful when it comes to making decisions. God has gone to great lengths to reveal his will, and as the good Shepherd, he is eager to provide ongoing guidance (John 10).

God has equipped people with a sound mind to make good inferences and discern God's leading. In 2 Timothy 1:7, the apostle Paul reminds Timothy that "God has not given us a spirit of fearfulness, but one of power, love, and sound judgment" (HCSB). God places a high premium on calculated judgments (Matthew 10:16) and expects us to be critical thinkers. In addition to reason, the Bible is profitable to equip children of God for every good work (2 Timothy 3:16-17). Christian decision makers must seek to apply relevant biblical truths and principles to every decision. When it comes to managing finances, the Bible has much to say about planning, saving, lending, investing, debt, giving, budgeting, work and prosperity. When Scripture is rightly interpreted, there is at least one scriptural principle for each decision waiting to be made. It is up to the individual to be a workman of the Word who rightly handles the Word of God (2 Timothy 2:15).

In addition to the Bible, the Spirit-filled believer has the mind of Christ and the Holy Spirit to discern right and wrong (John 10:27; 14:1–16:33; Romans 8:16; 1 Corinthians 2:16). Jesus and the Holy Spirit speak to the believer in ways that may seem unfathomable, and even strange, to the nonbeliever. A close analogy is "family speak," when insiders know and sense messages that are not immediately evident to outsiders. As discussed in chapter 2, Christians are new creatures who experience a regeneration that results in an actual adoption as a child of God. At the moment of believing, the Christian becomes an insider to the family of God (John 1:12; Romans 8:15). This intimate child-father relationship results in the Spirit bearing witness with our spirit (Romans 8:15-16). Jesus makes reference to this family-talk in John 10:27: "My sheep listen to my voice; I know them, and they follow me."

Another plumb line for knowing God's will when making decisions is the counsel of other believers. As shared in chapter 2, the Christian community is an important form of special revelation. Proverbs 11:14 and 24:6 state that "in abundance of counselors there is victory" (NASB). Proverbs 12:15 reminds us that "a wise man is he who listens to counsel" (NASB). Lest the reader miss the point, Proverbs 15:22 reiterates:

> Without consultation, plans are frustrated,
>   But with many counselors they succeed. (NASB)

The book of Proverbs also reminds us to be judicious when selecting our counselors. A friend is better when he or she wounds at times rather than providing only flattery (Proverbs 27:6; 28:23).

Believers also have prayer as a means to speak and listen to God. James 1:5-6 states that if any believer lacks wisdom to navigate the faith on earth, he or she can ask it of God, who will provide it when asked in good faith. God can provide the wisdom in one of many ways, but often it is revealed when a decision aligns with the Word of God, the leading of the Holy Spirit, the counsel of others and sound judgment.

AMBIGUITY AND GRAY AREAS

While applying the above insights from general and special revelation can result in fewer errors in our decision-making process, it does not mean the process will be easier. Most decisions of consequence are loaded with ambiguity and uncertainty. Most of the time, if the decision were clear and easy to make, it would have been made before it reaches the leader's desk. Rittel and Webber (1973) articulate that different types of problems require different approaches. Problems encountered in social planning are either "tame" or "wicked." Tame problems are routine in nature and can be solved in a linear fashion (e.g., what to do when the train is late). Wicked problems are complicated and have multiple and dynamic solutions (e.g., how to do triage when there is a train derailment). The more certainty, the more tame the problem. The more uncertainty, the more wicked the problem. Grint (2005) adds to the work of Rittel and Webber to suggest a typology of problems—ranging from critical, tame and wicked—which, depending on the degree of uncertainty, require a different response and decision-making process (p. 1477). Grint astutely points out the typology is not static, but rather "actively constructed" by the decision makers (p. 1470).

How a leader frames a problem will determine options for solutions. The point from Rittel and Webber (1973) and Grint (2005) is that the characteristics of wicked problems normalize ambiguity and uncertainty and that additional decision-making processes need to be implemented. Part of the wickedness comes from having multiple options that are equally good and permissible.

ETHICAL AND MORAL DECISIONS: NAVIGATING THE GRAY AREAS

It is late at night and you are in a hurry driving to your destination. The roads are deserted. Is it okay to proceed through a red light after confirming the intersection is indeed clear? Would your decision change if you were en route to the emergency room of the nearest hospital with a critically ill person in the back seat? Mitigating variables influence when one should yield to the spirit of the law versus the letter of the law. In the scenario above, failing to run the red light places the safety of the critically ill passenger at risk, creating a moral dilemma for the driver. With two "right" options, the driver is now navigating in the gray zone of decision making.

Can you think of any decision or human activity that is morally neutral? The clothes we wear (or choose not to) convey a moral message(s). The fact that our careless words will render judgment (Matthew 12:36) is a sober reminder that all of human activity has moral overtones. Even the person who claims that he or she is "morally neutral" can't ignore that he or she is taking a moral position. Once we recognize that all decisions have moral overtones, the question then becomes, what morals or values should inform the decisions? The premise of this book is that the Christian worldview is the legitimate framework for determining what values and virtues should take precedence when making decisions. As ambassadors for Christ, believers' decisions need to align with the priorities and mandates of the kingdom of God while honoring the array of values of their host country.

While all decisions are layered with moral messages, it is the moral dilemmas that consume and complicate decision making. While the right-versus-wrong choices (black-and-white decisions) are obvious and can result in "moral temptation," the real challenge is with those decisions that involve right-versus-right (Kidder 2009). In his book *How Good People Make Tough Choices*, Kidder astutely states that "those who live in close proximity to their basic values are apt to agonize over choices that other people, drifting over the surface of their lives, might never even see as problems." Kidder goes on to state that "sound values raise tough choices; and tough choices are never easy" (p. 1). These tough choices are not black-and-white. Rather, when discerning between equally good options, the decisions land in the gray area. For example, when do the needs of the individual outweigh the needs of the group, and vice versa? When does one err on the side of mercy or judgment? How does one balance short-term and long-term responsibilities and obligations?

Decisions become complicated when there are competing right factors and right ways when deciding a course of action. For example, saving enough to leave an inheritance for one's children (Proverbs 13:22) while re-lying on God for daily provision (Exodus 16; Matthew 6:9-15) and giving sacrificially (James 2:15-16) requires judicious planning, sometimes from paycheck to paycheck. Competing values are evident in companies that are incorporated to maximize profits, yet face options to implement costly eco-friendly policies or generous benefits packages to employees. The metaphor of steward leadership suggests that some attention to other items beyond the bottom line is warranted. How much more money should a CEO or president of an institution earn in relation to his or her colleagues who co-labor equally hard for the good of the organization? While the laborer is worthy of his or her wages, and top dollar attracts the best people, when a CEO or president, the first among equals, earns 150 percent more than the second highest paid position in the organization, the metaphor of leader as a steward of people and resources becomes strained.

So how does one decide in "right-versus-right" decisions or navigate the gray zone? The Supreme Court provides a powerful example for arbitrating between equally good competing values. Nine justices render a decision by hearing multiple sides of the issues, evaluating precedence and the intended and unintended consequences, and ultimately deciding by consensus. Even then the Supreme Court renders split decisions more often than not. If any-thing, when the sharpest judicial minds agonize over decisions and still disagree, this normalizes the tension, angst and controversies associated with making value-laden decisions.

Another example to guide "right-versus-right" decisions comes from

Scripture. The early church was looking for guidance with the freedoms that came with their new faith in Christ, even on what foods were acceptable. The early church wrestled with the appropriateness of eating food sacrificed to idols, lest they compromise their devotion to Christ and inadvertently legitimize beliefs contrary to the Christian worldview. In 1 Corinthians 6:12–10:31, the apostle Paul provides principles for the believer to discern if it is okay for him or her to eat certain food. The principles are didactic for making decisions in all kinds of gray areas, especially those things considered taboo in some Christian circles (e.g., is it okay to drink alcohol, play cards, gamble, go to movies, dance, etc?).

In this passage on Christian freedom, Paul identifies five criteria for discerning when a particular activity not specifically prohibited in the Bible is allowed. Paul opens the section on Christian freedom in 1 Corinthians 6:12 when he states that "all things are lawful for me, but not all things are profitable" (NASB). So we know that believers have great freedom and responsibility when making choices. The five criteria or principles for deciding what is profitable are:

1. *Mastery* (1 Corinthians 6:12): "All things are lawful for me, but not all things are profitable. All things are lawful for me, but I will not be mastered by anything."

2. *Stumbling block* (1 Corinthians 8:9): "But take care that this liberty of yours does not somehow become a stumbling block to the weak."

3. *Expediency* (1 Corinthians 9:23): "I do all things for the sake of the gospel, so that I may become a fellow partaker of it."

4. *Edification* (1 Corinthians 10:23): "All things are lawful, but not all things are profitable. All things are lawful, but not all things edify."

5. *Glory* (1 Corinthians 10:31): "Whether, then, you eat or drink or whatever you do, do all to the glory of God" (NASB).

While eating food sacrificed to idols is allowable, that does not mean it is profitable. It is okay as long as it does not *master me* ("I must have it!"). But even though the food does not master me, if it is a *stumbling block to other believers*, then it is not profitable for me to participate. A new believer may equate eating food sacrificed to idols (gambling, alcohol, etc.) with Christianity, and thereby wonder if Christianity is really different and stumble away from the faith accordingly. But what if I want to share the faith with those at dinner who are participating in a banquet with food sacrificed to idols? The law of *expediency* in this case may suggest a green light, even though the law of the stumbling block may suggest a red light. The law of *edification* guides me to do what edifies, or builds the body of Christ. Will my joining idol worshipers for a meal build up the body of Christ? If so, that is another green light that it may be okay to eat the food. The final criterion becomes the most revealing as it deals with motivation. Notice that Paul ends this section on freedom by concluding, "Whether, then, you eat or drink or whatever you do, do all to the glory of God." If the motive is to *glorify God*, then another green light appears. If the motive is to be popular with the group or get satiated, then a red light emerges.

Paul's method of principle-centered discernment does not mean that all green lights or red lights equate to a yes or no, respectively, for a particular decision. Rarely in the gray zone will one get all green or red lights. One has to evaluate what are the more salient of the issues for each situation. An example is when a friend of one of the authors of the chapter was visiting from out of town and was adamant about going to a bar to catch up on each other's life. Because the implication of a person in full-time Christian ministry going to a bar at night would be a potential stumbling block to prospective or new believers in the community to which he was ministering, there was a red light. At the same time, hanging out in a bar with an old friend would be a wonderful opportunity to have a captive audience to share the gospel. The law of mastery was moot since the author did not like alcohol and was not in the position of needing a drink. The motive was pure in wanting to glorify God, whether it meant going or not going to the bar. While others would have reached a different decision, the friend was invited to a bar twenty minutes away with a candid explanation similar to what was provided above. The fun aspect was that the author got to share the gospel with his friend at the bar that night.

Philosophers also refer to principle-centered reasoning as *ethical situationalism*, which is different from situational ethics. The latter states that the end justifies the means: it is okay to lie if it yields positive results. In contrast, ethical situationalism states that "objective moral principles are to be applied differently in different contexts, whereas ethical relativism denies universal ethical principles all together" (Pojman 2006, p. 56).

Jesus modeled principle-centered discernment or ethical situationalism repeatedly in his ministry. Notice that Jesus treated the woman at the well (John 4) differently than the money changers at the temple (Matthew 21:12). The specifics of the situation governed when Jesus took a more nurturing or direct approach in his dealings with people, all the time remaining unchangeable in his character and mission.

The lessons from the Supreme Court, 1 Corinthians and ethical situationalism are useful to evaluate relevant and competing principles, and objective values and virtues. A hard aspect of making decisions in the gray zone is working with individuals who choose to treat gray areas as if they are black or white. Principle-centered thinking is messy. It is much easier to minimize ambiguity by forcing issues and concerns into black-and-white categories. Unfortunately, to do so is to deny the nature of reality. When disagreement emerges, it is prudent to practice unity in the essentials, liberty in the non-essentials and charity in all matters. In all decisions, especially difficult decisions, wisdom is required.

Wisdom and Creativity

Ultimately, people want their leaders to make wise decisions. Unfortunately, stories of leaders' lack of discernment and sound judgment abound in the news. The frequent comments by subordinates of "What were they thinking?" and "Why did they do that?" reveal that wisdom is often perceived to be lacking from those in formal leadership roles. Schwartz and Sharpe (2010) document the decline in practical wisdom and its devastating consequences. The world needs people who judiciously discern and courageously implement innovative decisions at the right time and in the right way.

While wisdom "shouts in the street," even to the naive and foolish (Proverbs 1:20 NASB), it appears only a few take up the invitation to acquire it. Part of the problem is that the mystique often associated with wisdom gives the impression that it is reserved for the few. The loss of wisdom in deference to more utilitarian and pragmatic models of thinking has led to decisions and policies that defy even common sense (Schwartz and Sharpe 2010; Rooney and McKenna 2007). Decision makers have been conditioned to default to policy in lieu of nuancing out the issues associated with non-routine and "right-versus-right" decisions. Policy is good in that it provides direction for 80 percent of decisions; the wise leader recognizes that the other 20 percent of the decisions require additional deliberation.

An example where policy took precedence over wisdom is found in the expulsion of a student from her high school. A senior who had excellent grades and no behavioral problems showed up to school with a box cutter in her backpack. The principal believed that he had no choice under the policy of zero tolerance for weapons but to expel her. The backstory in this scenario is that the student worked evenings at a grocery store stocking shelves. She had forgotten to take the tool of her trade out of her backpack and realized her error after arriving at school. Fortunately the public recognized that the spirit of the law was not violated and pressured the school board to reinstate the student, even though she violated the letter of the law.

A discussion on wisdom is worthy of its own book. Parallel concepts to wisdom are creativity and expertise. *Creative, innovative, expert* and *wise* are often used synonymously to describe novel insights to routine and complex problems. While each concept is distinct, the literature on creativity, expertise and wisdom reveals that these qualities have much in common. Sternberg documents how wisdom, intelligence and creativity can be synthesized—that wisdom results "from the application of the successful intelligence and creativity toward the common good through a balancing of intrapersonal, interpersonal, and extrapersonal interests over the short and long terms" (2003, p. 188). For Sternberg, wisdom is at the top of the taxonomy of understanding.

So, in a nutshell, what is wisdom? In the Bible, the word for wisdom is used in association with someone who is especially skilled (Friedrich 1971). In Proverbs and Ecclesiastes, the concept is developed even further as one who is especially skilled at living. In the New Testament, wisdom is used to live strategically and skillfully as a Christ follower in a foreign land among multiple and competing pressures and responsibilities (Matthew 10:16). What makes someone especially skilled, an expert in his or her professional and personal life? The literature on expertise reveals that, in contrast to novices, experts recognize nuances and subtle patterns. Proverbs 9:10 says,

The fear of the LORD is the beginning of wisdom,
> and knowledge of the Holy One is understanding.

Wisdom is the ability to recognize multiple patterns and story lines and tap into the more relevant and transcendent ones at any point when making and implementing a decision. As to be expected, wisdom is inextricably connected to worldview. One's worldview defines what is ultimately right and how to act rightly. Discernment is choosing the better of many right things and many right ways. For example, when does the need of the group (equality) outweigh the need of the individual (liberty)? Does one make budget cuts equally across all programs or disproportionate cuts among different programs? As in the case of Solomon, how does one determine the truth when two conflicting and passionate claims to that truth are presented (1 Kings 3:16-18)? Solomon recognized multiple story lines at work when asked to discern the biological mother of an infant. Appealing to equity, he suggested splitting the baby in half. At the same time, he appealed to the more transcendent value of the preservation of life associated with maternal instinct as a more powerful story line to reveal the biological mother.

Hallinan states that "pattern recognition is the hallmark of expertise, allowing experts to anticipate events and respond quickly" (2009, p. 174). While wisdom is aligning life habits with the more important and relevant of all the existing story lines, Christian wisdom is tapping into the ultimate transcendent patterns revealed in the Bible. Ambassadors of Christ take seriously their role of knowing and representing the priorities and values of the kingdom of God in all of their decisions—taking every thought captive to the obedience of Christ (2 Corinthians 10:5). While it can take a long time to become an expert on life, Psalm 119:99-100 provides an accelerated lesson plan to gain wisdom beyond one's elders and teachers. The psalmist records,

I have more insight than all my teachers,
> for I meditate on your statutes.
I have more understanding than the elders,
> for I obey your precepts.

To become especially skilled at living, or wise, the necessary requirements include understanding and applying transcendent values that align with eternal patterns.

As mentioned, creativity is a close cousin to wisdom. While wisdom is leveraging relevant patterns (including eternal truths) to optimize outcomes consistent with what is good, creativity has been described as the "development of new mental patterns" (Joyce, Weil and Showers 1992, p. 220). Creativity is learning to think outside the box, breaking away from dominant patterns to discover hidden patterns by new connections. To be wise and creative is to make novel connections and implement practices that identify with the more important of the relevant story lines at work at any point of time. Wise decision makers take time to identify the relevant story lines and patterns (which will reveal competing values). Creative decision makers look for alternative connections between the various story lines.

Despite the mystique that wisdom is reserved for the few, wisdom is readily accessible to those who want it as it "shouts in the street," even to the naive and foolish (Proverbs 1:20 NASB). God is eager to supply wisdom to those who ask (James 1:5). Similarly, as people created in God's image, everyone is capable of creative thinking. Wallas (1926), Gordon (1961) and Sternberg (2003) document the creative processes and reveal how creativity is an acquired ability. An initial starting point in the creative process is just choosing to be creative—inviting the mind to look for unique connections not immediately evident. Since we see what we expect to see, changing what we expect when evaluating data becomes a foundation for discovering innovative solutions. The good news is that wisdom and creativity can be developed and are not reserved for the "gifted."

SUMMARY AND CONCLUSION

Decision making is fraught with human limitations and biases. There are multiple sources of interference when making inferences. Decision making becomes all the more complicated in the gray zone when having to discern the best of many good options. It is even a judgment call when deciding between what type of decision is warranted—systematic or intuitive. The quest for wisdom and creativity introduces another set of challenges and opportunities in the decision-making process.

To help improve the probability of making good decisions, one should

1. Engage in active listening.

2. Pay attention to what is not noticed.

3. Develop systematic data-gathering and decision-making processes.

4. Appropriately anchor and frame conversations.

5. Know when to hold, fold and walk away.

6. Keep it ethical.

7. Appoint a critic.

8. Give the benefit of the doubt when it comes to second-guessing decisions.

To improve the probability of making better decisions, one should

1. Identify relevant Scripture.

2. Follow the leading of the Holy Spirit.

3. Pray.

4. Seek the counsel of others.

5. Exercise sound judgment.

To make the wise and creative decisions, especially for those wicked problems that involve right-versus-right dilemmas, one should

1. Pray specifically for wisdom.

2. Choose to be creative and wise.

3. Identify relevant patterns, especially kingdom of God values and patterns, and make unique connections.

Regardless of the profession or the nature of the decision, a way to enhance decision making is to be an expert on the process. Auditing the decision-making process will help prevent or minimize biases and misleading information from influencing the decision at the expense of more salient issues. There are multiple resources found in both general and special revelation to compensate for human limitations. The theme of this chapter is that the more consequential the decision, the more systematic and thorough one should be in attending to the resources identified above.

A challenge with decision making under the Christian leadership model is managing kingdom of God priorities in an alien nation. A passage that summarizes well the nature of decision making is found in Matthew 10:16. As Jesus was sending out his disciples to go minister in the surrounding community, he cautioned them to be "shrewd as serpents and innocent as doves"

(NASB). In other words, be discerning, calculating, astute and judicious (an expert on decision making) and ethical (innocent as doves). Recognizing the various flaws inherent in the process and implementing the respective solutions is one step to developing a shrewd or judicious mindset. Keeping the ethical considerations in the forefront of every decision will also yield better decisions. Being both discerning and ethical will position Christians to represent God well in their formal and informal leadership roles.

REFERENCES

Ackoff, R. L. 1989. "From Data to Wisdom." *Journal of Applied Systems Analysis* 16: 3-9.

Avolio, B., and W. Gardner. 2005. "Authentic Leadership Development: Getting to the Root of Positive Forms of Leadership." *The Leadership Quarterly* 16: 315-38.

Bazerman, M. H. 2006. *Judgment in Managerial Decision Making,* 6th ed. New York: John Wiley & Sons.

———. 2011. "Bounded Ethicality in Negotiations." *Negotiation and Conflict Management Research* 4: 8-11.

Bazerman, M. H., and D. Moore. 2009. *Judgment in Managerial Decision Making.* Hoboken, NJ: John Wiley & Sons.

Bazerman, M. H., and A. Tenbrunsel. 2011. *Blind Spots: Why We Fail to Do What's Right and What to Do About It.* Princeton: Princeton University Press.

Blair, D. C. 2002. "Knowledge Management: Hype, Hope, or Help?" *Journal of the American Society for Information Science and Technology* 53 (12): 1019-28.

Blanchard, K. 2006. *Leading at a Higher Level: Blanchard on Leadership and Creating High Performing Organizations.* Upper Saddle River, NJ: Prentice Hall.

Burton, R. 2008. *On Being Certain: Believing You Are Right Even When You're Not.* New York: Saint Martin's Press.

Chugh, D., M. Bazerman and M. Banaji. 2005. "Bounded Ethicality as a Psychological Barrier to Recognizing Conflicts of Interest." In *Conflicts of Interest: Problems and Solutions from Law, Medicine and Organizational Settings,* edited by D. A. Moore, D. M. Cain, G. F. Loewenstein and M. H. Bazerman. London: Cambridge University Press.

Collins, J. 2005. "How to Make Great Decisions." *Fortune,* June 27, p. 102.

Damasio, A. 1994. *Descartes' Error: Emotion, Reason and the Human Brain.* London: Vintage.

Friedrich, G., ed. 1971. *Theological Dictionary of the New Testament,* vol. 7. Translated by G. W. Bromiley. Grand Rapids: Eerdmans.

Gladwell, M. 2005. *Blink: The Power of Thinking Without Thinking.* New York: Little, Brown, and Company.

Gordon, W. J. J. 1961. *Synectics: The Development of Creative Capacity*. New York: Harper & Brothers.

Grint, K. 2005. "Problems, Problems, Problems: The Social Construction of Leadership." *Human Relations* 58 (11): 1467-94. doi:10.1177/0018726705061314.

Hallinan, J. 2009. *Why We Make Mistakes: How We Look Without Seeing, Forget Things in Seconds, and Are All Pretty Sure We Are Way Above Average*. New York: Broadway Books.

Janis, I. 1982. *Groupthink: Psychological Studies of Policy Decisions and Fiascos*. Boston: Wadsworth, Cengage Learning.

Joyce, B., M. Weil and B. Showers. 1992. *Models of Teaching*. Boston: Allyn and Bacon.

Kahneman, D., P. Slovic and A. Tversky. 1982. *Judgment Under Uncertainty: Heuristics and Biases*. Cambridge: Cambridge University Press.

Kidder, R. 2009. *How Good People Make Tough Choices: Resolving the Dilemmas of Ethical Living*. New York: Harper Perennial.

Lee, D., and D. Hatesohl. 2012. "Listening: Our Most Used Communication Skill." *University of Missouri Extension*. Retrieved from http://extension.missouri.edu/publications/DisplayPub.aspx?P=CM150#three.

Lehrer, J. 2009. *How We Decide*. New York: Houghton Mifflin Harcourt.

Ley, K., and S. L. Chang. 2008. "Helping Online Faculty Eliminate Time-Wasting Challenges." Annual conference on distance teaching and learning, Board of Regents of the University of Wisconsin System, 1-7.

Neisser, U., and R. Becklen. 1975. "Selective Looking: Attending to Visually Specified Events." *Cognitive Psychology* 7: 480-94.

Nisbett, R. E., and L. Ross. 1980. *Human Inference: Strategies and Shortcomings of Social Judgment*. Englewood Cliffs, NJ: Prentice Hall.

Nutt, P. 2002. *Why Decisions Fail: Avoiding the Blunders and Traps That Lead to Debacles*. San Francisco: Berrett-Koehler.

Pfeffer, J. 2007. *What Were They Thinking? Unconventional Wisdom About Management*. Boston: Harvard Business School Publishing.

Pojman, L. 2006. *Ethics: Discovering Right and Wrong*. Belmont, CA: Thomson/Wadsworth.

Rittel, H., and M. Webber. 1973. "Dilemmas in a General Theory of Planning." *Policy Sciences* 4: 155-69.

Rooney, D., and B. McKenna. 2007. "Wisdom in Organizations: Whence and Whither. *Social Epistemology* 21 (2): 113-38.

Schwartz, B., and K. Sharpe. 2010. *Practical Wisdom: The Right Way to Do the Right Thing*. New York: Riverhead.

Simons, D., and C. Chabris. 1999. "Gorillas in Our Midst: Sustained Inattentional Blindness for Dynamic Events." *Perception* 28: 1059-74.

Sousa, D. 2006. *How the Brain Learns*. Thousand Oaks, CA: Corwin.

Sternberg, R. 2003. *Wisdom, Intelligence, and Creativity Synthesized.* Cambridge: Cambridge University Press.

University of North Carolina at Chapel Hill. 2011. "UNC Researchers Spot Six Demographic Trends That Will Transform U.S." *UNC News*, January 18, 2011. http://uncnewsarchive.unc.edu/2011/01/18/unc-researchers-spot-six-demographic-trends-that-will-transform-us-2/.

Wallas, G. 1926. *The Art of Thought.* New York: Harcourt, Brace, and Company.

9

CHRISTIAN LEADERSHIP AND FINANCIAL INTEGRITY

Temptation, Transformation and Transparency

R. Scott Rodin

—⚏—

*Whoever can be trusted with very little
can also be trusted with much, and whoever is dishonest
with very little will also be dishonest with much. So if you have not been
trustworthy in handling worldly wealth, who will trust you with true riches?
And if you have not been trustworthy with someone else's property,
who will give you property of your own?*

LUKE 16:10-12

*Jesus is making it unmistakably clear
that money is not some impersonal medium
of exchange. Money is not something that is morally neutral,
a resource to be used in good or bad ways depending solely
upon our attitude toward it. Mammon is a
power that seeks to dominate us.*

RICHARD FOSTER,
MONEY, SEX AND POWER

LEADERSHIP AND THE ROLE OF MONEY

Every Christian leader has a personal theology of money. They may never have thought about it in those terms or articulated it in a systematic way, but we all hold views and attitudes toward money that guide the way we earn it, invest it, spend it and give it. This personal theology may have been built purposefully on a solid biblical basis, but for most people it is a syncretic set of beliefs and attitudes that have been influenced more by worldly standards than solid biblical principles.

We assume positions of leadership because of our passion and calling to carry out a mission, achieve a vision and accomplish significant work. Whether leading a for-profit company or a not-for-profit ministry, we come into leadership with our eyes focused on some other prize than the merely financial. However, it is not long before we realize that our day-to-day work is dominated by decisions surrounding income and expenses, debt and investment, balance sheets and cash flow projections. Every decision we make as a leader has financial implications, and how we understand the place and role of money in our institutions may have a greater effect on our success as leaders than any other single factor.

This is a powerful and provocative statement but one that we believe to be true. Think back over the last four weeks in your leadership role. How much of your thinking and planning was dominated and influenced by the financial realities you face? How much conversation and strategy focused on securing more income, controlling expenses, setting or adjusting budgets, taking on or eliminating debt, managing investments? The discerning leader understands that because every decision he or she makes has financial implications, their own personal view of money will shape those decisions and with them the future of the entire organization.

In this chapter we will look at the temptations faced by every leader with regard to the role and function of money in their organization, the transformation that is our obligation and opportunity as Christian leaders, and the transparency that is the product of a Christian leader who has been set free to be a godly steward personally and a steward leader on behalf of their organization. We will develop a biblically sound theology of money and examine practices that will serve to guide Christians as we steward our financial resources.[1]

---

[1]For a splendid treatment of this subject in a systematic way, see Getz (2004).

Temptation: Facing Our Demons

In this section we will seek to understand the temptations about money we face as Christian leaders. Our beliefs and attitudes about finances are especially influenced in our American culture by six prevailing misconceptions of money and the temptations inherent in each.

The first temptation we face as leaders is viewing money in a detached, amoral way. Consider the following definition:

> Money is any object or record that is generally accepted as payment for goods and services and repayment of debts in a given socio-economic context or country. The main functions of money are distinguished as: a medium of exchange; a unit of account; a store of value; and, occasionally . . . , a standard of deferred payment. ("Money" 2013)

In this functional definition, money is amoral, a neutral medium for the exchange of value. It carries no inherent goodness or malevolence but serves the user equally whether he chooses to invest it for benevolent or malicious purposes. At face value this seems an obvious conclusion. Money is, after all, ink on paper or impressions on semiprecious metals. We don't value a quarter because of the material from which it is made but for its ability to secure for us about $.25 worth of goods and services. A piece of paper upon which a $100 bill is printed has no more value than the paper used to print this page. The value is bestowed on it by the arrangement of ink and what it denotes to the one who possesses it. There is nothing right or wrong with the piece of paper itself, or so the definition would lead us to believe.

The world of money and finance can be viewed erroneously as operating on the periphery of the true spiritual core of an organization. Consider the church that selects from among its most spiritually mature people those who will serve as elders with the responsibility for the spiritual vitality of the congregation. That same church will elect deacons to handle financial matters without any consideration of their spiritual maturity as long as they come with the requisite financial experience. We see the same attitude in not-for-profit organizations when chief financial officers and fundraising staff are hired with little regard to the depth of their spiritual maturity or their ability to integrate a robust and living faith with their work of managing and raising the resources for the organization. Whenever we separate the spiritual from the financial, we bear witness to this view of money as a morally vacuous medium of exchange. And we do so to our great peril.

In his three-year ministry, Jesus spoke more often about money than any other subject except the kingdom of God. What he said bore no resemblance to money as morally vacuous. Indeed he taught quite the opposite. Jesus' words in Matthew 6:24 should stop us Christian leaders in our tracks. The problem is, we have heard them too often and have downplayed their implications. Hear them again and test your theology of money against them: "No one can serve two masters. Either you will hate the one and love the other, or you will be devoted to the one and despise the other. You cannot serve both God and money."

Jesus is not setting up a dialectic between the sovereign God of the universe and a neutral medium of exchange. He is speaking of two rival spiritual forces that seek our absolute devotion. The words he uses are extreme and absolute: *master, love, hate, devoted, despised.* The only alternatives Jesus provides us with are love and hate, devotion and despising. There is no room for loving God and simply using money. Money is ascribed power that rivals the divine and demands from us our total love and allegiance. There is no denying the power that Jesus prescribes to money.

Richard Foster states, "According to Jesus and all the writers of the New Testament, behind money are very real spiritual forces that energize it and give it a life of its own. Hence, money is an active agent; it is a law unto itself; and it is capable of inspiring devotion" (1985, p. 26). The first temptation that must be overcome by every Christian leader is to view money as anything less than a significant spiritual force that constantly works to gain our allegiance and compromise our total trust in God and God alone.

A second temptation, and one that is a natural product of the first, is the seduction of tying our self-image and that of our organization to our financial status. This may seem less threatening than the first temptation, but beware. Consider the ways that organizations talk about themselves and measure success. While not-for-profit ministries may pride themselves on leading with mission-focused accomplishments, true success is almost always couched in financial terms. Pastors talk to other pastors about the size of their congregation, the success of the latest building project and whether their giving has gone up or down. Presidents of Christian schools, colleges and universities speak to alumni in terms of growing enrollment, new academic buildings and an increasing endowment. Owners of businesses speak to shareholders about profits, reinvestment and share prices. And for each of these, whether the pastor of a small church, the president of a community not-for-profit organization or the owner of a growing business, the financial success of their respective organization reflects heavily on their own self-image and reputation.

This connection between financial success and self-image starts at home. Our American culture idolizes the financially successful, and as a result has developed a culture that measures self-image in financial terms. While we may deeply desire to value our neighbor based solely on his or her integrity and contribution to the greater societal good, we find it hard to keep out of the mix ingredients such as the size of their house, the cost of their car, the places they vacation and the schools their children attend. When we are called to positions of leadership, this temptation only increases. Too often a Christian leader's self-worth is determined both by our personal financial status and the financial success of the organization we lead. When we allow our self-image to be determined by these factors, we have fallen prey to the second temptation.

The third temptation is to yield to the power that is inherent in all dealings with money. The apostle Paul warned his young colleague Timothy: "The love of money is a root of all kinds of evil" (1 Timothy 6:10). What tempts us is not the love of a neutral medium of exchange but the desire for the power that comes from the accumulation of wealth. With money comes power and with power comes control, and it is the power to control that we find so intoxicating. The opportunity to increase control, to become masters of our destiny, is a never-ending siren song that calls to us, promising us success and stature if we will but grasp it. Of course what happens is that it grasps us and soon our thirst for power that comes through the pursuing of wealth ends up controlling us. As Christian leaders we must fight every day this temptation to grasp at the power that comes from the accumulation of financial resources.

The fourth temptation is kingdom building. Loving one master and despising the other calls us to be one-kingdom Christians. Christ's call on our life is uncompromising and unequivocal. We are to deny ourselves, take up our cross and follow him. There is place for only one allegiance, one Lord, one Master. The abundant Christian life is only found in the total surrender of all we have and all we are to the one kingdom of God. For Christian leaders, Christ calls us to the total surrender of control and renunciation of the desire for the power that comes from success that is measured in any terms other than the building of the kingdom of God.

This kind of surrender is amazingly difficult! Our tendency, given our sinful nature, is to build, alongside the kingdom of God, our own little earthly kingdom where we get to play the lord and master. Our kingdom may include our time, some or all of our possessions, our relationships and our attitudes. Anything that has not been completely submitted and surrendered to Christ, any control that has not been thoroughly turned over to him, and any power that still wins our allegiance will be the stuff of our earthly kingdom. If we are honest with ourselves we will acknowledge that we are all kingdom builders. In our personal life we struggle with a desire to become masters in control over those parts of our lives that seem just too difficult to trust fully to God. As Christian leaders we struggle to satisfy employees, board members, donors, stakeholders, shareholders and business partners, while at the same time relinquishing control and placing all of our business or organization into the one kingdom of Christ. This struggle is seen in its greatest intensity in the way we deal with money in our institutions. As Christian leaders we must understand the struggle as a battle for lordship and we must help our colleagues to see the same.

The fifth temptation is to separate our personal spiritual journey from our work as Christian leaders. In our postmodern culture we are encouraged to compartmentalize the various parts of our lives. It is perfectly acceptable, if not encouraged, to live one life at home and another at the office. We are told that there is no metanarrative or overarching ethical standard that requires us to be consistent in the application of values across all areas of our lives. As this temptation seeps into the corners of our lives, it quietly encourages us to keep our personal faith separate from our public role as a Christian leader.

Surprisingly, this happens even in the church and the Christian not-for-profit world. In working with Christian fundraising professionals, I am often surprised at the resistance I face when I link their personal history of Christian stewardship, generosity and sacrificial giving to the success of their professional task of asking others to do the same. As Christian leaders our ability to help our organizations deal faithfully and effectively with money must flow from our own personal and ongoing spiritual transformation as followers of Christ whose hearts are rich toward God in all things and in all areas of our lives.

The sixth temptation is to play the owner and not the steward. Our earthly existence can be understood on four planes: our relationships with God, with ourselves, with our neighbor and with the creation itself. On all four planes we live in relationships that were distorted and destroyed in the fall and completely restored in the life, death and resurrection of Jesus Christ. These relationships have now been given back to us as precious gifts from the Master with the command to steward each to his glory. There is not one item on any plane that we ever own for one moment of our earthly existence. It all belongs to God. The previous five temptations may be wrapped up and subsumed under this one powerful Christian concept: we are stewards, not owners. Stewards understand that the Master is the owner and that the steward's job is to use the Master's gifts for the Master's purposes.

When we pretend to be owners, we return to the original sin in Eden and grasp at an alien ownership that will only serve to put us in bondage. The Christian leader must never forget that these two things are inseparable—ownership and bondage. And just as inseparable are stewardship and freedom! That is the choice set before us every moment we choose to serve as a leader. If we believe we own our employees, our clients, our facilities, our students, our inventory or our profits, we will serve as leaders in absolute bondage. With that bondage comes fear, anxiety, relentless pressure, discouragement and despair. It is from this place of bondage that all five of the temptations listed above will call to us louder and louder, offering us freedom through the accumulation of wealth and the supposed control and power that it can offer. Ownership and bondage simply yield deeper bondage.

The Christian leader must make it a daily discipline to refuse the temptation to ownership and assume with joy and privilege the mantle of the godly steward in every area of his or her life. As a steward we can handle money in a way that robs it of its corrupted power and places it in the service of the Master. And we can lead our people to do the same.

TRANSFORMATION: THE JOURNEY OF THE CHRISTIAN LEADER

There are five indistinguishable marks of the journey of transformation of every Christian with regard to money and possessions. Each of these marks will transcend the individual life of the Christian leader and have an indelible impression on the organization they're called to lead.

This process aligns with what we described in chapter 5 as the movement from X^1 to X^2 that occurs in an organization. In this process X^1 represents a clear assessment of the current status of the organization, and X^2 is the desired status to which the organization aspires. Between X^1 and X^2 are the obstacles that are encountered by any organization seeking to achieve its vision. We illustrated that these obstacles range in scope and level of difficulty, and while X^2 can be defined it is never fully achieved, for whenever an organization approaches it, the parameters change and new obstacles emerge. This is the dynamic quality of vision in an organization. The same is true for the individual Christian life. We define our spiritual X^2 as complete conformity to Christ, which, of course, we will never achieve this side of heaven. We also assess our X^1 and understand our need for spiritual transformation. This sets us on a journey with a clear goal and a set of obstacles along the way.

In this section we will set these two journeys side by side and demonstrate that as we face and overcome the obstacles in our own journeys of moving from our current state to complete conformity to Christ, we also, as Christian leaders, help move our organizations through a similar set of processes, facing similar obstacles on our journey toward a similar goal. Even more importantly, the progress of our organization is wholly dependent upon the process in our own lives. In other words, we can only lead others if we are progressing on the same journey. We will define the steps and challenges of this journey as death, dethroning, delivery, discovery and doxology. Figure 9.1 below illustrates the interconnectedness of our individual journeys and that of our organizations along these five steps from our X^1 to our desired X^2.

Death. In Dietrich Bonhoeffer's famous book *The Cost of Discipleship*, he makes this startling statement: "When Christ calls a man he bids him come and die" (1957, p. 73). In doing so he was simply restating Jesus' own words, "Whoever finds their life will lose it, and whoever loses their life for my sake will find it" (Matthew 10:39). The Christian life begins with the death of self, or it does not begin at all. The apostle Paul tells us boldly, "Since, then, you have been raised with Christ, set your hearts on things above, where Christ is, seated at the right hand of God. Set your minds on things above, not on earthly things. For you died, and your life is now hidden with Christ in God"

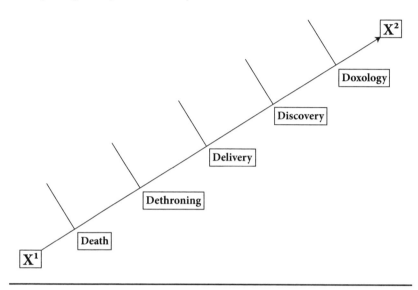

Figure 9.1. Transforming/Adaptive Leadership

(Colossians 3:1-3). Earlier in Colossians he reminds us, "Since you died with Christ to the elemental spiritual forces of this world, why, as though you still belonged to the world, do you submit to its rules?" (Colossians 2:20).

To lose our life, to die in such a way that our life is hidden with Christ in God, is to start the journey of our complete transformation from our sinful, self-centered worldview to the fully committed child of God conformed to the image of Christ. In one sense it is a once-and-for-all event. It happened fully for us in the completed work of Christ. Just as Christ does not have to die again and again, so our death to sin has happened once in Christ and, as such, it is "finished." However, in another sense it must be recollected on a daily basis. Our ongoing battle with our sinful nature requires that we re-affirm the finality of this event and claim the freedom that is ours as a result. This work of recollection and reclaiming is the ministry that every Christian leader brings to his or her organization.

In dealing with finances we lead with integrity when we help our organization remember that we have put to death the desires to follow the basic principles of this world. Christian leaders help their people name those principles, recognize them whenever they surface and come against them with the full force of absolute death in regard to them. This is the first plank in an organizational theology of money that every Christian leader must help fashion and enforce. Organizations must collectively embrace this death as their first step toward communal transformation.

Dethroning. Death alters our worldview fundamentally. From the vista of our absolute death to the things of this world, we will be able to see the parapets of our earthly kingdom. As individual followers of Christ the next step is a total relinquishment of our attempts to play the lord and master over this kingdom. We take off our crown, step off our throne, tear down the walls and dismantle the defenses that have protected our stuff as our stuff. This requires a process of naming the things in our kingdom, repenting of our kingdom-building ways and placing them one by one at the feet of Jesus. This can only be accomplished by the ongoing work of the Holy Spirit in our lives, and it is a process we will undertake until God takes us home. As Christian leaders we must serve our organizations by helping them walk through the same steps with regard to finances and possessions. This process will require us on both the personal and corporate level to identify and reject three lies that the enemy seeks to whisper in our ears with regard to our two-kingdom lifestyle.

The first lie is that these two kingdoms are somehow *compatible*. Our sinful nature combined with our prevailing American culture will provide a formidable defense and protection of our earthly kingdom. "Surely," we will hear ourselves say, "there is no harm in some things remaining in a kingdom over which we continue to exercise control. Surely the Lord will not care if a few things remain as ours to do with as we please."

This is especially hard in our professional life. We run our organizations on the business school model that assigns all components of our work to individual responsibility that requires us to control, manage and direct every part of our organizational life. Success or failure in our outcomes is traced back to the quality of our individual or team performance and our ability to control and manage the means of production that brought about these outcomes. It is difficult for the Christian leader to find a place in this process for a one-kingdom approach to the operation of a business or ministry. The difference may seem subtle between responsibly carrying out our work using our God-given talents and seeking to control and manipulate our work for our own ends. It is, however, one of the great spiritual battlefields in the life of every Christian institution. So much is at stake when we step off the throne of our own kingdom. For most of us, including the Christian leader, the greatest threat is to our self-image. We build earthly kingdoms in order to prop up the image we wish to portray to the world around us. This usually includes success, competency, relevance, charisma, wisdom and courage. Leaders can use their organizations as their own personal kingdoms and manage their people in order to bear witness to this image.

We must not underestimate the power of this temptation, not just for leaders but for every person in our organization. We are all seeking personal affirmation from our work, the admiration of our peers and the reassurance that we are a valuable part of the community. When people in our organizations tie the measurable outcomes in their work performance to their self-image and sense of importance, the foundation has been laid for the construction of an impenetrable earthly kingdom. Christian leaders face the challenge of helping the people they serve understand the danger in this linkage. In its place we are called to be image bearers of Christ and find our satisfaction in our work solely in the faithfulness with which we employ our skills and bear that image. This shift from a performance-based self-image to a faithfulness-inspired self-image will produce the kind of freedom that is necessary for organizations to undertake a thoroughgoing process of de-throning. It all begins with the heart of a leader who is moving successfully along that same journey. Only such a leader can face this first lie straight on and name it for what it is.

The second lie is that we can *compartmentalize* these two kingdoms. The story line here is simple: be faithful in your spiritual kingdom and God will not really care what you do in your earthly one. This is the postmodern philosophy that encourages an eclectic approach to the application of ethical values in the different spheres of our lives. It is perfectly acceptable to hold to one set of values in our spiritual kingdom while at the same time applying a modified set of values to our earthly kingdom. The importance, so say the postmodernists, is to be true to each set of values within their sphere without the pressure of pursuing a consistency of ethics across the totality of our lives.

In organizational life this is most often seen in a compartmentalization of the mission and program part of our work from the financial and fundraising side. As we pointed to above, there is a temptation for Christian organizations to spiritualize their mission and secularize their operations. If we fail to recognize the spiritual forces behind money, it will be easy to fall prey to this two-kingdom lie. Christian leaders are challenged to articulate and apply the core values and ethics in every area of their organizations. Again, leaders can only accomplish this if the same consistency is being pursued in their personal lives.

The third lie regarding retaining your earthly kingdom is that we can placate God and justify our earthly kingdom through a series of *transactions*. The logic is as follows: by overachieving in the spiritual work we undertake, we buy ourselves the space to ignore or live comfortably with the compromises we have made in constructing our earthly kingdoms. It is a sort of sleight-of-hand approach—keep God happy with the good spiritual work we are doing and he may not notice the compromises we make in the other parts of our lives. We buy God off through our good work on his behalf.

This may sound harsh but as Christian leaders we must look for this attitude in our own hearts and in the attitudes and actions of the people in our organizations. Here more than in any other place, we will face the difficulty of leading our people through a process of identifying, naming and owning the earthly kingdoms that we have built in our organizations. The temptation to downplay these kingdoms and justify them in the face of all the good work we are doing is enormous. Christian leaders must be winning this battle in their own hearts, and then they must lead with courage in helping their organizations refuse to compromise at any point in this dethroning process.

Faithful Christian leadership will include naming these three lies, leading with transparency and vulnerability with an uncompromising approach to building a one-kingdom organization.

Delivery. In spiritual terms, *delivery* means to be freed from the restraints and shackles of old ways of thinking. It is, as the apostle Paul put it, a taking off of the old self and a putting on of the new self, "which is being renewed in knowledge in the image of its Creator" (Colossians 3:10). Delivery results in a new set of attitudes and perspectives that significantly alter our worldview and allow us to make decisions with a new set of tools at our disposal. Both individually and corporately it means viewing money in its true perspective and being able to deal with it without being influenced by it. This is a real, tangible freedom that allows us to handle, invest, earn and spend money effectively while remaining unaffected by the power and control it offers. As individual Christians we must hunger and thirst for this delivery that only comes through God's Spirit working in us. As Christian leaders who are being delivered, we must help shape and form the new attitudes and perspectives that will guide the way our organizations deal with finances. Spiritual delivery in a community context is hard work. It can only be carried out successfully by leaders who are experiencing that delivery every day in their own lives.

Discovery. God's way of doing everything is seldom, if ever, the same as the world's way. The values of the kingdom of God are antithetical to the values of the world. For this reason, as we continue our journey from death and dethroning through our delivery we will open ourselves up to discover ways of dealing with money and finances that otherwise would have been impossible. Through prayer, discernment and a heart newly tuned to the will of God, our journey will be filled with the joy of discovery of God's way of leading our organizations. This includes fresh thinking about important issues such as the role of faith in developing budgets, the proper use of debt, a God-pleasing approach to giving and asking, the tension between trusting God and building endowments, and the true meaning of transparency and financial accountability. There are three key components to this process of discovery, and the successful leader must know them and follow them tenaciously.

First, the leader must establish and hold fast to the influencers that he or she will use to undertake this investigation. There will be a strong push by many voices to hold sway over the process, especially the always-present politics of scarcity. Those that believe we are in a competition for limited resources will force the discussions along those lines. Motivated by fear and faction, they will "advise" the organization to deal with money as a sacred commodity, and in so doing they will put the organization in bondage to the old wineskins marked by attitudes of absolute ownership and control. The successful leader will need to raise up the one voice of Scripture interpreted and applied by the community under the guidance of the Holy Spirit, and not let any other voice compete with it.

Second, the leader must be willing to lead the organization through the hard task of dismantling the systems that may be shown to be unbiblical or not in alignment with the direction the organization will choose to go as a result of the discovery process. Fear of this kind of systemic change will keep many organizations from embracing what they discover. Be prepared for the pushback when the implications of the discovery become known. Discovery will often require sacrifice and change, and every leader knows the challenges of both to organizational life.

Third, the leader and his or her organization must be prepared to develop new vocabulary and tools for what they discover. Most discoveries transcend old language and cannot be measured by the former methods and tools. For instance, when an organization discovers what God may be calling them to regarding how they handle debt, they may need to measure success and growth in different ways and use language to communicate that change. A Christian college that has historically measured success by student enrollment may take on massive debt to fund sustaining growth. If the measurement of success is changed to decreasing the amount of debt per student, at least as one measurement, the discussion changes, and so does the strategy for the use of money. Without new vocabulary and tools for measurement, it will be difficult for the leader to embrace the discovery of how God may lead them to use money in their organization.

Organizations, like individuals, must be freed in order to have these discovery conversations. As Christian leaders we are called to proclaim freedom in Christ, to help organizations move through the process from death and dethroning to delivery and discovery. It is in this discovery phase that we have the attitudes and tools to discern God's will and the courage and freedom to carry it out.

Doxology. God's work done God's way by God's people always results in worship and praise. In our personal lives it is manifest in a heart that is increasingly rich toward God. It results in joyous generosity and sacrificial giving. As we experience this transformational process in our own lives we, as Christian leaders, have the opportunity to help our organization develop a culture of generosity and joyful giving. When we are truly freed in our relationship to money, when we are fully serving one master, then as an organization we can be used by God in marvelous ways.

Doxology requires a kingdom perspective. Here we come to a most critical aspect of Christian leadership. What will elicit your applause? As a leader and as an organization, what will you choose to lift up and celebrate? If our measurements for success, whether personal or communal, are focused only on the external, the visible and the quantifiable, we will find it almost impossible to be people of doxology as the natural result of the often messy process of death, dethroning, delivery and discovery. Such a process as we have outlined here will yield much that is cause for celebration and praise to God, but it will look different to us. It will require that we lift up kingdom values as our sole guide. Jesus celebrated changed lives, broken yokes, reestablished justice, reconciliation, peace and love. He rejoiced when kingdom work was done, even when it looked to everyone around him that his ministry was failing. He did not measure his success in numbers of followers, size of budget for his work or even mission impact. He sought to be kingdom focused, rejoicing in the work that served kingdom purposes for kingdom ends. Our doxology will come naturally and fully when we watch for signs that kingdom values are guiding our organizations, and the fruit of our work is aligned with the fruit of the Spirit of God.

These are the steps of godly personal and organizational transformation. While the process is never-ending, there are measurable milestones that tell us we are moving along the continuum and growing in our personal role as stewards in the kingdom of the triune God of grace. The same is true for our organizations. As leaders we are able to measure the process of moving from death to dethroning, and from delivery to discovery. The pressures and temptations to slide backwards are enormous. This work will demand the very best of us, and it begins not with what we do but with who we are. We need not be perfect but we must be in process, continually being conformed to the image of Christ in all areas of our lives and especially in our relationship to money and the things of this world. Then we trust that God will use us and our peers and colleagues in our organizations to help lead our community through the same process to the glory of God.

TRANSPARENCY: THE CHRISTIAN LEADER'S APPROACH TO
RAISING, SPENDING, INVESTING AND BORROWING MONEY

As Christian leaders help their organizations move from their X^1 along the continuum to X^2, they pass the mileposts of death, dethroning and delivery and find themselves in the discovery phase with a new set of lenses with which to approach the way they raise, spend and borrow money. We will conclude this chapter with some implications for each.

Raising money in the kingdom of God. Over the past fifteen years there has been much written on the uniqueness of fundraising for Christian organizations, including *Revolution in Generosity*; *Rich in Every Way*; *Stewards in the Kingdom*; *The Ministry of Development*; *God and Your Stuff*; *The Treasure Principle*; *Neither Poverty nor Riches*; *Money, Possessions, and Eternity*; *Heart, Soul, and Money*; *Living on Purpose*; *The Chief Steward*; *The Sower*; *The Spirituality of Fundraising*; *40 Day Spiritual Journey to a More Generous Life*; *Secrets of the Generous Life*; *The Seven Deadly Sins of Christian Fundraising*; and *A Christian View of Money*.

Every Christian leader who seeks to handle money in a God-pleasing way should become familiar with these works. One thread that runs throughout all of them is the idea that as we grow in our relationship to Jesus Christ we will develop hearts that are rich toward God. Personal spiritual growth and joyous, generous giving go hand in hand.

Christian leaders involved in fundraising must understand this critical relationship. It is a one-way movement that cannot be reversed. A growing and deepening faith will always result in a more generous heart. This is what we call transformational giving. As the heart is transformed the pocketbook follows. The opposite direction is what we refer to as transactional giving. Here the focus is on the gift and, as such, every means and device can be used to secure the transfer of assets from the donor to the ministry. The goal shifts from the transformation of the human heart to that transaction of a financial exchange. For this reason a large gift to an organization does not automatically mean that it came from a generous spirit. It may simply mean that the right techniques were used to bring about the transaction.

Let's go back to our movement from our X^1 to our X^2. If an individual is stuck in the death and dethroning process, they will not be in a position to know the full joy of a generous heart that is rich toward God. Too often the fundraising approach to people in this situation is purely transactional, and the opportunity is missed to help such an individual on their journey. Instead, our goal should be to be used by God as an instrument for the donor's further transformation to delivery, discovery and doxology. When we treat people only as sources of funding rather than cojourneyers in our walk of faith, we rob ourselves of opportunities for ministry and we cease doing the work of truly Christian fundraising. The same is true of our organizations and especially our development departments. If we are stuck between death and dethroning, we will find it difficult to plan and execute fundraising programs that are truly transformational. If we do not know the freedom of the delivery of our spirit from owner to steward, we will treat others as owners and our fundraising techniques will follow suit.

Transformational fundraising is the product of an organization that is passionate about the X^2 of complete conformity to Christ. Such organizations are led by individuals who share the same passion and who are embarked on the same journey. And these organizations, led by these individuals, will conduct fundraising programs that lift donors up and journey with them toward their own spiritual X^2. The result is a view of fundraising as ministry, donors as cojourneyers, the Holy Spirit as the true fundraiser and total trust in God's abundant provision. For this reason Christian leaders must define the X^2 for their organization in ministry terms and not purely financial terms.

We must lead our organizations to the discovery phase of our collective journey and expect to find new paradigms for measuring success that may appear nonsensical to the secular world. Even further, we must help our organizations discover what it means to bear witness *as an organization* to the values and priorities of a godly steward. What does it mean to build an organization from a steward respective? What would be the implications if our X^2 for our organization were to exhibit transformational, faithful stewardship in every area of our organizational life? What would be the impact of such a vision on our fundraising, our human resource policies, our budgeting process, our investment policies, our attitude toward debt, our relationship with our supporters, our use of natural resources, the facilities we build and how we use them? These are questions that confront us at the discovery stage of our transformational process.

Our role as leaders is not to have the answers to these questions but to ensure that our organizations mature to the point where these issues form the agenda of our daily life together.

Spending resources. In my years serving in both staff and leadership positions for not-for-profits and as a consultant in the same field, I have observed three significant tensions that exist when it comes to spending resources: faith versus fiscal responsibility, investing versus saving, and borrowing versus waiting.

Faith versus fiscal responsibility. The first tension is between exercising faith in God's provision and developing careful budgets grounded in financial constraints in order to assure fiscal responsibility. Let me illustrate this tension by the following true story. I attended a board meeting of a prominent theological school that had been struggling with ongoing debt for a number of years. Each year the school leadership would present what they considered to be a conservative budget that also included an element of faith. Each year, despite the hard work of everyone on the team, the school continued to run a six-figure deficit.

At this particular board meeting the leadership was again presenting their budget for next fiscal year, and it contained both the conservative projections requested by the board and the faith element that the leadership considered vital to the operations of a Christian organization. As the debate ensued one distinguished board member and longtime Christian leader stood up and gave a stirring oration calling on the board to step out in faith and approve the budget believing that God will surely be faithful and meet the financial needs of the school. All heads nodded in agreement and hearts swelled with encouragement. As he took his seat the chairman of the board, also a highly respected man of God and Christian leader, stood and looked around at all of his colleagues and in a somber voice of absolute conviction said, "Are we proposing that we keep trusting God until we go bankrupt?"

Everyone sat in stunned silence. Two highly respected men of God had just framed the issue in no uncertain terms. Was it foolhardy to adopt a budget with an element of faith given the organization's inability to meet similar budgets in the past? Or was it a demonstration of a lack of faith to only pass a budget that was attainable purely on human effort? In every Christian organization where I have worked, this tension between trusting

God and the responsibility for financial planning has surfaced, sometimes as a pounding storm!

For the Christian leader this tension must be preserved and not solved. To jettison either alternative leads to an unacceptable position: blind trust with no financial accountability or financial planning without prayer, discernment and faith. It is in the midst of this tension that the best decisions are made. However, the tension itself must be managed carefully. Remember, we are dealing here with money, and all we have said above will come into play. Issues of power, control, undue influence, a scarcity mentality and fear can steer this tension in the wrong direction. For the Christian leader, three things must guide the process at this point.

First, the tension must be framed on equal ground. That is, those advocating for a more faith-driven response must not be labeled as less fiscally responsible than the others. Alternatively, those seeking a more fiscally driven course must not be labeled as less spiritual than the others. This "camp" mentality forms almost immediately when this debate arises. As leaders we must create a level playing field where both sides can articulate their views and concerns without such labels. This will allow both sides to hear each other, and it leaves open the possibility of being persuaded without the threat of losing one label and inheriting another.

Second, Christian leaders must help everyone involved remember the journey they are on from death and dethroning to delivery and discovery. It is easy and quite common for old attitudes toward money to resurface regardless of how much work has been accomplished in helping an organization through this journey. Whenever money is at issue, fear, power and control are hovering around the edge. The leader must name these temptations and gain full support for the work of setting them aside so that the issue can be discussed at the discovery point in the transformational process. This will prove especially difficult if some people in the debate have not made similar progress in their personal transformation. This may require the Christian leader to ask some people to withdraw from the discussion. Even the most well-meaning Christian colleague will have a difficult time in this debate on behalf of their organization if they are personally still struggling between death and dethroning in their own attitude toward money. The discerning Christian leader will need to assure that the

people around the table of this debate have the spiritual maturity to warrant
their involvement.

Third, the end goal that God is seeking is not the perfect budget but a
process that nurtures the transformation of each person involved and glo-
rifies God in its outcome. The most expertly crafted financial plan will not
serve the kingdom of God if it is built on a process that devalues people,
breeds disunity and harms relationships. Effective Christian leadership will
keep this higher goal in mind and gain consensus from all involved toward
this one outcome. This does not mean there will not be serious and perhaps
heated discussion, occasional frustration and even hurt feelings. What it
does mean is that reconciliation and a restoration to full fellowship will be
the highest priority for all involved.

There is no one solution to this tension. There are times in the life of an
institution where the leadership may not find it wise to budget expenses
beyond what can conservatively be expected from its sources of income.
There are other times when leadership may feel specifically called by God to
step out in faith and put plans in place far beyond the capabilities of its
current financial resources. Both are legitimate in their time and place, but
more important will be the integrity of the process that was used to arrive
at either decision.

Investing versus saving. The second tension is illustrated by the following
story. A downtown rescue mission in a midsize California town had faithfully set aside a contingency fund from the proceeds of each fiscal year
budget for the past twenty years. The fund had grown to considerable size,
which gave board members and those in leadership great comfort in
knowing that they had the resources to carry them through difficult times.
However, the fund was seen by some as a hedge against a downturn in dona-
tions, where others saw it as a strategic investment fund to grow the ministry
at the right time. When a facility adjacent to the current location became
available for sale, those who regarded the fund as available for investment
made the proposal that a significant portion of it be used to purchase the
facility and expand the ministry. Their argument was that surely God had
entrusted these extra funds to the mission over all these years for such a time
as this. What good was it, they asked, to have these funds sitting in the bank
when they could be directly employed in God's work? The other group re-

coiled in horror. After all these years of faithfully setting aside funds to be sure the mission would continue in bad economic times, now this group wanted to spend almost all of it and expose the mission to great risk. Once again camps were established and labels crafted as the debate ensued.

This tension between saving money and investing money raises many of the same issues as the first tension. Those who seek to build endowments and savings accounts are often labeled as untrusting and wanting to lay up treasures on earth. Those who seek to employ funds in ministry are seen as reckless and irresponsible, exchanging short-term gain for long-term risk and vulnerability. Here again the Christian leader is called upon to establish and maintain a process where careful decisions can be made and relationships preserved. While the three guiding principles above are applicable in this situation as well, there are two additional thoughts that should serve as a guide to the Christian leader in this debate.

The first is a return to the owner/steward distinction. When an excess of money is at issue, the temptation to play the owner increases significantly. It is easier to be a steward in times of need and more tempting to be the owner in times of plenty. It will be important for the Christian leader to help all members in this debate reaffirm their commitment to faithful stewardship and their complete rejection of a spirit of ownership. In this sense the funds in question become completely impersonal—that is, no one's pride or reputation are tied up in how the funds are ultimately used. I have seen faithful men and women of God who carefully set aside funds over a long number of years slowly adopt a total ownership attitude toward those funds. The overwhelming desire to "protect" what has been so carefully saved is sometimes indicative of this ownership attitude. It will be important here for the Christian leader to help everyone return to a true steward mindset with regard to the funds in question.

Second, the Christian leader will need to help the organization return to its guiding mission. The mission of every organization, whether for-profit or not-for-profit, is in some sense to serve, to act, to accomplish something for the greater good. No organization has a mission statement that simply says "to survive." Yet we often make financial decisions as if our survival were more important than our mission. This again reveals an ownership mentality. There is a difference between a strategy of setting aside funds to help an organization navigate through a downturn in income and a desire to build an endowment that enables an organization to survive even if it proves faithless in carrying out its mission. Even though the leaders who build the endowment in the latter example do not intend for it to be a vehicle that enables the organization to stray from its mission, it has proven to be the outcome for many such organizations. This debate must be driven by mission with the full commitment to a steward's heart and undertaken by spiritually mature men and women who will value relationships over outcomes and recognize the danger signs of dealing with an excess of money.

Borrowing versus waiting. Christian leaders often face the tension between borrowing to support short-term ministry goals and putting those goals off until the funds are available without going into debt. Supporters of the former view see the strategic use of debt as an ally in building ministry. Supporters of the latter view point to scriptural evidence and practical experience to argue that debt should be avoided at all cost. As in the other examples above, there is no right or wrong answer that covers every organization in every situation.

The challenge for the Christian leader is again to understand the underlying powers at work in this debate. Debt can be used to help us build our earthly kingdoms. Some would argue that debt presumes upon the continuing provision of God in order for the organization to complete its debt retirement obligation. Such a presumption takes away from the ongoing prayerful discernment that should be required of every ministry in deciding its income and expenditures. Ministries become "locked in" to a long-term obligation that reduces their ability to be agile in discerning God's will and moving accordingly. The larger the debt the less agility an organization has, and the less it will be able to respond to changes in direction as God may lead. However, the careful use of debt has allowed many organizations to take advantage of immediate opportunities to serve a greater clientele, expand ministry and improve critical facilities in a timely manner. For these, the decision not to take on debt would move the organization backward and significantly impinge upon its ability to carry out its mission.

Both arguments are valid in their time and place. While Scripture warns of the perils of debt, it neither denounces it nor prohibits Christians from borrowing.[2] The question again goes back to the heart of the Christian leader and those making the decision. Stewards respond differently than owners to the use of debt. When the money to be borrowed is rendered powerless by those considering the decision, and when issues of self-image, reputation and importance are set aside, often the decision becomes clear. The Christian leader is responsible to name all those powers and temptations that will cloud the decision. Such a leader will gain full consensus from all those involved toward a process of clearing away the static that buzzes around the periphery of such decisions so that they may truly discern the will of God through a God-pleasing process.

CONCLUSION

Let us summarize what has been said as we conclude. As leaders we must first face our demons regarding money and help our organizations do the same. That means we must address and conquer the temptations of (1) seeing money in a detached, amoral way; (2) tying our self-image to financial success; (3) giving in to money's power that seeks to control us; (4) using it to build our own kingdoms; (5) separating our personal journey from that of our role as leader; and (6) playing the owner and not the steward.

Which of these temptations do you struggle with the most? Which have you ignored, even though they exist in your organization, or in you? Develop strategies today to address with honesty the temptations you face, and with the help of your peers and colleagues, help your organization do the same.

In facing these temptations we enter into the journey of transformation of the godly steward leader. That journey will take us through the five steps of death, dethroning, delivery, discovery and doxology.

Where are you on that journey? Are you stuck at any one place? Have you counted the cost of moving ahead, and the even greater cost of staying where you are or moving backward? What transforming work must you do to lead your organization through that process to the place of true doxology?

In all of these issues pertaining to money, the real bottom line is the disposition of the heart and not the dispensing of the asset. Christian leaders

---

[2]The issue of debt for Christians continues to be widely debated. Some of the best and most balanced approaches have come from Crown Financial and the work of Ron Blue and Kregg Hood (see especially Hood 2003, 2004).

who deal with finances with the utmost integrity have reached that point of discovery and doxology in their own transformation, and they have the vision and courage to lead their organization toward the same. Remember the words of Jesus, "Whoever can be trusted with very little can also be trusted with much" (Luke 16:10).

REFERENCES

Alcorn, R. 2001. *The Treasure Principle: Unlocking the Secret of Joyful Giving.* Colorado Springs: Multnomah.

———. 2003. *Money, Possessions and Eternity.* Carol Stream, IL: Tyndale House.

Blomberg, C. 1999. *Neither Poverty nor Riches: A Biblical Theology of Possessions.* Downers Grove, IL: InterVarsity Press.

———. 2000. *Heart, Soul, and Money.* N.P.: College Press Publishing.

Bonhoeffer, D. 1957. *The Cost of Discipleship.* New York: Macmillan.

Borg, R. 2008. *The Chief Steward.* N.P.: Xulon Press.

Foster, R. 1985. *Money, Sex and Power.* New York: Harper & Row.

Frank, J. 2012. *The Ministry of Development.* Kohler, WI: Design Group International.

Getz, G. 2004. *Rich in Every Way.* West Monroe, LA: Howard Publishing.

Hood, K. R. 2003. *Escape the Debt Trap.* Fort Worth: Prime Source Providers.

———. 2004. *From Debt to Life.* Gainesville, FL: Bridge-Logos.

Kluth, B. 2006. *40 Day Spiritual Journey to a More Generous Life.* Sandy, UT: Aardvark Global Publishing.

"Money." 2013. *Wikipedia,* last modified June 24. http://en.wikipedia.org/wiki/Money.

Nouwen, H. J. M. 2010. *A Spirituality of Fundraising.* Nashville: Upper Room Books.

Rodin, R. S. 2000. *Stewards in the Kingdom: A Theology of Life in All Its Fullness.* Downers Grove, IL: InterVarsity Press.

———. 2007. *The Seven Deadly Sins of Christian Fundraising.* Colbert, WA: Kingdom Life Publishing.

———. 2010. *The Steward Leader: Transforming People, Organizations and Communities.* Downers Grove, IL: InterVarsity Press.

Rodin, R. S., and Hoag, G. G. 2010. *The Sower: Redefining the Ministry of Raising Kingdom Resources.* Winchester, VA: ECFA Press.

Sine, C., and Sine, T. 2002. *Living on Purpose: Finding God's Best for Your Life.* Grand Rapids: Baker Books.

Vincent, M. 2006. *A Christian View of Money.* Eugene, OR: Wipf & Stock.

Willmer, W. 2002. *God and Your Stuff.* Colorado Springs: NavPress.

———. (ed.). 2008. *Revolution in Generosity: Transforming Stewards to Be Rich Toward God.* Chicago: Moody Publishers.

10

SUSTAINING THE LEADER

Timothy G. Dolan

—ɯ—

My greatest challenge is turning a church around that is more than 100 years old, and doing it with integrity. All of the stuff I learned about the church growth movement I have thrown out the window. If I tried to do in my church what the church growth movement tells me to do (like throw away the hymnals) my church would be destroyed. My struggle is knowing how to turn the church around. It takes a long time—eight miles—to turn an aircraft carrier around in the open ocean, and it takes a long time to turn the church around. I see myself as the "first lieutenant" and Jesus as the "captain." For the first twelve years of my ministry, I did not understand leadership. I am now realizing that our church has done some things in terms of outreach in urban environments, but we are only seventy-five people, and we are old and weak. And things are not changing. My challenge is to think strategically—and especially how to get people to go with me.

If it is true that four out of five churches are either on a plateau or declining, then that means that four out of five pastors are pastoring churches that are on a plateau or declining. I have a strong church growth background. There is an assumption that if your church is not growing, you are a failure by denominational standards. I told someone two weeks ago, "I am a failure." I took a church of 150 members and made it 125. I am now working on making it 100 members. This whole issue of resistance to change is at the very heart of what I am wrestling with in my life right now. Seven years ago when I came to this church I had no idea how much my church defined itself by its traditions. I am the leader. I know where to go, but every change I have made has alienated somebody. People like some things I have done. It's not always seen as my fault. I know there is just so much psychological pain that a church culture can absorb. The question is, am I leading this church or destroying it? The other issue is, am I going to survive it, or will I be a casualty?

QUOTATIONS FROM AUTHOR'S INTERVIEWS WITH PASTORS

THE CHANGING CONTEXT FOR CHRISTIAN LEADERSHIP IN THE TWENTY-FIRST CENTURY

Permanent whitewater. The comments above, made to me during interviews with two different Christian leaders, strikingly illustrate some of the challenges Christian leaders face at the beginning of the twenty-first century. Pastors, laypeople and Christian leaders in all kinds of organizations increasingly find themselves buffeted by rapid social and technological change, decreasing resources and uncertain futures. Some organizations are healthy and growing; many others (the vast majority?) are not. Some organizations are unified and cohesive; others are deeply divided over painful issues. Increasingly, many Christian leaders in all kinds of organizational contexts find themselves struggling with limited financial and human resources, internal conflict and an ever-changing world that threatens to overwhelm them and the organizations they serve.

Many observers of contemporary American society are convinced that the rapid changes in attitudes, beliefs, behaviors, mores, economic uncertainty and technology we are experiencing—and the challenges they create—will continue to increase in number and intensity over the coming years (e.g., Vaill 1996; Conner 1998). Peter Vaill uses the metaphor of navigating whitewater on a turbulent river to describe the situation facing so many leaders and managers today. Vaill, and many others, believes that we live in a world increasingly characterized by what he calls "permanent whitewater." There is every reason to believe that these changes will continue to adversely affect the health and vitality of Christian and all other kinds of organizations in the years to come. Darrell Conner goes so far as to suggest that society is not in the middle of dramatic change, but only on the cusp of it. Conner believes that even with all of the rapid changes that are happening, now is a sea of stability compared to what leaders will experience in the future.

These rapid changes are a particularly significant set of challenges for congregations and Christian organizations. A *Faith Communities Today* 2008 survey of American congregations, conducted by the Hartford Institute for Religion Research, discovered that most American congregations are struggling with a "persistent and broad based downward trend in congregational vitality" (Roozen 2009, p. 2). Although the author of the report found some reason for hope, he concludes, "The clear and consistent short-term direction [among American congregations] is negative—including worship attendance growth, spiritual vitality and sense of mission and purpose" (p. 5). Roozen discovered that congregations continue to struggle with declining attendance at worship, eroding financial and spiritual vitality, and increasing uncertainty concerning their mission. The Hartford study focused exclusively on congregations, yet many other Christian organizations are also grappling with similar issues. Most significantly, these relentless changes and complex leadership challenges continue to take a heavy emotional, physical and spiritual toll on the men and women who lead and serve Christian organizations.

Even cursory attention to television news or a newspaper makes clear that many Christian leaders are struggling to stay emotionally and spiritually alive and healthy in the midst of their leadership responsibilities in both Christian and non-Christian organizational contexts. The truth is, being an effective leader today is becoming more difficult all the time, and the challenges and opportunities for Christian leaders are significant.

Whitewater casualties. Archibald Hart (1984), in his classic book *Coping with Depression in the Ministry and Other Helping Professions*, describes a number of challenges Christian leaders face, especially those who serve in "helping" professions (social workers, teachers, counselors, pastors, nurses, leaders of nonprofits, etc). Some of these challenges include depression, burnout, loneliness and having few clearly defined boundaries. Hart posits that loneliness is a constant companion for leaders, especially those in the helping professions. Rodney Hunter defines "leadership loneliness" as "a subtle type of loneliness known only or primarily by people whose work it is to relate in some intimately yet technically specialized fashion, or in some authority relationship with other people—service professions and the leaders and administrators of organizations" (2005, p. 6). Hunter suggests that loneliness is a difficult topic because leaders often are ashamed to admit they feel lonely. Hunter writes, "No one wants to be thought of as lonely in our gregarious American society, especially religious leaders who identify themselves with the virtues of love and community. To admit loneliness is tantamount to admitting a kind of failure, an inability to live out what we preach" (p. 5).

Stress is another area that has been identified as a major source of problems for Christian leaders. Hart (1984) believes that not all stress is bad for us. In fact, some stress (eustress) is not only acceptable but actually necessary for our systems to function properly. If we had no stress at all, we would be dead! Stress turns negative when it becomes chronic and we are unable to manage it. Unmanaged stress often morphs into "dis-stress." Because they are dedicated to God, their work and the needs of others, many Christian leaders often experience a high level of dis-stress. Hart believes that the fast-paced, highly technological world in which we live today has created a "marked increase in the incidence and severity of stress related disorders, including depression" (p. 5).

Hart describes depression as the "dominant mood of our age" and a "major occupational hazard" (1984, pp. 5, 12) for Christian leaders. While depression can play a positive role in our lives—warning us that something is wrong and needs attention—Christian leaders in helping professions are especially vulnerable to it. Some forms of depression occur as a response to loss of some kind, either real or imagined. Christian leaders in helping professions often deal with loss in their work, and a sense of loss often leads to depression. According to a recent US Congregational Life survey of Presbyterian pastors, many of them were "at risk for feeling depressed, in crisis and burned out" (Scanlon 2010, p. 1).

Perhaps the most visible of all Christian leaders are pastors. One might be tempted to think that these spiritual leaders are somehow immune to the pressures and challenges Christian leaders face in other kinds of organizations. Research demonstrates that pastors not only experience similar kinds of challenges, but also that those experiences can be exacerbated because of the spiritual expectations that accompany their positions. For example, overwork is another issue that plagues many Christian leaders. A telephone survey of Protestant pastors in America discovered they are working longer hours than ever before, often at the expense of their health, their family relationships and, ironically, their relationship with God (Kelly 2010). In addition, dis-tress, and the harm it creates, has become for some a major health problem. Eric Frazier suggests that the level of dependence many people have on their pastors "is adding to the stress of [pastors'] jobs and helping to fuel a health-care crisis among the nation's clergy" (2007, p. 1). Frazier goes on to report that "experts say clergy members of all faiths and denominations are literally working themselves sick; their health-care claims are rising so fast that church budgets are straining under the weight" (p. 1).

A recent study on clergy physical health confirms Frazier's observations. Paul Vitello (2010), writing in the *New York Times*, summarizes the study that was conducted by the Clergy Health Initiative at Duke University Divinity School. He reports that members of the clergy "suffer from obesity, hypertension, and depression rates higher than most Americans. In the last decade, their use of antidepressants has risen, while their life expectancy has fallen. Many would change jobs if they could" (p. 1).

George Barna reports that divorce among "born again" Christians (including all kinds of Christian leaders) is "statistically identical to that of non-born again adults" (2008, p. 1). Internet pornography has become a pervasive moral and ethical problem in the United States, and Christians are not immune to this problem. Although accurate statistics on porn addiction among Christians are difficult to come by, Michael Foust suggests that "porn's usage among Christians is significant enough that a growing number of ministries and Christian publishers are releasing materials designed to encourage mental purity and to help those with addictions" (2010, p. 2).

Conflict also has become an increasing reality throughout society. While constructive conflict can be healthy and even useful, destructive conflict has a way of tearing at the very fabric of the community and the leaders who serve its members. Once again, Christian organizations are not exempted from this pervasive social issue. The *Faith Communities Today* study (Roozen 2009) reports that the level of conflict in congregations in 2008 was virtually identical to what it was in a similar study in 2000. Roozen notes both negatives and positives in this finding when he writes, "The bad news is that conflict remains nearly as pervasive in 2008 as it was in 2000. The good news is that the reach of conflict has not increased across the last eight years" (p. 4). We all too often hear about a Christian leader who has succumbed to a nasty internal conflict, sexual temptation or some other moral failure commonly found in the culture at large—and the results are usually devastating, not only to the Christian leader and his or her family, but also to his or her organization.

In his seminal book *Margin: Restoring Emotional, Physical, Financial, and Time Reserves to Overloaded Lives*, Richard Swenson (2004) suggests that a major problem underlying many of the challenges Christian leaders face today is what he calls "overload." Swenson defines overload as a state of chronic overage that leads to various kinds of dysfunction. He states that overload occurs "whenever the requirements upon us exceed that which we are able to bear" (p. 54). It is Swenson's contention that we live in an increasingly overloaded world, caused in part by unrelenting change and never-ending "progress." New things are coming at us faster and faster all the time. There is simply too much to do and too little time to do it. As a result, leaders today are often overloaded and exhausted—working harder than ever before yet enjoying it less and less. Swenson refers to the way we live today as "hyper living." Like the accelerated speeds that catapult the starship Enterprise into the outer reaches of the universe on reruns of the popular television series *Star Trek*, it seems like much of our world and our lives have now accelerated into "warp speed." And we are not sure how to slow them down.

The research group Conference Board conducted a survey of American workers' attitudes toward their jobs. According to the survey, only 45 percent of Americans were satisfied with their work in 2009. While that might seem relatively high, it is actually the lowest job level satisfaction recorded since the Conference Board began researching the topic in 1987, when the job satisfaction rating was nearly 70 percent (Aversa 2010, pp. 7-8). A number of reasons were given as to why job satisfaction is at such a low ebb, including a faltering economy, soaring health Insurance premiums and slower than hoped for wage increases. But certainly overload also plays into it, as more and more organizations downsize, leaving frustrated workers trying to accomplish the same or more work with fewer resources.

Swenson (2004) blames much of the pain of overload today not only on the acceleration of change but also on the increasing complexity of technology. Technology overload has become a fact of life for all of us. Until recently, our family had four different remote controls all programmed for the same television. These four remotes did four different things. Even though I am an educated person, there have been many times when I have been unable to turn on the television or play a DVD. This is especially true if my children tinkered with these remotes in any way. If they changed even one small setting on any of the remotes, it usually meant doom for me. It is helpful technology, but often I am stumped by it.

Ironically enough, even in the midst of all these troubling realities, a number of studies indicate that pastors and other Christian leaders are relatively satisfied with their work. Even though leadership of Christian organizations can be tough and demanding, many leaders report that they are satisfied overall with the work they do (Carroll 2006, pp. 161-62). But the relentless push of progress, the pace of change and the complexity of technology still take a heavy toll. In his book *Sabbath*, Wayne Muller writes, "Even when our intentions are noble and our efforts sincere—even when we dedicate our lives to the service of others—the corrosive pressure of frantic activity can nonetheless cause suffering in ourselves and others" (1991, pp. 1-2).

In light of the complexities of leadership today, how might Christian leaders keep from becoming—as the pastor in the quote at the beginning of this chapter feared—a leadership "casualty"? What must Christian leaders do to keep themselves emotionally, physically and spiritually healthy? What does it take for Christian leaders not only to survive in their lives and their work but actively thrive over the long haul?

SURVIVING AND THRIVING IN A
WORLD OF PERMANENT WHITEWATER

In the remainder of this chapter, I want to highlight several helpful practices. I believe these are some things leaders can do to help them survive and even thrive in this turbulent age. These include: increasing personal margin, cultivating greater emotional and spiritual accountability, engaging in lifelong learning, and developing a healthier spiritual life by practicing spiritual disciplines.

Increasing personal margin. If one of the main problems Christian leaders are facing today is overload, then what can leaders do about it? According to Swenson (2004), one important thing we must do is create more margin in our own personal lives and in the lives of our families and the organizations we are privileged to lead. Swenson defines margin as "the space between our load and our limits. It is the amount allowed beyond that which is needed. It is held in reserve for contingencies or unanticipated situations. Margin is the gap between rest and exhaustion, the space between breathing freely and suffocating. Margin is the opposite of overload. If we are overloaded we have no margin" (pp. 69-70).

If you have ever missed or nearly missed a flight because you did not give yourself enough time to get to and through the airport, you know what it is like not to have enough margin. When I go to the airport, I usually try to leave plenty of time to get checked in, go through security, use the restroom and get to my gate. There have been times, however, when I did not leave enough time to do all these things. The result? I was forced to frantically run through the airport hoping and praying I did not miss the flight. Any way you look at it, that is operating with too little margin! Getting to the gate with plenty of time to wander around the concourse, buy a newspaper, use the restroom and maybe enjoy a snack or two is giving myself plenty of margin.

There will be times when, out of necessity, leaders will not experience positive margin. When I was writing the dissertation for my PhD, working full time and fulfilling my duties as a husband and father of three school-aged children, I was not always in positive margin. There was simply too much to do and only so many hours in the day to do it. I was often stressed and stretched too thin. Given the circumstances, it was acceptable for me to live with very little margin in my life—but only for a while. I knew this "marginless" existence as a doctoral student would only be for a relatively brief season.

The problem is not so much *being* in negative margin as it is *staying* in negative margin. Leaders can handle not having enough margin for a short period of time. Realistically, there will be times in our personal lives, our work and our families when we will slip into negative margin. We can't help it. Living with negative margin is a problem when it becomes *chronic*—a way of life for us. When that happens, it becomes harmful over the long haul.

Unfortunately, it appears that many leaders today live their lives most of the time in negative margin. Swenson (2004) suggests that severe, chronic, negative margin is one of the leading causes of burnout. To be healthy and productive over the long haul, Christian leaders need to find ways to operate with plenty of margin. Swenson writes, "Margin grants freedom and permits rest. It nourishes both relationship and service. It allows availability for the purposes of God. From a medical point of view, it is health enhancing. It is a welcome addition to our health formulary: Add a dose of margin and see if life doesn't come alive once again" (p. 69).

Jesus provides a great example of someone who paid attention to margin—making sure his life was full, but not overfull. Luke tells us that as Jesus grew in popularity with the common people, they badgered him and pressed in on him for more teaching and healing. Jesus, of course, was happy to serve the people. But Luke implies that sometimes all this ministry got to be too much. When it did, Jesus "often withdrew to lonely places and prayed" (Luke 5:16). On other occasions, we are told that when the work he was doing threatened to spill over from load to overload, Jesus simply dismissed the crowds and "went up on a mountainside by himself to pray" (Matthew 14:23). What do we learn from Jesus? We learn that even though his calendar was chock-full of important appointments and things for him to do, Jesus took time for margin. He knew he would be much more useful to the Father and others if he spent time in self-care. Pursuing margin, for Jesus, was not simply for the purpose of getting physical rest and renewal, but also for reconnecting with the Father in order to draw help and strength from him. Jesus knew that maintaining his relationship with the Father was absolutely essential if he was to accomplish all that he had been sent to accomplish, and so he paid special attention to this important form of self-care. Wayne Muller writes,

> Jesus did not wait until everyone had been properly cared for, until all who sought him were healed. He did not ask permission to go, nor did he leave anyone behind "on call," or even let his disciples know where he was going. Jesus obeyed a deeper rhythm. When the moment for rest had come, the time for healing was over. He would simply stop, retire to a quiet place, and pray. (1991, p. 25)

One of the great benefits we have as Christian leaders is not only the *example* of Jesus but also the continuing *presence* of Jesus with us through the Holy Spirit. Before he ascended into heaven, Jesus promised his disciples that he would send the Spirit, who would give them power to be his witnesses in the world (Acts 1:8). The Spirit would also give his disciples strength to face every kind of trial and tribulation they might encounter, including many of the things we still face today (John 16:5-15).

The point is, Christian leaders have not only the example of Jesus to follow when we get in over our heads, but also the resources of Jesus himself through the continuing presence of his Spirit living and active in us. If this experience of gaining and maintaining enough margin was important for Jesus, why is it not more important to us?

Take better care of ourselves. Swenson (2004) mentions a number of other things Christian leaders can do to gain more margin, including sleeping longer, eating better and getting more exercise. A recent Centers for Disease Control study indicates that 41 million workers don't get enough sleep at night. According to the study, many workers get fewer than six hours of sleep (Jaslow 2012). Doctors tell us that the average person needs about eight hours of sleep each night. How many people actually get that much? According to several studies, not many of us!

As a university professor, I used to get emails from students with assignments attached to them at 1:00 or 2:00 in the morning. When I got these emails, I had a pretty good idea that these students are probably not getting enough sleep (and when they do finally sleep, it might be in class!). Sleeplessness contributes to all kinds of problems in our society, including accidents on the job, lost productivity and a host of mental and physical problems that affect our mood, relationships and ability to perform our work. Many problems could be prevented if people received more rest. Getting more sleep means learning to be more disciplined in the use of our time—especially paying attention to the amount of time we watch television, use computers and do other things that tend to keep us up at night.

Exercise is another area Christian leaders need to pay attention to if they want to be healthier and happier. For many years now, I have tried to exercise at least one hour every day. This exercise usually takes the form of walking, swimming or working out at the campus fitness center. Even when I travel, I try to stay in accommodations that have exercise equipment. If they don't have exercise machines, I usually look for the nearest, safest road to walk on. There is rarely a day when I wake up in the morning and ask myself if I should exercise that day or not. It is just something I do automatically. I don't say this to pat myself on the back or suggest that I have a corner on exercise. I don't. I emphasize it simply to suggest that there will always be good, even valid, reasons not to exercise. That is why exercise needs to become an ingrained habit. This kind of regular ongoing exercise habit not only helps me feel better physically, but it also feeds me mentally and emotionally. I am convinced that it helps me think clearer and do better work.

When I worked at Whitworth University, the director of the campus fitness center regularly saw me working out in the center. He asked me one time if I enjoy exercising. He looked a bit shocked when I candidly admitted to him that I really do not enjoy it, especially riding exercise bikes. I don't exercise because I like it, but because I am convinced it is good for me and the people I serve. So I have gotten into the habit of doing it. Of course, if you can get exercise by doing something you like, that is even better!

Some leaders, for various reasons, are not physically able to exercise. But even leaders who have physical limitations or who are very busy can work some form of exercise into their daily routine. For instance, instead of using the elevator in your office building, take the stairs. My mother-in-law used to pride herself on always being able to find parking right next to the front door of a store. While this is helpful and maybe even necessary for people who are older or have handicaps, most people would do well to park farther away and walk. Even brief periods of exercise like these can pay significant physical, emotional and spiritual dividends in the long run. In her book *Sacred Rhythms*, Ruth Haley Barton describes her journey of learning to care for her body as an act of leadership and expression of faith.

> There is a very real connection between care of our body, our ability to continue deepening our relationship with God and our capacity to faithfully carry out God's purposes for our life over the long haul. I began to slowly shift my living patterns, eating better, drinking more water, getting more rest rather than resorting to the short-lived benefits of caffeine, and working my way slowly into a more active lifestyle that included walking, running and biking. (2006, p. 83)

In his first letter to the Corinthians, the apostle Paul reminds us that our bodies are important to God and are given to us to be used for his service: "Do you not know that your bodies are temples of the Holy Spirit, who is in you, whom you have received from God? You are not your own; you were bought at a price. Therefore honor God with your bodies" (1 Corinthians 6:19-20).

Use time more effectively. Using time more intentionally and effectively is another way Christian leaders can gain more margin in their lives and work. Because they are committed to serving others, many Christian leaders are not very comfortable saying no. But I am convinced that learning to say no is a key leadership skill. Conscientious leaders tend to pile on more and more responsibilities until they become overloaded and resentful. The principle is: don't take on anything new unless you let go of something else. Of course, this is much easier said than done, especially if it is your boss who is telling you that you need to take on something else!

We have a policy in our family that we do not answer the telephone (or respond to text messages) during the dinner hour. Having grown up in a family where my attorney father regularly answered the phone during dinner (and subsequently spent significant amounts of time away from the dinner table), my wife and I decided early on that our family mealtime was too precious to let it be interrupted. As it is, 99 percent of the calls are not urgent anyway and can be easily answered at a time that is more convenient.

As I was sharing the contents of this chapter with a colleague, he commented that, in his opinion, one of the traps Christian leaders fall into is the false idea that they are indispensable and always need to be available. Unfortunately, technology has made it possible for leaders to be "on call" all the time, wherever they are. There is no downtime unless leaders insist upon it. *How can people live without us?* we wonder. We have already noted that— even thought he took ministry with others very seriously—Jesus was not always available.

According to the study that was mentioned earlier in this chapter about clergy health, one of the best things a Christian leader can do to improve his or her emotional and physical health is take more time off from work. Paul Vitello writes, "As cell phones and social media expose the clergy to new dimensions of stress, and as health costs soar, some of the country's largest religious denominations have begun wellness campaigns that preach the virtues of getting away. It has been described by some health experts as a sort of slow-food movement for the clerical soul" (2010, p. 1).

One of the things I have always tried to do in the various leadership roles I have had is to take adequate time away from work. Contrary to the practice of several people I know, I always try to take as much vacation time as I have coming to me. I remember Professor Archibald Hart saying in a Doctor of Ministry class that if a person takes a month vacation, he or she will actually get two weeks of vacation. What he meant, I think, is that it takes at least a week to really unwind and get away from our work mentally and emotionally. And usually we start to gear up again the week before we return to work. So if a person takes four weeks, he or she actually gets two weeks of real vacation! Whether this is true or not for everyone is certainly open for discussion. But the point is, taking adequate time away from the pressures and stresses of work can do wonders for one's emotional, spiritual and physical well-being.

Discipline our use of technology. Learning to be more disciplined in the management of various technologies, especially those that connect us to email, social networks, games, internet searches, work and television, is another way to help get control of our time. Some studies have indicated that the average adult spends four hours a day, or twenty-eight hours a week, watching TV (Herr 2007). Anyone who works with teenagers or college students knows that young people spend even greater amounts of time consuming popular media and using various social networking technologies.

Increasing numbers of people are chronically attached to their portable wireless devices. More and more parishioners check their email and do text messaging during worship services and other religious functions. Now that technology can go wherever we go, we need to be more intentional and disciplined with our use of it—and getting away from it when necessary.

One of the things I have always admired about the Old Order Amish is their inherent caution when it comes to the use of technology. As I understand it, one of the reasons they tend to resist many forms of technology is out of concern for how it will affect their common life together. Instead of mindlessly adopting the latest technology, as it seems so many people do today, they ask what I call the "Amish question": How will this technology promote greater dependence on one another or lead to greater independence? For the Amish, any technology that leads to greater self-reliance is suspect because it takes away from their core value of shared community.

Of course, technology can be a positive thing. Used wisely and judiciously, technology can enrich our lives, our relationships and our ability to lead others. But one of the questions Christian leaders continually need to ask themselves and the people they lead is this: Does this technology promote health and social capital or take away from it? The blurring of work and leisure has become an increasing problem as cell phones and tablets have proliferated. All of this has made it difficult to establish boundaries between personal/family time and being available 24/7. Establishing firm boundaries and enforcing discipline to keep them is the key to taking better control of our time. My advice generally is, as much as leaders are able, they should leave work at work. Begin your own assessment of the potency or your electronic boundaries with this maxim, and develop firm boundaries that make sense for you and your situation. Once established, live by them!

Live within our limits. Swenson (2004) suggests a number of other creative ways to gain more margin in our lives, including planning more time for hobbies and recreation, spending more time with family and friends, and learning to respect, and live within, the limits God has set for us. Ruth Haley Barton (2008), in her book *Strengthening the Soul of Your Leadership*, reminds leaders: "Our unwillingness to live within limits—both personally and in community—is one of the deepest sources of depletion and eventual burnout. That's the bad news. The good news is that there is something

deeply spiritual about living and working within our God-ordained limits—
or to put it another way, living fully and acceptingly within our own set of
realities" (pp. 111-12).

Leaders must also be careful to pay attention to the limits of those with
whom we live and work. In our desire to gain greater margin for ourselves,
we sometimes unintentionally contribute to the loss of margin for others.
We need to do a better job of evaluating whether that evening phone call or
email to a colleague, that additional weekend meeting or that request for a
coworker to get something for you during their vacation is necessary.
Learning to respect our own margin and the margin of others is one way
leaders can add health to their own lives and the lives of others.

What intentional steps can you take to gain more positive margin in your
work, family and time with God? How can you contribute to the margin of
others? How disciplined are you with your use of time and technology? How
well do you take care of yourself and others?

Cultivating greater emotional and spiritual accountability. Another
way that Christian leaders can thrive in a world of permanent whitewater is
by taking greater advantage of resources that help promote emotional and
spiritual well-being.

Therapists and spiritual directors. In early 2010, I had the opportunity to
spend three weeks alone in a cabin on beautiful Puget Sound in Washington
State, participating in a three-week therapeutic "intensive." The purpose of
this intensive (or "journey," as it is called) was to get away from the normal
everyday distractions to focus on some of the emotional and spiritual issues
in my life, especially as they relate to my family of origin. Each morning
during those three weeks I met for an hour and a half with a very skilled
therapist/spiritual director. I then spent the rest of the day in solitude—
taking long walks, writing in my journal, "talking" to significant others in
my family of origin and praying.

Imagine being alone in a rural cabin for almost three weeks with no cell
phone, computer, internet, TV, movies, radio, magazines, newspapers,
books (except for the Bible) or any other distractions. You would think one
would get bored and lonely pretty fast. But that was not the case for me. I
was alone, but never lonely. It was actually one of the most profound and
moving experiences in my life. During those three weeks my therapist/

spiritual director was able to help me feel, embrace, and express thoughts and feelings that had been long buried. I came to a much deeper awareness about who I am as a person and where I need to grow as a Christian, husband, father and leader.

My experience on this intensive reminded me that being an emotionally and spiritually healthy Christian leader today is so vitally important and yet often so difficult to accomplish. I have long held the conviction that Christian leaders should have regular access to a skilled therapist and spiritual director. My intensive convinced me of this even more. It might be that leaders will never feel the need to use it; but it should be available to them nonetheless. Pastors, especially early in their ministry, should have this resource routinely included as part of the call process. Along with pension and health insurance, pastors should be provided with access to a therapist and/or spiritual director. In some cases, it might be one and the same person. It is my conviction that all Christian leaders, wherever they serve, can benefit from this kind of intentional, ongoing support.

Unfortunately, this kind of mental and emotional support is often seen by followers as a sign of weakness rather than strength. "What's wrong with our leader that he or she needs a therapist?" There is often considerable stigma attached to a leader's seeing a counselor. But the truth is, no leader is as emotionally and/or spiritually healthy as he or she can or should be. Leaders are human. Most of us have family-of-origin challenges, marital and/or family issues, relationship conflicts, emotional or spiritual struggles, and so on, and we need help and support from time to time. If leaders had regular access to a therapist and spiritual counselor as part of their job benefits, it would not be seen as something negative but simply as part of the business of leading others. Leaders would not need to feel ashamed or embarrassed when they access this support. It would just be assumed that this is part of the deal.

Some Protestant Christian leaders are not always comfortable with the idea of "spiritual direction." Spiritual direction, for some, sounds a bit too mystical or Catholic. Even though this may be true for some, spiritual direction has a long history in the Christian tradition and has been finding increasing acceptance in Protestant circles, as evidenced by the proliferation of books and seminars on the topic in recent years.

Marjorie Thompson, in her classic book *Soul Feast: An Invitation to the Christian Spiritual Life*, defines spiritual direction as "the guidance one person offers another to help that person 'grow up in every way . . . into Christ' (Eph. 4:15). A spiritual guide is someone who can help us see and name our own experience of God" (1995, pp. 103-4). Thompson believes that anyone who has a heart for God and depth of spiritual maturity can provide this kind of spiritual guidance to others.

In his book *Working the Angles: The Shape of Pastoral Integrity*, Eugene Peterson comments that spiritual direction takes place "when two people agree to give their full attention to what God is doing in one (or both) of their lives and seek to respond in faith" (1987, p. 150). Peterson suggests that the role of spiritual directors is not to apply truth but to "discover particular temptations and actual graces" (p. 157). Peterson argues that in times past, it was expected that leaders, especially pastoral leaders, would not only provide spiritual guidance to others but would also have access to spiritual guides themselves. He writes, "Having a spiritual director, whether called by that name or not, was assumed in the job description" (p. 166). Sadly, this is not a reality for most pastoral leaders today. Peterson argues that having a spiritual director is not only useful but indispensable for the ongoing spiritual health of Christian leaders. Of course, it is not only pastors who need this kind of spiritual accountability, but all Christian leaders.

What kind of ongoing emotional and spiritual support do you have as a leader? Are there resources available that you are not seeking? Why?

Mentors. In addition to a good therapist/spiritual director, I believe that one of the best things Christian leaders can do to sustain themselves in leadership is to avail themselves of good mentors. Randall O'Brien defines a mentor as "one who shares wisdom with another, preferably but not always in a one-to-one relationship" (2011, p. 290). Similarly, Stanley and Clinton define mentoring as "a relational experience through which one person empowers another by sharing God-given resources" (1992, p. 13). Mentors are similar to spiritual directors in that they tend to be people who have "been there, done that" and can help guide and direct others down the sometimes rocky path that all leaders must travel. Spiritual directors tend to focus more on the interior spiritual life of leaders, while mentors usually provide insight and guidance in a number of areas.

Mentoring is something that is helpful not only when we are young, but throughout our lives. Each stage of our lives, and each leadership transition we experience, brings new adjustments and challenges and therefore new learning that needs to take place. It is my observation that the most effective leaders tend to be those who have been, and still are, mentored by someone else. They are also people who have made a commitment to mentor others. Being in a mentoring relationship (either one-on-one or in a group setting) is one critical way leaders develop life skills and greater leadership capacity. In his book *Mentoring*, Walter Wright observes: "One of society's significant needs is the continuous development and maturation of its leaders. Based on many years of mentoring and being mentored, I believe this give-and-take relationship is the most effective way to guide people with leadership gifts toward their potential" (2004, p. vii).

Unfortunately, as I look back on my life, I can identify only one or two people who have been any kind of real mentors for me. There have been a few people who have served as role models, but not many that I would describe as the kind of mentors that make a lasting impact on the heart and soul. I believe this is as much my fault as the fault of others. This realization has led me to a renewed determination to seek out those leaders who can help mentor me through the next phases of my life and work.

I recently heard a Christian leader give an eloquent tribute to a seminary professor who mentored him while he was in seminary. This man came to seminary, as he described it, "a mess" both spiritually and emotionally. Apparently, this leader grew up in a very dysfunctional and abusive home. When he arrived at seminary broken and confused, this seminary professor befriended him; and through his care, compassion and focused attention, was able to have a profound impact on the life of this future Christian leader. It was one of the most sincere and heartfelt tributes to the influence of another man that I have ever heard. As I have reflected on his talk, I have been reminded that the best thing we can give to ourselves, and to others, is the gift of time and focused attention.

Certainly the primary way Jesus trained and equipped his twelve disciples for the work he wanted them to do was through intentional, ongoing mentoring. He carefully prodded, encouraged and guided these ordinary men to become extraordinary leaders. Except for the one who betrayed him, all of them went on to become significant leaders and greatly influenced the early church.

Do you have friends and mentors who nourish and nurture you as you seek to be the leader God is calling you to be? Are you, in turn, committed to mentoring others?

Support and accountability groups. Another way a Christian leader can seek emotional and spiritual support and accountability is in a group setting. In my experience, real emotional and spiritual growth often happens best in groups. When I was a young pastor fresh out of seminary, I had the opportunity to be involved in a small therapy/spiritual support group for pastors. We met once a week, early in the morning, with a skilled therapist/spiritual director. We sat in a circle and took turns sharing what was going on in our lives and ministries. It was a confidential group, and I was surprised at times, maybe even shocked, at the level of pain and heartache that was sometimes expressed. Unfortunately, I was very new in ministry and did not really appreciate, or take full advantage of, this great gift. I had not really experienced yet some of the difficulties and loneliness that come with leadership. I found out recently that after twenty-six years, this group is still meeting. If I did not live in a different city now and had the opportunity, I would jump at the chance to be in that group again.

In their book *The Leader's Journey*, Herrington, Creech and Taylor affirm the value of this kind of intentional ongoing support for leaders: "Personal transformation happens best in the context of a loving community that extends grace and truth. . . . We have found the context of the peer group and the guidance of an effective coach to be powerful places of disclosure and discovery" (2003, pp. 8, 10). If you, or other leaders you know, are not currently connected to a support group, then I would highly recommend it. It will pay huge benefits to you personally and professionally.

In my research on small support groups for pastors, I discovered that the best groups meet on a regular basis, have a clearly defined purpose, are facilitated by a highly skilled facilitator and are committed to strict confidentially. No leader will ever open up with other leaders unless he or she is convinced that what he or she has to share will not get back to a supervisor, denominational executive or someone else who could use that information in a negative way. Leaders, generally, have so few places where

they can go that are truly safe for them to share the challenges and loneliness of being a leader.

What individual or group do you regularly connect with that holds you
accountable, feeds your soul, provides a sounding board for you and helps
you find direction in your life and ministry?

Engaging in lifelong learning. I am convinced that one of the best ways
to help Christian leaders survive and thrive over the long haul is to encourage them to be lifelong learners. One-time, stand-alone educational
events (workshops, seminars, short courses, etc.) can be helpful, especially
for learning a specific skill or application of a skill. But I have come to believe that the most transformative learning often takes place in small groups
that meet regularly over an extended period of time. These kinds of learning
experiences are intentional, systematic and ongoing. These groups not only
help leaders develop new leadership skills, but they also provide emotional
and spiritual support.

This small group model is variously referred to in the literature as
learning communities, learning cohorts or learning clusters. In his book *A
Work of Heart: Understanding How God Shapes Spiritual Leaders*, Reggie
McNeal stresses that the goal of these learning clusters is not simply the
acquisition of knowledge, but the development of leaders. He argues that
as leaders are changed, the churches and Christian organizations they lead
will also be changed. McNeal states, "A critical intellectual capacity for
twenty-first century leadership success will be the ability to build knowledge
together with other colleagues. The rate of information growth, coupled
with the collapse of the Christendom paradigm, makes it no longer possible
to prepare for ministry challenge through traditional preparation processes." McNeal goes on to suggest that, contrary to traditional learning
styles that are "linear, didactic, privatized, and parochial," learning in community is "nonlinear, layered, and experimental. It is also just in time"
(2000, pp. 131-32).

There are several key pieces to these learning communities or clusters.
According to McNeal, these pieces include peer mentoring, mutual encouragement and support, opportunities for dialogue and reflection, and self-
directed learning. McNeal believes that Christian leaders are facing challenges today that arise so quickly that they need to be continually learning

in order to keep up. However, due to the nature of the kind of learning that needs to take place, it cannot be accomplished as a solitary activity.

Many continuing educators agree that effective lifelong learning is best done in tandem with others. D. Bruce Roberts believes that creating ongoing peer groups for Christian leaders makes clear the assumption that "learning for the practice of ministry is never finished, but is important for it to continue" (2010, p. 158). So many of the models for lifelong learning that are available today are designed for "lone rangers"—individuals who attend on their own, learn on their own and then go back to their place of leadership alone. While it can be helpful, this kind of learning generally is not as life-giving or transforming as learning done with others.

My own research on the use of learning clusters as a means to provide continuing education for Christian leaders has convinced me that the most effective and transformational learning most often occurs in community with others, as opposed to independent study (Dolan, 2010). Meeting together regularly in groups, input into the content of one's learning, opportunities for group interaction and significant group mentoring all play a vital role in the success of this form of continuing education (Roberts 2010, pp. 163-80). Lifelong learning, especially done in tandem with peers and mentors, not only stimulates leaders spiritually and intellectually, but also contributes greatly to the ongoing health and vitality of their leadership.

How intentional are you in regards to your own intellectual and skill development? Do you have an intentional plan of lifelong learning that helps sustain your leadership and ministry over the long haul?

Developing a healthier spiritual life: Solitude, prayer and sabbath. Study after study has confirmed that Christian leaders generally struggle to maintain a healthy spiritual life. Yet without a life that is deeply grounded spiritually—a life that pays attention to what Ruth Haley Barton (2006) refers to as "sacred rhythms"—leadership quickly deteriorates into busyness at best, and insignificance at worst.

I once watched a series on public television titled *The Emotional Life.* It was hosted by Dr. Daniel Gilbert, who is a professor of psychology at Harvard University. The series focused on understanding social relationships, resolving negative attitudes and searching for happiness. In one of the episodes, Dr. Gilbert identified optimism and "deep religious faith" as two of the top three characteristics of highly resilient people (Gilbert 2010). Resiliency, generally, has to do with how quickly leaders are able to bounce back from problems and setbacks. Leaders who are highly resilient tend to be able to recover more quickly from the inevitable irritations and conflicts they encounter on an almost daily basis. Deep religious faith is at the center of highly resilient Christian leaders.

There are many spiritual disciplines that the Christian tradition encourages Christian leaders to practice. These disciplines are long-standing and time-tested spiritual attitudes and practices that can help leaders get in touch with and stay connected to God in the crucible of daily living. In his classic book *Celebration of Discipline* (2002), Richard Foster divides the spiritual disciplines into three categories: inward, outward and corporate. First are what he calls the *inward* disciplines—practices like meditation, prayer, fasting and study. These disciplines are probably familiar to most Christians and focus primarily on developing our more personal or private relationship with God. Second, Foster describes the *outward* disciplines, which include practices like simplicity, solitude, submission and service. These disciplines tend to be more visible than the inward disciplines and have much to do with our motivations and the attitude by which we live our lives as believers. Third, Foster describes the *corporate* disciplines, which include confession, worship, guidance and celebration. These corporate spiritual disciplines focus less on our personal relationship with God and more on our common life together.

I believe that three of the most helpful spiritual practices, especially in the noisy, distracted world Christian leaders serve in today, are solitude, prayer and Sabbath. Solitude simply means creating space for God. Ruth Haley Barton defines solitude in this way: "Solitude is a place. It is a place in time that is set apart for God and God alone, a time when we unplug and withdraw from the noise of interpersonal interactions, from the noise, busyness, and constant stimulation associated with life in the company of others" (2006, p. 32). We live in a world of constant noise and distraction. There are very few places people can go today and not be bombarded by constant noise. This is one of the reasons why I usually do not listen to the radio when I am alone driving in my car. Those few minutes alone in the car give me time to think, pray and meditate. In a word, they give me much-needed solitude.

Taking time each week to practice prayer and Sabbath is also very important. I have not always been as consistent as I would like in observing the Sabbath. My intentions are good, but the follow-through is not always there. Because we live in a 24/7 world, Christian leaders need to find ways to experience genuine Sabbath. Muller writes, "The practice of Shabbat, or Sabbath, is designed specifically to restore us, a gift of time in which we allow the cares and concerns of the marketplace to fall away. We set aside time to delight in being alive, to savor the gifts of creation, and to give thanks for the blessings we may have missed in our necessary preoccupation with our work" (1991, p. 26). In our increasingly distracted world, real Sabbath will not happen unless leaders make it a priority.

What does your practice of solitude, prayer, Sabbath and other spiritual disciplines look like?

SUMMARY

"Am I going to survive it, or will I be a casualty?" This question, posed at the beginning of the chapter by one of the pastors I interviewed, is a question many Christian leaders are asking today. At first glance, it does seem like leaders galore, many of them Christian leaders, are indeed becoming casualties. And there is every reason to believe that being a leader is not going to get easier any time soon. That's the bad news. The good news is that there are many concrete things leaders can do to get emotionally and spiritually healthy and stay that way. There are choices leaders can make that will help them not only survive but also thrive in their leadership capacities and become the kind of leaders God is calling them to be.

REFERENCES

Aversa, J. 2010. "Fewer People Report Feeling Satisfied at Jobs." *Spokesman-Review*, January 5. www.spokesman.com/stories/2010/jan/05/workers-whistle-less.

Barna, G. 2008. "New Marriage and Divorce Statistics Released." Barna Group website, March 31. www.barna.org/barna-update/article/15-familykids/42-new-marriage-and-divorce-statistics-released#.UhI1UGRYI4w.

Barton, R. H. 2006. *Sacred Rhythms: Arranging Our Lives for Spiritual Transformation.* Downers Grove, IL: InterVarsity Press.

———. 2008. *Strengthening the Soul of Your Leadership.* Downers Grove, IL: InterVarsity Press.

Carroll, J. 2006. *God's Potters: Pastoral Leadership and the Shaping of Congregations.* Grand Rapids: Eerdmans.

Connor, D. 1998. *Leading at the End of Chaos: How to Create the Nimble Organization.* New York: John Wiley and Sons.

Dolan, T. 2010. "Making Sense of Ministry: A Clergy Cluster Project." In *A Lifelong Call to Learn: Continuing Education for Religious Leaders,* edited by R. Reber and D. Bruce Roberts. Harndon, VA: Alban Institute.

Foster, R. 2002. *Celebration of Discipline: The Path to Spiritual Growth,* 3rd ed. San Francisco: HarperSanFrancisco.

Foust, M. 2010. "Internet Porn a Wide-Ranging Problem, Even in the Church." *Baptist Press,* April 6. www.bpnews.net/bpnews.asp?id=32644.

Frazier, E. 2007. "Easing Their Burdens: New Efforts Seek to Assist Stressed-Out Clergy Members." *The Chronicle of Philanthropy,* November 29. http://philanthropy.com/article/Easing-Their-Burdens/61022/

Gilbert, D. 2010. *This Emotional Life.* PBS television series, produced by Kunhardt McGee Productions.

Hart, A. 1984. *Coping with Depression in the Ministry and Other Helping Professions.* Waco: Word.

Herr, N. 2007. "Television and Health." The Sourcebook for Teaching Science. www.csun.edu/science/health/docs/tv&health.html.

Herrington, J., R. R. Creech and T. Taylor. 2003. *The Leader's Journey: Accepting the Call to Personal and Congregational Transformation.* San Francisco: Jossey-Bass.

Hunter, R. 2005. "Loneliness in Ministry: Pastoral Theological Perspectives." Austin Seminary *Communitas* 2: 5-14.

Jaslow, R. 2012. "41 Million American Workers Don't Get Enough Sleep, CDC Says." CBS News Online, April 27. www.cbsnews.com/8301-504763_162-57422902-10391704/41-million-american-workers-dont-get-enough-sleep-cdc-says.

Kelly, M. 2010. "Pastors' Work Hours Tallied in New Survey." *Baptist Press,* January 6. www.bpnews.net/bpnews.asp?id=31993.

McNeal, R. 2000. *A Work of Heart: Understanding How God Shapes Spiritual Leaders.* San Francisco: Jossey-Bass.

Muller, W. 1991. *Sabbath: Finding Rest, Renewal and Delight in Our Busy Lives.* New York: Bantam Books.

O'Brien, R. 2011. "The Leader as Mentor and Pastor." In *Christian Leadership Essentials: A Handbook for Managing Christian Organizations,* edited by D. S. Dockery. Nashville: B & H Academic.

Peterson, E. 1987. *Working the Angles: The Shape of Pastoral Integrity.* Grand Rapids: Eerdmans.

Roberts, D. B. 2010. "Energizing, Supporting, and Sustaining Religious Leaders Through Peer Learning Groups." *A Lifelong Call to Learn: Continuing Education for Religious Leaders*, edited by R. Reber and D. B. Roberts. Harndon, VA: Alban Institute.

Roozen, D. A. 2009. *Faith Communities Today 2008: A First Look*. Hartford, CT: Hartford Institute for Religion Research. http://faithcommunitiestoday.org/sites /all/themes/factzon4/files/FACT2008sfLook pdf

Scanlon, L. 2010. "Congregational Snapshot: Presbyterian Churches, Members Respond to Survey." *Presbyterian Outlook*, October 7. www.pres-outlook.com /news-and-analysis/1/10508.html.

Stanley, P. D., and R. Clinton. 1992. *Connecting: The Mentoring Relationships You Need to Succeed in Life*. Colorado Springs: NavPress.

Swenson, R. 2004. *Margin: Restoring Emotional, Physical, Financial, and Time Resources to Overloaded Lives*. Colorado Springs: NavPress.

Thompson, M. 1995. *Soul Feast: An Invitation to the Christian Spiritual Life*. Louisville, KY: Westminster John Knox.

Vaill, P. 1996. *Learning as a Way of Being: Strategies for Survival in a World of Permanent White Water*. San Francisco: Jossey-Bass.

Vitello, P. 2010. "Taking a Break from the Lord's Work." *New York Times*, August 1. Retrieved at www.nytimes.com.

Wright, W. 2004. *Mentoring: The Promise of Relational Leadership*. Secunderabad, India: OM-Authentic Media.

For Further Reading

McNeal, R. 1998. *Revolution in Leadership: Training Apostles for Tomorrow's Church*. Nashville: Abingdon.

Postscript

In the preface, we editors stated, "Our hope is that this book will demonstrate that the word *Christian* in front of the word *leadership* proposes something substantially different and quantitatively better." We have, in fact, shared with the reader many tried and true methods of developing leadership skills. We have also identified and documented many biblical examples that shed light on God's role in shaping the life of those who were chosen to take on the mantle of leadership. We also noted that all who espouse to become Christian leaders have the benefit of biblical revelations that provide insight not found elsewhere. On the surface, given the resources and tools available to emerging Christian leaders, one would assume that embracing the model of a Christian leader would be an easy task. Unfortunately, this is rarely the case.

As professors and administrators at Christian universities, we are often called to speak on matters related to leadership. Once during a lecture on servant leadership, where one of us used Christ as the example of the epitome of a servant leader, a young man in the audience asked the following question: "Sure Christ was a great leader, but in the end he was put to death and even denied by his followers, those who were closest to him. I wouldn't mind being a leader but Christ's example of leadership isn't very inspirational for mere mortals. Who wants to be denied and crucified?"

The young man's comments brought giggles and laughs from the audience, but he did have a point. Certainly Christ's death and resurrection was part of God's plan and, absent those unique circumstances, we should all try to emulate the life of Christ. Yet that young man's question is unsettling. It requires us to look deeper for alternative biblical examples of successful Christian leaders to whom people could more easily relate. It is one thing to wear "WWJD" apparel and ask ourselves "What would Jesus do?" when confronted with challenges, but does that really translate into a model for leadership?

Perhaps there are alternative biblical leaders who could give others hope that peril or death might not be the fate for those modern Christians who become leaders. Unfortunately, the Bible provides very little evidence of leaders, Christian or otherwise, who have an easy way of things. Most leaders in the Bible are unappreciated, challenged at every turn and often denied by the very individuals they try to lead. Moses, for example, was questioned and challenged in spite of the numerous miraculous occurrences associated with his ministry. How could anyone doubt Moses and his God after all that he had done? We can't begin to imagine how devastated and disheartened he must have felt when he saw the golden calf (Exodus 32:19).

Moses was one of the lucky ones. The Bible is filled with examples of early leaders who experienced unimaginable suffering and death as a result of their purposeful Christian faith. John the Baptist, who is referenced in the canonical Gospels, the one who recognized Jesus as the Messiah and baptized him, is a prime example of a Christian leader who, like Jesus, suffered a senseless and horrible death. The ministry and leadership of John and his disciples was worthy of note, so much so that in John 5:35, the Gospel records that John was as "a lamp that burned and gave light." John's success led to his imprisonment and ultimately his death, followed by the presentation of his severed head to the king on a platter. John and his followers, most biblical scholars agree, were a perceived threat to the king. John was a great leader, no question about it, but a beheading is an equally uninspiring alternative to crucifixion for emerging Christian leaders.

It is important to note, however, that suffering leaders are not unique to the Bible. Mohandas Ghandi, Martin Luther King Jr. and Nelson Mandela, three of the most heralded and recognizable leaders of the twentieth century, all spent considerable time in jails and prisons, alienated from their families and followers. King, like many before and since, died in the service of his cause.

George Washington, considered by most Americans to be the father of our country, was defeated and forced to sign humiliating terms of surrender the very first time he engaged in combat, a little known fact about his early colonial career as an officer in the militia. During the American Revolution, he not only braved enemy fire but also suffered through a near revolt and mutiny of his own troops during the winter of 1783, when Congress refused to appropriate funds to pay the army.

When addressing his officers during that darkest of hours of the Revolutionary War, General Washington reached in his coat pocket and said the following words before beginning to read: "Gentlemen, you will permit me to put on my spectacles, for I have not only grown gray, but almost blind, in the service of my country" (Brattebo and Malone 2002, p. 54). His officers were so touched that talk of the mutiny ceased and some who were present wept not only from the powerful personal example and oratory of their leader, but because of the sacrificial leadership they all would have to conduct for their great cause.

We observe almost daily the price paid by those who step into the role of leader. The effects of stress and pressures on those who lead are often readily apparent. We have all seen, for example, how rapidly our political executives appear to age while in office. American presidents, according to Dr. Michael Roizen, chief wellness officer at the Cleveland Clinic, effectively age twice as fast while in office as the rest of us do. He believes that the stress and loneliness associated with serving as a national and world leader plays a major role in aging (Hanna 2011).

In short, the role of leader of any organization, whether Christian or secular, is often lonely, trying and frustrating, and the physical and emotional toll of these key positions cannot be denied. Even if you are almost perfect as a leader, as was our Lord and Savior, and you do everything right, you will at some point find yourself alone, as did Christ. Ask anyone who has held a position as leader within the church or any organization and they will confirm this truth. If you answer God's call to be a leader, you will undoubtedly ask yourself the following question at some point: "Is it really worth it?"

We hope that as a partial answer to this question, there are some significant reasons to be optimistic. First, Christian leadership has meaning and purpose. In both Christian and secular organizations, Christians who conduct leadership can discover the sacred calling for their organizations and work to make them effective for God's kingdom work. It is indeed "worth it" when we discover how God has called us to transform our organizations so that they help to transform our broken world. Second, we are never in this alone. Leadership is never a one-person show. A symphony conductor cannot merely wave a baton to make music. The music emerges when trained musicians are all working to the same end to bring their instruments to life, transforming notes on a page into a symphony. While the position of leader requires specialized skills associated with unique responsibilities, and may draw lots of attention, the leader is not capable of conducting leadership on his or her own. Trained, committed followers must join their skills with others to achieve a mutually shared transforming purpose. Leadership is always collaborative, and Christian leadership enjoys one more key collaborator: God, as he guides us through the Holy Spirit.

As we close our study of Christian leadership, it seems appropriate to reflect on the life of the apostle Paul. He is perhaps the most quoted and referenced early leader of the church, and the first great missionary to the Gentiles. He and his missionary partners were largely responsible for the early growth and expansion of the church beyond the Holy Land, and he still brings untold numbers to the faith daily through his scriptural legacy. Through it all he and his companions endured unimaginable challenges as they introduced others to Christ. They were shipwrecked, tortured, persecuted and imprisoned repeatedly.

During his mission work, Paul at one point traveled with a man named Demas, who with others also ministered to the Romans. Demas was with Paul during his imprisonment in Rome. Some time later, however, Paul referred to Demas in his writings, noting that "because he loved this world, [he] has deserted me and has gone to Thessalonica" (2 Timothy 4:10).

Here, in this seemingly otherwise insignificant biblical reference, Paul lays out for us the challenge that is unique to those called to Christian leadership. Along with the other corporate or organizational goals that we are expected to meet or exceed, Christian leaders also have a responsibility to follow the teachings of our Lord and Savior in our every thought, word and deed, and in doing so bring others to Christ. Demas loved this world, as so many do. Demas abandoned the mission, and when Paul was brought to court even those loyal to him took off. But Paul was not alone.

> At my first defense, no one came to my support, but everyone deserted me.
> May it not be held against them. But the Lord stood at my side and gave me

strength, so that through me the message might be fully proclaimed and all the Gentiles might hear it. And I was delivered from the lion's mouth. The Lord will rescue me from every evil attack and will bring me safely to his heavenly kingdom. (2 Timothy 4:16-18)

Great Christian leaders are never alone as they learn to be, first and foremost, great followers. They follow the teachings of our Lord and Savior Jesus Christ, always seeking the true promise of the kingdom of God.

We wrote this book because Christians are called to work in this world to help advance God's kingdom, and that work is never easy and often uncomfortable. Leadership is a collaborative, intentional effort that requires dedication and hard work. The people who do this work are in positions in every part of organizations (not just the folks at the top). Even so, all Christians have been gifted by God and designed for a purpose. We all need to understand our gifts, understand our organizations and their purpose, and step into our calling to Christian leadership.

References

Brattebo, D. M., and Malone, E. F., eds. 2002. *The Lanahan Cases in Leadership, Ethics, and Decison Making.* Baltimore, MD: Lanahan Publishing.

Hanna, J. 2011. "Do Presidents Age Faster in Office?" CNN. www.cnn.com/2011 /POLITICS/08/04/presidents.aging/index.html.

Contributors

Gayne J. Anacker (PhD, University of California, Irvine) is professor of philosophy and dean of the College of Arts and Sciences at California Baptist University in Riverside, California. He also serves as vice president for academic affairs for the C. S. Lewis Foundation.

John S. (Jack) Burns is professor of leadership studies at Whitworth University in Spokane, Washington, where he coordinates the Interdisciplinary Leadership Studies Program. He has taught leadership studies since 1985 and has developed leadership studies programs at two universities. He has served as director of an Eisenhower Leadership Program Grant, and has published several articles and book chapters on leadership pedagogy, organizational theory and leadership theory. He received his PhD in higher education administration and MA in counseling from Washington State University.

Timothy G. Dolan (PhD, Gonzaga University) currently serves as director of the doctor of ministry program and associate professor of pastoral leadership and ministry at Denver Seminary. Prior to joining the faculty of Denver Seminary, he spent fifteen years as the director of the Institute for Clergy and Lay Leadership Development at Whitworth University. For six of those years he also directed Whitworth's master of arts in theology program.

Richard C. Langer (PhD, University of California, Riverside) is professor of biblical studies and theological integration and director of the Office for the Integration of Faith and Learning at Biola University in La Mirada, California.

Chris McHorney (PhD, University of California, Riverside) is professor of political science and chair of the Department of History and Government at California Baptist University in Riverside, California.

Ronald K. Pyle (PhD, University of Washington) is professor of communication studies at Whitworth University in Spokane, Washington.

John R. Shoup serves as dean of the School of Education at California Baptist University in Riverside, California. He teaches leadership and educational history and policy at the graduate level, and has presented and conducted research and workshops on leadership development and best practices and educational policy. Shoup has also served as a school principal and in various social service settings. He has a PhD in education with an emphasis in institutional leadership and policy studies from the University of California, Riverside. He also has a master of divinity and a master of arts in counseling psychology from Trinity Evangelical Divinity School in Deerfield, Illinois.

Donald C. Simmons Jr. (PhD, University of Denver) is president of The Obion Group in Omaha, Nebraska, a leadership consulting firm that advises nonprofits, churches and Christian colleges. As founding full-time director of the McGovern Center for Leadership and Public Service at Dakota Wesleyan University, he also served as dean and professor at DWU before founding The Obion Group. He holds a certificate of ministry from Truett Theological Seminary, Baylor University, and is actively involved in church planting and prison ministry, as well as international mission programs in Kenya and Belize.

R. Scott Rodin (PhD, University of Aberdeen) is president of Rodin Consulting Inc. and a senior fellow of the Association of Biblical Higher Education. He has served as counsel in fundraising, leadership, board development and strategic planning to hundreds of organizations in the United States, Canada, the Middle East, Great Britain, China and Australia. He also served as president of the Christian Stewardship Association and president of Eastern Baptist (now Palmer) Theological Seminary. He is the author of ten books, including *Stewards in the Kingdom, The Steward Leader* and *The Third Conversion*.

Finding the Textbook You Need

The IVP Academic Textbook Selector
is an online tool for instantly finding the IVP books
suitable for over 250 courses across 24 disciplines.

www.ivpress.com/academic/textbookselector